Post-Communist Aesthetics

In this book, Anca Pusca seeks to extend the aesthetic and cultural turn in international relations to an analysis of post-communist transitions in Central and Eastern Europe. Building on the philosophy of Walter Benjamin and Jacques Rancière, the work investigates how post-communist film, photography, theatre, art, museumisation and architecture have creatively re-engaged with ideas of revolution, communism, capitalism and ethnic violence, and how this in turn has helped people survive and reinvent themselves amongst the material and ideological ruins of communism. The work illustrates how popular culture has effectively targeted and re-interpreted the classical representations of the transition in order to question:

- The origin – focusing on practices of re-staging, memorialising and questioning the 1989 revolutions.
- The unfolding – focusing on the human and material consequences of significant changes in processes of production and consumption.
- The potential end – focusing on the illusions and disillusions surrounding the 'transition' process.

A unique take on the influence that popular culture has had and continues to have on how we understand the post-communist transitions, this work will be of great interest to students and scholars of cultural and visual studies, Eastern European politics and international relations.

Anca M. Pusca's current research seeks to re-conceptualise the aesthetics of change within the context of today's EU and its candidate states, by tracing spatial, architectural and visual representations and responses to the EU's most important policies: from immigration, monetary and the common agricultural policy to constitutional reform. She lectures at Goldsmiths, University of London.

Popular Culture and World Politics

Edited by **Matt Davies**, *Newcastle University*,
Kyle Grayson, *Newcastle University*,
Simon Philpott, *Newcastle University*,
Christina Rowley, *University of Bristol* and
Jutta Weldes, *University of Bristol*

The *Popular Culture World Politics* (PCWP) book series is the forum for leading interdisciplinary research that explores the profound and diverse interconnections between popular culture and world politics. It aims to bring further innovation, rigor, and recognition to this emerging sub-field of international relations.

To these ends, the PCWP series is interested in various themes, from the juxtaposition of cultural artefacts that are increasingly global in scope and regional, local and domestic forms of production, distribution, and consumption; to the confrontations between cultural life and global political, social, and economic forces; to the new or emergent forms of politics that result from the rescaling or internationalization of popular culture.

Similarly, the series provides a venue for work that explores the effects of new technologies and new media on established practices of representation and the making of political meaning. It encourages engagement with popular culture as a means for contesting powerful narratives of particular events and political settlements as well as explorations of the ways that popular culture informs mainstream political discourse. The series promotes investigation into how popular culture contributes to changing perceptions of time, space, scale, identity, and participation while establishing the outer limits of what is popularly understood as 'political' or 'cultural'.

In addition to film, television, literature, and art, the series actively encourages research into diverse artefacts including sound, music, food cultures, gaming, design, architecture, programming, leisure, sport, fandom, and celebrity. The series is fiercely pluralist in its approaches to the study of popular culture and world politics and is interested in the past, present, and future cultural dimensions of hegemony, resistance, and power.

Gender, Violence and Popular Culture
Telling stories
Laura J. Shepherd

Aesthetic Modernism and Masculinity in Fascist Italy
John Champagne

Post-Communist Aesthetics

Revolutions, capitalism, violence

Anca M. Pusca

Routledge
Taylor & Francis Group

LONDON AND NEW YORK

First published 2016
by Routledge

2 Park Square, Milton Park, Abingdon, Oxfordshire OX14 4RN
52 Vanderbilt Avenue, New York, NY 10017

Routledge is an imprint of the Taylor & Francis Group, an informa business

First issued in paperback 2020

British Library Cataloguing in Publication Data
A catalogue record for this book is available from the British Library

Library of Congress Cataloging in Publication Data
Names: Pusca, Anca, author.
Title: Post communist aesthetics : revolutions, capitalism, violence / by
Anca M. Pusca.
Description: Abingdon, Oxon ; New York, NY : Routledge
is an imprint of the Taylor & Francis Group, an Informa business, [2016] |
Series: Popular culture and world politics
Identifiers: LCCN 2015021635
Subjects: LCSH: Post-communism--Social aspects--Europe, Eastern. |
Post-communism--Social aspects--Europe, Central. | Popular
culture--Europe, Eastern. | Popular culture--Europe, Central. | Europe,
Eastern--Social conditions--1989- | Europe, Central--Social
conditions--1989-
Classification: LCC HN380.7.A8 P87 2016 | DDC 306.0947--dc23
LC record available at http://lccn.loc.gov/2015021635

ISBN: 978-0-415-52300-4 (hbk)
ISBN: 978-0-367-59769-6 (pbk)

Typeset in Times New Roman
by Taylor & Francis Books

To Gloria

Contents

Illustrations

Foreword

Thinking about popular culture and world politics together is not new. We can read almost any important political thinker as having an acute interest in how they are related and how they shape and limit each other. Indeed, if we take each of those four terms as contestable, rather than fixed by definitional fiat, it is hard to think about them separately: whatever else "popular" might mean, it ultimately refers to a people and their agency; culture is notoriously plural and hard to pin down so it tends to describe spaces that cannot be reduced to particular identities; the world is increasingly taken as a unit of analysis (as in 'globalisation') but is difficult to specify in cultural or political terms; and politics, well, is there a more contested or contestable concept? Does it imply a 'people' who might have a particular kind of agency or be governable? Is it shaped by 'whole ways of life' or systems of producing and distributing meanings? Does it have a proper scale or space?

The diversity of approaches to these questions and to the intersections – or continuum (Grayson, Davies, Philpott, 2009, Pop Goes IR? Researching the Popular Culture–World Politics Continuum, *Politics* 29(3): 155–163) – of these terms in the Popular Culture and World Politics book series signals how fruitful it can be to cross the disciplinary boundaries that bracket one or two of the terms while deferring (or ignoring) the others. Each of the volumes published in the series shows, in distinctive ways, how the premises behind theories of international relations rely on versions of common sense that become deeply problematic when played out in other genres of writing, as well as how the common senses produced in the practices of popular culture affirm as well as deconstruct the ontological assumptions behind thinking about world politics. Each volume, again in its own way, rises to the post-positivist challenges in international relations by exploring different ways of responding to the 'how can we know' question through examining evidence that escapes the notice of more rigid epistemologies. And each arms the reader with an expanding sophisticated methodological toolbox, drawing on lessons from the fluidity and litigiousness of cultural relations against the locking down and foreclosure of the political needed to render the latter predictable and manageable.

Anca Pusca enters into these intersections and continuums accompanied by one of the most important thinkers about popular culture and world politics of the twentieth century: Walter Benjamin. Benjamin's work has been taken up in critical international relations theory and research much less than some of the thinkers identified with French post-structuralist thinking; however provocative and clarifying the engagements with the latter have been, a careful stroll through the ruins of the post-Cold War with Benjamin is long overdue.

For Benjamin, artefacts such as ruins are not only the material condensations of the unfolding historical forces that produce them but they are also glimpses into the structure of the present and possible futures. The end of the Cold War and the collapse of communism produced just such a collection of ruins. These ruins lie across world politics. The collapse of the formal certainties of secular conflicts across a bipolar world stabilised by a nuclear standoff, certainties that constrained political possibilities in the Cold War, yielded a bewildering tableau shaped by the return of the repressed. Assertions about the 'end of history', 'democratic peace', and 'globalisation' contended with 'clashes of civilisations', a 'global war on terror', and 'unknown unknowns' as accounts of the world political present and possible emergent problems. International relations was itself revealed as a historical artefact, stripped of its timeless certainties about whatever power might be and however it might be pursued or deployed or contained.

Pusca focuses her reflections on the post-socialist context of Eastern Europe as a site of these condensations of the collapse of and possible presents and futures of world politics. The 'popular' configures this space through the dissolving of the 'people' of the communist people's democracies and the re-emergence of the people across manifold sites: living in and amongst the ruins of industries and monuments, for example, or through the dialectic of visibility and invisibility that has helped define the Roma as people. Through these tropes we can see the differing, conflicting connotations of the popular in contention: across the continuums from the ideology of popular democracy to the inscription of a population to be contained and governed, from the self-expression of a marginalised identity to its mass-mediatisation.

Culture in the plural must figure here, not only in terms of the multiple identities that come out of the fracturing of the communist people but also in terms of the cultural objects that speak to and through these emergent subjectivities. Thus photographs, films, and performances encounter museums, decoration, or erasure, forgetting, and decay to produce different registers for living culturally. How this expressive and ephemeral emergence and subsidence is shaped and perceived calls for analysis through dissident methods. Pusca draws on the tradition of aesthetics – as an account of the perceivable, as the sensitivity of the perceiving body to its surroundings and environment – to discern such methods. So from Jacques Rancière and the aesthetic moment as a disruption of the 'distribution of the sensible' to Benjamin as a *flâneur* and collagist, the methods for discerning and analysing the culture and the *popular* culture of post-communist ruins are made in the analysis by all the observers: the viewers of the photographs or films, the performers on the streets, the graffiti or mural artists, the writers and readers of the book are all implicated and imbricated in the cultural project.

Grasping these multiple subjects of popular and cultural analysis situates the project in the world. But where is this world? Here again, Pusca's invoking of Benjamin places the familiar world of international relations – the world of the international system, of interstate conflict and cooperation – in its material spaces and objects. The world is thus not merely the container for international, popular, and cultural relations: it is the material manifestation of history and social change. As such, the evanescence of the comfortable certainties of the world as we inhabit it is revealed as they yield to other, different transitory forms. Pusca, with Benjamin, invokes Paul Klee's painting of the Angel of History to glimpse this world as it passes. Time – history and temporality – cannot be abstracted from this world so its location – the where of popular culture and politics – is necessarily discerned in its movement.

Thus politics – world politics – is revealed in its transitions. The bodies and objects in movement, the *flâneur* strolling through the collapsing ruins of yesterday's firmaments, produce ever changing and ever shifting social relations. As Pusca points out, even 'transitology', the study of transitions, has been transitory as the living memory of the communist past fades and gives way to new certainties – themselves fated to fade and rot. But this is not a pessimistic view for it shows how politics is always possible, how a possible politics is always emerging from the world as it is reconfigured in the everyday work of putting things together, shoring things up, finding new resources and means to live in the world.

Popular culture and world politics live in, around, and through each other, a chiasm (as Merleau-Ponty described it) where each is the condition of possibility for the other. The artist, the *flâneur*, and the reader, as much as the diplomat, the banker, or the general, or as much as the scholar, the think tank, or the policy, are the subjects of this drama. They all stand in the pages of this book, driven by history, viewing what passes, and leaving objects and traces to be recovered and rebuilt.

Matt Davies
Newcastle University

Acknowledgements

I wrote this book in my head over and over again for the last four years, but have only managed to get it on paper now. If it weren't for a few, very patient, encouraging and inspirational people, it may never have happened. Thank you Matt Davies, Kyle Grayson and Simon Philpott for inviting me to be part of your exciting book series on World Politics and Popular Culture in the first place, and for creating such a welcoming forum for discussion and a home for those of us interested in questions of popular culture and aesthetics. You have each been an inspiration of kindness, friendship and intellectual creativity. Thank you to Nicola Parkin and Lydia de Cruz for their guidance, patience and support, and for believing that this project will indeed materialise. Thank you to Susan Buck-Morss, Svetlana Boym and Tim Edensor for being such an inspiration and for allowing me to borrow and play with some of their ideas. Thank you to Dan Perjovski, Dumitru Gorzo, Tamas Dezso and Vaclav Jirasek for allowing me to use their stunning photographs as illustrations, and to all the artists, directors and performers that have opened up such interesting new ways of looking at the communist past and its aftermath. I can only hope to do your work justice. Thank you to Mustapha K. Pasha for continuing to be my mentor and friend throughout all these years. Thank you to Goldsmiths for being the best intellectual home that I could hope for, and to the Manhattan College library for so generously hosting me while away from home. Thank you to Gloria for coming into my life and being the most amazing thing one could hope for, and to Noel for putting up with everything. And finally, thank you to Walter Benjamin, for opening up the possibility for what has been my most exciting intellectual endeavour so far.

1   Introduction

What/why/how post-communist aesthetics?

What is post-communist aesthetics?

The concept of post-communist aesthetics already carries strong connotations for both those interested in questions related to post-communism and the experience of the 'transition' in Central and Eastern Europe as well as for those interested in the relationship between ideology/politics and aesthetics. Bringing these two audiences together is not always easy as both the concept of 'post-communism' as well as the concept of 'aesthetics' are heavily invested with their own set of connotations and meanings. Post-communism, through the very presence of the 'post', implies a certain temporal trajectory that takes you through and beyond a particular ideological era – communism – which is understood as clearly bracketed by set historical events. The 'post' puts the emphasis on the 'end' of an era – the closing 'bracket' event – and the beginning of another. The moment of 1989 and the revolutions that marked it represent, in this case, the definitive end point of communism, and everything that comes after emerges as a time of intense change and transition whose trajectory is ongoing.

By adding the concept of 'aesthetics', the discussion is in a way both narrowed – by focusing it on the 'aesthetic' angle – as well as opened – by introducing a series of potentially new interventions. Those who expect this to be largely a discussion of post-communist art will be to a certain extent disappointed: although the book does look at specific forms of artistic expression such as photography, film, theatre, performance art and architecture, it does so within a very specific context. It looks at how some of these artistic expressions openly engage with and challenge the meaning of key historical moments – such as the moment of 1989, as well as key experiences of the transition, such as the collapse of major state owned industries and the communities associated with them during the early transition period, the rise of intense commercialisation and the new structures/architectures that came along with that, and the radical stratification of society which served not only to create deep inequality but also to connect that inequality to violence against other races and ethnicities.

'Aesthetics' in this case is understood not so much as being about a certain (art) object and its perception – what Rancière calls 'the sensible', but rather about what he calls a 'politics of aesthetics' – 'a refiguration of the forms of visibility and intelligibility of artistic practice and reception' (Rancière 2009: 6) as well as 'the staging of a dissensus – of a conflict of sensory worlds' (Rancière 2009: 12). To exemplify this, Rancière gives the example of the worker's gaze as captured by one of the workers' newspapers that emerged during the French Revolution of 1848: a joiner who lays the floor in a palace is described as stopping for a moment to enjoy the view from the open window; his perspectival view is unlike that of the palace owners in that it places both his body as well as his uniquely shaped capacity of perception in an unlikely circumstance, turning the short moment of enjoying the palace view into a political act and, as Rancière would argue, a form of political resistance. The dissensus is created by the unexpected presence and enjoyment of a particular way of seeing – the perspectival view – by a worker who is usually confined to closed spaces, obstructed views and a work ethic that does not afford contemplation.

From this perspective, post-communist aesthetics is understood as a unique set of circumstances, events and interventions, which disrupt normal/expected forms of perception and visibility and create/open a space where new and often unexpected meanings, interpretations and opportunities emerge. This can happen both intentionally – through targeted interventions, as well as spontaneously through the odd juxtapositions created by the process of historical change itself. These circumstances, events and interventions are usually guided or afforded by a series of specific technologies – this books focuses in particular on the technologies of photography and film; as well as by particular material embodiments of the process of historical change – in this case, the focus lies mainly on different architectural forms such as the large industrial platforms and building estates often associated with communism, as well as the open-markets, garage architecture, shopping malls and excessive publicity often associated with the transition to capitalism.

The book follows and retraces a series of different 'gazes', which afford different fields of vision and ways of perception: the gaze from 'within', often associated with those who are undergoing the 'transition experience'; the gaze from 'outside', associated with those who examine the transition while being either physically or politically removed from it – in the sense that they are not directly/personally affected by it or that even when affected they can remove themselves from within it at will; and the 'oblique' gaze, generally associated with those who find themselves in between the 'inside' and the 'outside', such as emigrants and different ethnic groups whose 'belonging' has always been challenged – this book discusses mainly Roma/Gypsy groups.

Neither of these three gazes represents a unified field of vision: each is in turn splintered along class, ethnic and intellectual/political/ideological inclinations. The idea of the book is not to represent each of them in an equal fashion, nor to try in any way to offer a comprehensive view, but rather to acknowledge their presence and differences within the specific context of the circumstances, events and interventions chosen to showcase the 'dissensus' and through them challenge the creation of a set 'storyline' for the experience of 'transition'. While prioritising views from 'within' and to a certain extent 'oblique' views – also the author's view – as challengers of 'outside' views that have generally dominated academic discussions surrounding the post-communist 'transition' experience, the book also acknowledges that the separation between them is largely imaginary, as many 'outside' views have been effectively internalised, while 'inside' views are often so fragmented that they cannot provide a coherent picture.

Each of the chapters that follow seeks to challenge, in different ways, the prevalent storyline of the post-communist transition: the 'heroism' and 'democratic intentionality' of the 1989 Revolutions at the beginning of the transition; the 'necessity' and 'positive' impact of economic restructuring following the revolutions; the embracing and celebration of consumerism and its culture as something necessarily new; and the common association of the 'problems' of the transition and integration into the 'West'/European Union with marginalised and vulnerable groups such as Roma/Gypsy minorities. They do so from the perspective afforded by the passing of a certain amount of time – in this case over two decades: looking back onto the early stages of the 'transition', largely the 1990s and early 2000s as particularly intense moments of change uniquely prone to a certain sense of 'blind sidedness'. The 'present' – largely the mid to late 2000s up to today – emerges as a period with a much stronger sense of 'clarity' and confidence to explore and question the past, particularly by a generation for whom 'communism' is now a distant memory.

The 'looking' back is often literal here, with each chapter focusing on a series of interventions that prioritise the sense of 'seeing' as key to the experience of the transition, and '(en)frame' what we see by zooming in on a particular, often emblematic, aspect of change. The second chapter for example looks at different forms of visually re-staging the moment of 1989 through: television – particularly through the inclusion of new visual shots and perspectives of the first televised revolution; film – by focusing on the success of the so-called Romanian 'New Wave'; early street performances and a more recent 'New Wave' in theatre; as well as street monuments. Each of these re-stagings strategically disrupt the perceived unity in meaning of 1989 – in particularly its heroism – as well as its limited temporal timeframe. Through each of these re-stagings the 'moment' of 1989 emerges as a much more elastic timeframe that has often been strategically (mis)used to attach desired connotations to certain spaces and people.

The third chapter zooms in on some of the most emblematic material remains of communism: the now dilapidated industrial platforms that sustained the communist economies and the towns and people that were ruined along with them. By focusing on a series of photographic, film and performance interventions which seek to engage with and bring forward this unique patrimony, the chapter re-prioritises the now marginalised and overlooked former heroes of communism, seeking to afford them new meaning. The photographs, film and artistic performances bring these spaces alive by showing that there still is life amongst the ruins, that even when dilapidated, these spaces continue to be deeply invested emotionally, and that those living among them cannot just be erased.

The fourth chapter turns our eyes towards the future by looking at how communism laid the foundations for unusually strong consuming desires and how, in turn, these were expressed and sustained by increasingly sophisticated architectures/spaces of consumption: from open-markets, to garage architecture, to hypermarkets and shopping malls, and more recently, gated communities. The chapter adopts the pace and perspective of a nineteenth-century flâneur stepping into the twenty-first century: the novelty of the first sidewalks, the arcades, and panoramas is replaced by that of publicity panels and bright colours that hide the grey of former communist flats, and the opening of new shopping spaces that create the illusion of equal access to both new commodities and new lifestyles. By focusing on the now famous Painting Tirana project – which saw most of Tirana, Albania painted in bright colours; as well as the Czech Dream documentary – which filmed the fake opening of a new hypermarket with 'unbelievable' prices, the chapter challenges some of the unique forms in which capitalism has not only been internalised across transitioning Central and Eastern Europe but also taken to its consumerist extremes.

The fifth chapter examines the problematics of the increased visibility of Roma/Gypsy minorities across Europe and how this newfound visibility is negotiated in different ways by both majority groups – which often use it as a way to instigate further violence; and Roma minority groups – which creatively, although at times controversially, use it to demonstrate a new found control over their changing identity and their portrayal. By looking at the new kind of visual and physical spaces that Roma minorities occupy – from 'nomad' camps and slums, to palaces, reality TV shows and international photography and art exhibits, the chapter compares and contrasts the effects of what appears to be a radical shift in how Roma minorities are 'seen' and choose to be 'seen'.

Post-communist aesthetics is thus about exploring new ways of 'seeing' and 'experiencing' the transition through a series of creative interventions which seek to position the viewer/reader at certain key vantage points and afford them the ability to look both back and forth in time, to experience often unseen corners of the transition on an equal footing with the more prevalent images, and to put themselves in the shoes of often marginalised or mundane characters which tend not to make the news. Different readers will 'see' different things as they go through the book: some might recognise similar experiences of change or 'transition' as those happening in other parts of the world, while others might see a completely new face of the post-communist transitions. Although written in text, the book employs similar montage techniques as documentaries, juxtaposing case-studies, images and discussions in order to elicit different reactions, but also carefully chooses the issues, images and sites that it sets its eyes on as key entry points into understanding the experience of the transition.

Why post-communist 'aesthetics'?

By prioritising not only the 'experience' of the transition but also the potential for a new kind of 'politics' embedded in certain aspects of this experience, the book offers an opportunity to re-think key moments of the transition and experience unique spaces endowed with what Foucault calls heterotopic powers (Foucault 1967). Very much inspired by Walter Benjamin's *Arcades Project*, this is a much more humble attempt to find the remaining *passages* spread across the post-communist landscape which continue to afford glimpses into the past as well as the future. Like Benjamin's project, this is not an attempt at 'grand theorising', or offering an overarching understanding of post-communist transitions. Very much intended as a fragmented argument that functions as a constellation of ideas, which resist a singular interpretation, the chapters offer at most an example of how some of these ideas and spaces could be arranged and interpreted, without giving a definitive explanation.

While this goes against the spirit of most theoretical endeavours in the discipline of international relations, and certainly comparative studies, resisting in many ways the most basic demands that each of these disciplines place on the creation of relevant 'text', including the increasingly pressing demand for 'impact', the book nonetheless hopes to spark relevant discussions and thoughts without seeking to arrange them into pre-drawn disciplinary and theoretical boxes with pre-conceived conclusions. While some might argue that this constitutes an easy way out of important disciplinary debates that nonetheless need to be acknowledged – we are after all in the business of acknowledging and debating with each other; as well as an easy way out of having to ultimately draw some kind of conclusion – the book does actually have a conclusion, which functions however more as a furthering the discussion as opposed to offering a decisive final word; the book hopes to nonetheless offer a strong enough theoretical and methodological structure to justify its purpose.

The theoretical framework of the book is largely built upon the work of two critical thinkers: first is Walter Benjamin's unique understanding of history and social change which challenges on the one hand the 'location' of history in historical texts – suggesting instead that material objects, spaces, architecture and images are much more likely to capture and reveal key aspects of history (Benjamin 1968); and on the other the linearity of historical time – for him, the past, present and future can co-exist, even if briefly, brought together by the very same materials and spaces mentioned above (Benjamin 1998). Materials, spaces, images, become in a sense history itself, absorbing us not only metaphorically but physically: certain sites – for him, the arcades, for us movie theatres, former industrial platforms, open markets, shopping malls, migrant camps – serve to not only open up spaces where history stops, but also often entrap within them entire (forgotten) sections of society.

Second is Jacques Rancière's unique understanding of the relevance of 'aesthetics' in terms of its ability to create/point to unique and unexpected disassociations of experience, that create new opportunities for 'seeing' things differently. For him, this is largely a question of class, whereby the working class creates for itself ways of engaging with the sensible that would otherwise not be afforded by their position: writing poetry, philosophising, gazing reflectively and aimlessly (Rancière 1989, 2004). For the purpose of this book, this goes well beyond the working class to point to the fast, shocking and often strange sensorial awakening that followed communism, the distortions in both consumerist and political desires that it created, and perhaps more importantly, the often dual, complicit and reflective, character of the spaces in which these often frustrated desires were expressed.

Through Walter Benjamin and Jacques Rancière, the book develops a theory of experiencing change which focuses on different ways of 'seeing' and '(en)framing' that are often mediated by the changing politics of space and the changing attitude towards technologies such as photography and film; the act of walking as related to the reflective yet aimless attitude of the flâneur and the kind of spaces that engender the possibility for flânerie today; and the importance of desires, illusions and disillusions in helping to experience/imagine change often before it has actually materialised.

The process of 'transition' is one of intense change, yet also one where change materialises at a different pace, and in different ways, depending on the spaces that one inhabits. While some spaces seem trapped in time, others are fast propelled into the future. Many of these spaces are not separated by clear borders anymore: the rural/urban, industrial/commercial divides are often too simplistic to capture what is happening. One may step out of the past and into the future within the space of a few minutes. The contrast, while striking at first, is often normalised through daily routines to a point where it becomes invisible. Continuous, fast-paced change though is often exhausting: the constant necessity to adjust, to find new routines, to cope, to move forward, narrows our ability to 'see', to 'focus', to 'reflect'.

There are in fact few opportunities to exercise these functions in the middle of a 'transition'. The tail end of a 'transition' however affords a whole new series of opportunities. This is in many ways, along with the initial revolutionary moment, the most exciting moment of a transition: things are once again questioned, key moments of the past re-staged and re-enacted to open up lost meanings, the future once again presents more than one possibility. It is precisely this moment that the book tries to capture. The moment is often short-lived, and today (2015) we are perhaps coming towards its end. As most of post-communist Europe, although certainly not all – see Ukraine, Moldova, Serbia – gets close to finally declaring the 'transition' period over, there is a unique opportunity in this 'here' and 'now' to rethink the experience of the 'transition' and reconsider its legacy.

By zooming in on some of these attempts to rethink and reconsider and hinting at other spaces where similar acts could be attempted, the book does not necessarily offer a 'model' through which this could be done. Instead, it simply highlights some of the creative spaces, acts and diversions that have created room for reflective thinking. These are in no way exhaustive, nor could they be, many are focused on the environment that the author is most closely familiar with – Romania – and are limited by the ultimately subjective choices that the author made. Although each specific choice can be justified theoretically and methodologically, ultimately, there are many other case-studies that could have been picked. This is hopefully where the book will, in an odd way, make its more lasting contribution: by creating an intellectual space where other relevant spaces, acts and diversions can be discussed.

How does one 'do' post-communist aesthetics?

There certainly is no single or prescribed way of engaging with post-communist aesthetics. One can only talk about the specific approach chosen for this book and why it felt like the most appropriate one. As explained earlier, the book was initially envisioned as a much more humble contemporary equivalent of Walter Benjamin's *Arcades Project*, which would focus on the post-communist spaces of Central and Eastern Europe. As such, adopting a method similar to that of Benjamin seemed like the most intuitive thing to do. Benjamin's method(s) however are in many ways not straightforward. They are shaped on the one hand by a particularly difficult life trajectory and a love–hate relationship with established academia that saw Benjamin often marginalised as an intellectual, and on the other by access to a particular set of materials, largely within the Bibliothèque Nationale de Paris, and increased pressure to creatively mould this material in order to produce non-traditional yet money earning outputs – radio shows, short magazine essays, dictionary entries.

At the Bibliothèque Nationale, Benjamin discovered a series of volumes on the Topographie de Paris, which were organised as collages of images from the popular press – mainly caricatures – as well as famous first photographs of Paris. These volumes played a critical role in how Benjamin conceptualised his *Arcades Project*. They offered both a creative and highly effective layout using the technique of collage/montage, which allowed for interesting juxtapositions, as well as room for reflection with a light touch guiding hand yet without a strong prescribed sense of direction. These images complemented Benjamin's everyday encounters with Paris itself during his daily walks, his thinking on practices of flânerie, as well as his earlier philosophy of the relationship between text, material and history. The Bibliothèque Nationale provided a safe space for Benjamin to work, removed from the hustle and bustle of the city, yet still very much in the middle of it.

Although there is no contemporary equivalent to the Topographie de Paris that would apply to post-communist Central and Eastern Europe, the volumes represent a unique approach to the study of the city and its transformation over time, by focusing on not only some of its emblematic spaces, places and peoples, but also on how the city and its people, in their unprecedented boom, were 'captured' and 'seen' in the middle of these intense processes of change. Judith Wechsler argues that by recording aspects of everyday life that would otherwise go unrecorded, these images and caricatures were essential in transforming how one looked at the city – popularising the emblematic bird's eye view of the nineteenth century and panoramas as a form of distancing that encouraged reflection – as well as how one looked at its inhabitants – with caricatures becoming an important form of classification of character and morals (Wechsler 1982: 20).

What Benjamin recognised in these volumes is the clear emergence of a new way of 'seeing' that uniquely characterised the nineteenth century, and he went on to look for other creative ways of explaining not just how this new mode of perception emerged, but also, the kind of spaces and technologies that continued to shape it. In the process, he developed an interesting new theory of experience and perception which relied on the relationship between what he called Erfahrung – meaning between travelling and standing still; Erlebnis – between living and death; Empfindung – between finding and loss, and Gefühl – between feeling and touch (Elsaesser 2009: 293). The modern nineteenth-century city for him reflected both intense change and transformation – a whirlwind of 'progress' that pushed everyone into the future; as well as a place still very much impregnated with the past. Klee's drawing of Angelus Novus, which Benjamin purchased and kept in his possession throughout his life, most accurately evoked this contrast: the angel of history, with his face towards the past, is pulled backwards into the future, his wings immobilised by the strength of progress, his feet now barely touching the wreckage of the past which keeps piling up.

What does all of this tell us about Benjamin's 'method(s)'?

First and foremost, it presents us with a unique take on the concept of 'experience' and, in particular, the experience of change. Howard Caygill explains Benjamin's philosophical foundations of his concept of experience in light of a basic disagreement with Kant's two main assumptions: that there is a distinction between the subject and the object of experience, and that there can be no experience of the 'absolute' (Caygill 1998: 1). Going back to Benjamin's early writings on perception, fantasy and colour, Caygill argues that this disagreement is directly related to Benjamin's unique understanding of (historical) space and time as well as his unique understanding of origin, as addressed earlier:

> it is crucial for Benjamin's argument that space and time (Kant's forms of intuition) be regarded as modes of configuration whose plasticity, or openness to other forms of patterning, can 'decay' or be otherwise 'transformed'. Space and time which feature as the givens of transcendental philosophy become modes of configuration which can be understood speculatively as providing the contours of but one among many possible configurations of experience.
>
> (Caygill 1998: 5)

Space and time are thus not constant throughout history. In fact, they are the best 'reflectors' of historical change: with every great moment of change, our relationship to both our lived space as well as our perception of time changes. Benjamin's genius lies in his attempt to track precisely how this relationship changed throughout the nineteenth century by focusing on the lived space itself, the relationship to time in light of new technologies and new experiences, and the physical and psychological transformation of the subject: the stress of modern times as expressed through experiences of shock, the dreams of modern times as expressed in fashion and architecture. All of this, he found concentrated within the Parisian arcades: a microcosm that imitated and captured, perhaps better than anything else, the major transformations of the nineteenth century.

Benjamin's transition from philosophy to cultural history is increasingly felt in his essays following the rejection of his habilitation and partially inspired by his nomadic lifestyle while in exile in Paris and his travels to Italy and Russia. His fascination with the Paris Arcades, triggered most likely by the reading of Aragon's volume *Le Paysan de Paris*, marks Benjamin's increasing conviction that cultural history is one of the best ways to access and examine the concept of 'experience' and historical changes in our perception apparatus. Adopting a language significantly different from his previous, philosophical writings, Benjamin shifts gears only to the extent that he has found a different medium/methodology of examination. Cultural history and its relationship to the arts and aesthetic theory provides him with a series of new tools through which to reassess the relationship between experience and 'truth'.

The majority of these tools rely on the prioritising of the visual/image over text. Caygill tracks Benjamin's development of these tools back to his earlier essays on colour, where Benjamin argues that colour provides an important alternative to text and the graphic line on which written text relies. Unlike text, colour communicates itself rather than any kind of essence, its objectivity being related not to form but rather to a certain idea of 'pure seeing' which creates no object/subject separation – children for example, experience this kind of pure seeing (Caygill 1998: 84–85). Colour is for Benjamin not just paint on a canvas, but rather a material/physical element that shapes all of our external perception: from buildings, to printed images – such of photography and film – to nature. Just like words, colours and images help to organise experience, yet they do so intuitively as opposed to rationally. This is not to say that colour/images cannot be manipulated in a rational manner.

Benjamin's transition into cultural history and aesthetic theory should however not be viewed as a jump into another discipline. As Caygill well argues, his point of departure and main concern: the relationship between experience and truth, remains the same. Benjamin is as much of a philosopher as he was when writing about Kant. His methodology however has turned towards what he would label as the marginal:

> The eye for this marginal domain is for Benjamin characteristic of the 'new type of researcher' who seeks the meaning of a work not by inserting it within historical or formal narratives, but by examining the

disarticulations of form and content and thus uncovering the 'composition' or tracing the translation of what is exterior to the work into the medium of art.

(Caygill 1998: 91)

For Benjamin, most modern human creations fall into the medium of art: from architecture and city planning, to industry, technology, visual and material reproduction. The job of philosopher is thus similar to that of an art critic: untangling the relationship between the work of art, its medium and what lies exterior to it. Most importantly then, the philosopher's job is not to untangle historical text, but rather to immerse himself/herself into daily life, into the rhythm of the city as the modern centre of human activity, and into the nature and usage of modern objects/production. The philosopher gazes/ looks outwards to things as opposed to text/books alone. Unlike text, things are capable to return our gaze: 'Things perceive us; their gaze propels us into the future, since we do not respond to them but instead step among them' (Benjamin cited in Caygill 1998: 8).

Caygill argues that the examination of the work of art as human creation – Benjamin focuses mainly on architecture and fashion as two examples – develops in Benjamin along three separate dimensions:

The first regarded the work as a site for experimentation and the invention of new modes of experience while the second saw it as an occasion for tactile critical enjoyment by analogy with architecture; to these is now added the view that the work of art is a form of cathartic inoculation against the psychotic development of the energies generated by technology.

(Caygill 1998: 114)

These three dimensions capture the potential and relevance of Benjamin's unique methodology to how we interpret periods of intense change/transition today: 1) experimenting with/inquiring into the development of new modes of experience; 2) analysing the relationship between these new modes of experience and critical reflection/enjoyment; and 3) understanding the extent to which different works of art (broadly speaking) serve to reflect on and unpack/momentarily slow down the modern experience of shock as a result of intense change.

Tracking new modes of experience

Benjamin used a creative collecting and archiving system as his main work-method. This included experimenting with different writing styles, sorting and organising techniques, as well as a fascination for the material, texture and surface on/through which his work was laid out, such as particular types of paper, notebooks or pens. As Marx *et al.* explain:

Benjamin's mode of working is marked by the techniques of archiving, collecting, and constructing. Excerpts, transpositions, cuttings-out, montaging, sticking, cataloguing and sorting appear to him to be true activities of an author. His inspiration is inflamed by the richness of materials [...] Benjamin believes that [...] peculiar to the collector is a relationship to objects which does not emphasize their functional, utilitarian value – that is their usefulness – but studies and loves them as the scene, the stage of their fate.

(Marx *et al.* 2007: 4)

As a representative of the phenomenological tradition, Benjamin places much of his emphasis on 'things' and 'material objects' as opposed to 'human subjects'. Experience for him is a particular kind of interaction with the 'material' around us, and is not limited to the human subject alone. Objects and materials experience history alongside living beings, and carry within themselves stories that are otherwise erased and distorted in the human mind. Objects have a revelatory function: at the right time, under the right circumstances, the stories captured within these objects are revealed. Three of Benjamin's main concerns are thus: to explain the circumstances under which such stories become visible, the 'objects' that are more likely to reveal them and whether/how this visual experience should/can be translated into text. According to this, perhaps over-simplified account, Benjamin appears to be no different from an archaeologist. While his inspiration did partially come from his fascination with archaeology, Benjamin does however remain very much interested in the human subject, despite his overwhelming focus on objects. How, thus, are objects connected to the human subject?

Benjamin describes the relationship between the two as a form of double-watching/mutual observance: the human observes the object and vice-versa. The object becomes not only the material embodiment of human imagination and creation, but also of human destruction and hesitation. The object is thus the ultimate human 'text': history and the story of human 'progression' is written into the very creation, use and destruction of such objects. In his first major book-length manuscript, his habilitation, Benjamin chooses to examine objects that are placed within an 'allegorical' context: the theatre, and more importantly, a particular form of historical theatre: German tragic drama (Benjamin 1998 (originally 1963)). The 'objects' on the theatre stage are all evocative fragments of 'time': signalling in this case the transition from the sixteenth to the seventeenth century.

Benjamin goes on to argue that the fragmentary nature of theatre: through its different props, scenes, sets and characters, as well as through its ability to manipulate space/the scene in order to transgress time, creates an interesting model for understanding real-life architectures. In fact, his later, unfinished project on the Parisian Arcades, follows to a large extent his previously examined model of the German tragic theatre: the scene in this case is the city, and more specifically, the shopping arcades, and the characters are no longer actors but rather the city's inhabitants. Just like the theatre stage and its props became a way to re-enact, re-live and re-imagine sixteenth-century history, the Parisian arcades and their props, for Benjamin, play a similar role in remembering the nineteenth century.

In many ways thus, theatre props and shopping arcades become for Benjamin material 'essences' that capture, more so than other objects, a particular historical experience, a sense of 'truth', that can only be expressed 'visually' as opposed to 'textually'. These 'essences' are however much unlike Husserl's essences: they do not simply exist within 'things' themselves but are instead determined by direct changes in human perception apparatus. As humans are increasingly silenced by war, violence and shock, language is replaced by visuality and text by images. Objects become unlikely translators and bearers of historical memory. To arrive at these material 'essences', Benjamin does not follow the classical phenomenological method of 'bracketing'[1] as described and implemented by Husserl and his followers, but rather develops his own mechanism of selection: in his case the 'bracketing' is not an arbitrary choice to focus on a particular phenomenon/object, but rather intuitively imposed by the nature of historical/material transformation itself: the object reveals itself as essence (essential) through its ability to capture all of the classical historical planes: the past, the present and the future. An 'essential' object is thus one which breaks the human silence on a particular subject and expresses, through its very form, the 'stream of becoming and disappearance'.

If new modes of experience are ultimately linked to the emergence of key evocative 'things' and 'spaces' as well as the emergence of new modes of 'seeing' in direct relation to those 'things' and 'spaces', then the challenge for one who sets out to apply Benjamin's method(s) is to: 1) first figure out how to identify such 'things', 'spaces' and new modes of 'seeing'; and 2) decide how to engage with them. What Benjamin tells us is that these 'things' and 'spaces' reveal themselves to you through both your own direct experience as well as that of others, captured increasingly in images – photography, film, caricatures. There is no 'complete' list of things or spaces that one needs to exhaust in order to capture the emergence of a new mode of experience. Nor is there a 'correct' list of things: the choice is ultimately relative, yet needs to be evocative enough to speak to others as well.

The 'spaces' that he chooses are imbued with meaning, evoking a unique experience of time: most of them are in some form or another of decay, at odds with ideas of the 'modern', yet reminiscent of a past glory. For those familiar with the post-communist landscape, many of these spaces reveal themselves fairly easily: they represent the cornerstones of the communist experiment, the very symbols on which it was built – the former industrial platforms, the large housing complexes, the public squares, the commemorative monuments, the former houses of culture. Just like the decaying arcades of the nineteenth century, all of these spaces, although in decay, are for the most part still populated and inhabited. Caught in the midst of an intense transformation, many of them have undergone either superficial facelifts – such as painting of façades; or more radical re-constructive work – such as industrial complexes turned into museums or shopping malls.

Yet not all of Benjamin's spaces belong to the 'past': he is equally fascinated with the emergence of new spaces that symbolise the future, that pull people into a new world, just like the storm that pulls the angel of history in Klee's painting. For him, these spaces were the new movie theatres, the street with its motorcars and hustle and bustle, the world fairs. In the post-communist environment, the future is often confused with symbols of the 'west' and spaces that seek to bring the 'west' in. Not surprisingly, these are often represented by spaces such as: shopping malls, new housing complexes and gated communities, new office spaces, colourful publicity panels and airports as gateways to the 'west'.

Each of these spaces, whether old or new, is for the most part experienced in two different modes: direct exposure, most often by walking through these spaces as well as through different forms of street performances and theatre; and indirect exposure through different modes of representation – most often television and film, but also photography and other forms of visual art. The 'new modes of perception' engendered by post-communism are on the one hand a result of a significantly increased and diversified exposure to the technology of television and film, which served to create a new sense of nationhood, with television becoming the most important source of information throughout the 'reform' process, and to provide an essential escape mechanism through the airing of Western shows; and on the other a result of an increasingly divided way of experiencing change, with some stuck in environments that showed little if any change – mainly rural areas and small industrial cities, but also increasingly impoverished areas of larger cities – while others experienced radical change – capital cities, city centres, new financial centres.

Each of the chapters that follow seeks to creatively engage with some of the most emblematic of these spaces and the new modes of perception through which they are experienced. Change, for Benjamin is thus not a factor of a clearly measurable time, with historical moments that have a set start and end date. An interpretation of the experience of the 'transition' to capitalism, although often addressed in terms of set periods of time: 5 years, 10 years, 20 years, 25 years after, is, if one were to use Benjaminian lenses, less about specific segments of time, and more about the 'things' that come into appearance and the 'things' that disappear. The process of change is thus measured less in time and more in palpable, perceptible things and material transformations.

Experiencing and reflecting upon change

Benjamin is above all fascinated by processes of change, which he seeks to understand differently from the traditional historicism of his time: for him, history does not progress along a clearly marked temporal line, but rather unfolds rhythmically in a constant ebb and flow that links the past, present and future. To analyse change, Benjamin does not rely on the identification of 'key moments' or the bracketing of particular time periods, but rather on the 'process of becoming and disappearance' as marked in his carefully chosen objects of study. Just like tragic drama becomes emblematic of changes occurring at the end of the sixteenth century in Germany, the Parisian arcades become emblematic of nineteenth-century France. The process of becoming and disappearance is marked not temporally but physically and spatially: it is the object that comes into being and physically disappears, leaving behind ruins, memories and 'wish-worlds' for the future. Benjamin's notion of change and history cannot be disconnected from his understanding of the concept of origin, which is:

> not intended to describe the process by which the existent came into being, but rather to describe that which emerges in the process of becoming and disappearance. Origin is an eddy in the stream of becoming, and in its rhythmic movement it swallows the material involved in the process of genesis.
>
> (Benjamin cited in Caygill 1998: 57–58.)

If one accepts this particular understanding of origin and history, then the study of change no longer relies on carefully identified key temporal moments (revolutions, coups, wars), but rather on the way in which these moments have been physically marked into our surrounding environment: change has to be visible in order to be internalised, just like it has to be understood and inter- preted in order to be acted upon. A mere declaration of change, such as 'we are now independent!' or 'our country is at war' or 'the economy is experiencing its sharpest downfall since 1929' is not enough to mark that moment as sig- nificant in history. In fact, Benjamin seems to suggest that not only can we not identify change until it is exhibited physically, materially and spatially, but also that we cannot understand it, until the process leads to the physical/ material/spatial and perhaps also visual destruction of what lay there before. The material melange of the city and the arcades, in particular, provides Benjamin with a visual expression of history's ebb and flow: the recent ruin marks not only the moment of disappearance but also that of becoming. Stripped bare, a building unveils the very process of its construction, its bat- tered existence and faded glory at the moment of decline. Stripped bare, a building also unveils the dreams that supported it before its structure even existed, the 'wish-worlds' it has helped create and the models it provided for the future.

As Katherine Arens nicely explains, Benjamin seeks to identify precisely those 'centres around which all other period understandings of that city are organized, within that era's economic rationales' (Arens 2007: 48). Change is concentrated in the image and materiality of the city, to the extent that key centres of the city, such as arcades, are able to preserve within their own physical transformation both the economic as well as the social and political rationales of a particular time. Uncovering these rationales through an examination of the material body of the city becomes Benjamin's challenge and method.

This intricate relationship between change and materiality/visuality creates a number of different opportunities for both positive and negative manipulation of change (and its interpretation), but more importantly, an opportunity for understanding the extent to which the present as well as the future rely on our ability to visually/physically recognise them as such. This detaches ideas of the past, present and future from clearly determined temporal moments and instead, attaches them to individual (and collective) processes of perception and recognisability: the past is the past to the extent that we recognise it a such and the same goes for the present and the future: 'every present day is determined by the images that are synchronic with it: each "now" is the now of a particular recognisability' (Benjamin quoted in Arens 2007: 51) This implies that change is ultimately a moment of change in perception that is triggered both by a material/visual reflection of change as well as by an individual and collective 'perceptual' adjustment to that change: what we until recently recognised as the present, we now recognise as the past, and what we until recently thought of as the future, we now think of as the present.

Each chapter in the book seeks in its own way to address this idea of a collective adjustment to change, and how different collectives experiencing different degrees of marginality are able to utilise creative means to make sense of the process of change. Many of these collectives are organised or shaped by interventions that often come from a generation whose senses have come to maturity largely in the post-communist period: the New Wave across central and eastern European film – all led by a series of young directors; a museumisation and preservation movement that sees communist patrimony, such as old industrial plants and platforms, as valuable beyond their reinvestment value – also largely led by student movements from architecture and humanities schools; an urban regeneration movement that seeks to recover public spaces from an aggressive commercialisation and privatisation process that has taken over most cities – for the most part led by young architects and public sector workers; as well as a coalition of younger as well as more established photographers and documentary directors who are beginning to address issues related to different forms of marginalisation, including the prevalent issues of ethnic based marginalisation of Roma groups.

Thinking about change through images/works of art

Perception and visuality play a key role in Benjamin's work and influence his unique methodology in at least two different ways: 1) the object of study is often a material/visual object as opposed to text; and 2) Benjamin's reflection on this material/visual object of study seeks to take a form that is significantly different from traditional 'philosophical text'. For Benjamin images/visuality become text. Understanding images in light of the initial Greek meaning of the word: likeness, similitude, resemblance, as opposed to its contemporary meaning of representation (Weigel 1996: 20), Benjamin develops an intricate system of classification and interpretation of images that relies on a number of important concepts including that of 'thought-image', 'wish-image' and 'dialectical image'.

Thought-images are the process by which the 'now' is translated and becomes interpretable/readable 'text'. Differentiating between images and text, Benjamin suggests that thought-images are more primal than language: they undergo a different mental translation process by which images are automatically transformed into an 'idea' or a 'thought' that need not necessarily have a linguistic/textual expression. Thought-images are thus not the verbalised thoughts triggered by a particular site, but rather individual 'world images' that form an individual's instinctive opinion of the present or what he/she sees. Thought-images lie at the basis of Benjamin's attempt to transcribe and discuss these images in a formal, written form that escapes the normal conventions of 'philosophising'. Suggesting that thought-images follow a similarly fractured and collage-like format to that of the actual process of seeing itself, Benjamin seeks to transcribe them into his own version of textual collage that makes use of citations, different writing styles, photographs and calligraphy in order to express breaks, changes in vantage points and temporal jumps.

Unlike thought-images, wish-images are both a mental as well as a visual/physical expression of individual and collective desires (or manipulation of those desires). According to Benjamin, wish-images:

> are images in the collective consciousness in which the old and the new interpenetrate [...] in them the collective seeks both to overcome and to transfigure the immaturity of the social product and the inadequacies in the social organization of production [...] what emerges in these wish images is the resolute effort to distance oneself from all that is antiquated – which includes however the recent past.
>
> (Benjamin 1999: 4)

Fashion and architecture are for Benjamin two important domains in which wish-images become particularly visible (Weigel 1996: x). Fashion, which Benjamin describes as the tiger's leap into the past, is also the tiger's leap into the future. Both fashion and architecture become mechanisms of creative material entrapment: through them and their imitation of our bodies, we explore our inner physical and mental desires and in turn, express them outwardly/materially through new fashion/architecture (Weigel 1996: 19). Weigel thus argues that the city, fashion, interiors, objects, architectures, are for Benjamin the dream-writing of the collective (Weigel 1996: 35).

All images are dialectical according to Benjamin, who argues that: 'image is dialectics at a standstill. While the relation of the present to the past is a purely temporal, continuous one, the relation of what-has-been to the now is dialectical: it is not progression but image, suddenly emergent' (Benjamin cited in Schwartz 2000), they only arrive at readability at a particular point in time (Weigel 1996: 109). Judging from his own choice of dialectical images to examine, it seems that this particular moment is more often than not the moment of ruin, destruction and disappearance (or push into the marginal domain). The 'reader' of dialectal images is however not just any person: he/she is generally a marginal figure himself/herself: the child, the flâneur, the homeless, the whore. Marginalised by society, and text, these characters appear as unlikely readers/translators of 'now-time'. The choice for the marginal character seems to be imposed by Benjamin's desire to write 'text' differently: not only through unusual 'images' but also through unusual 'eyes'. For him, traditional text reflects not only the limitations of language but also of the person writing. Writing in images seeks to forgo the need to translate into language the untranslatable as well as the tendency to privilege a particular writer/seer.

By arguing that thoughts and ideas, as expressed through language are nothing but organisational devices, Benjamin places the possibility of attaining 'truth' clearly outside of language and text and instead, within the revelatory potential of the material world/objects. This radically shifts not only the role of social sciences in general, but also the role of the intellectual/researcher, from that of a writer that seeks 'truth' to that of a collector/critic that unintentionally stumbles upon 'truth'.

The condition of 'transition' widens the scope of marginality significantly, to include large sections of the population as unlikely readers/translators of 'now-time'. The immediate surrounding environment along with the changes that it undergoes becomes deeply imbued with both 'thought-images' and 'wish-images' which, more often than not, reveal themselves through 'aesthetic' interventions that manage to, at least temporarily, slow down the pace of change by creating a space where certain key aspects of change can be absorbed and reflected upon.

These interventions can be as simple as painting the city's facades, or as complex as repurposing/reclaiming abandoned symbolic buildings and spaces, photographing marginalised spaces and exhibiting them both locally as well as internationally, re-staging key historical moments through film and theatre and imagining different scenarios, interrupting the fast flow of traffic through street performances that reflect on changing/dying traditions and force the eye to focus on unlikely spaces/things/images. This book offers a collage of such interventions seeking to arrange them into a kaleidoscope of ideas and themes that can be recombined through a simple turn of the eye.

Where does this sit within the broader literature on world politics, popular culture, and the 'aesthetic' turn?

The aesthetic turn in IR has now turned almost 15, since its official proclamation by Roland Bleiker in a December 2001 article in the *Millennium* journal (Bleiker 2001a). The turn has led to a series of interesting debates on the relationship between art and politics (Bleiker 2001b); the role of the image (Lisle 2011), photography and film in war (Der Derian 2001); the impact of new technologies of seeing on practices of surveillance (Wise 2004), security, gender and more broadly, our experience of space and time (Moore and Shepherd 2010); the relationship between popular culture and politics (Grayson, Davies and Simon 2009); the relationship between literature, poetry, cinema and politics (Holden 2003, 2010); the examination of the everyday (Davies 2008), the aesthetics of the 2008 financial crisis (Davies 2012). It has also triggered an intellectual return to the philosophy of Kant through a re-examination of his concept of the sublime (Shapiro 2006), Gadamer and hermeneutics (Moore 2006), Walter Benjamin and methodology (Pusca 2009), amongst others.

Instead of coagulating into a unified movement, the aesthetic turn has instead splintered into a number of related initiatives with their own disciplinary and methodological concerns, including: a movement focusing on the wider relationship between popular culture and world politics, a new materialist turn (Salter 2015), and a wider critical methodological turn (Aradau and Huysmans 2014). What each of these 'turns' have in common however is: 1) an interest in going beyond the usual 'objects' of study – such as states, institutions, transnational movements, world leaders – within IR, and finding new ways of looking at the 'international' through other 'things' – images of different kinds, architecture, borders, weapons – and through other 'acts' – art performances, new ways of 'looking and seeing', getting across borders; 2) a desire to expand the ways in which the 'international' can be analysed, by acknowledging that 'methods [are] performative rather than representational' (Aradau and Huysmans 2014: 598) and as such directly involved in construing and promoting different forms of political life; and 3) a critical attitude towards positivism in its different forms.

This 'splintering' of the aesthetic turn has perhaps a lot to do with the very concept of 'aesthetics' and the hesitation of many scholars to be subsumed under it: with a rich philosophical tradition and a wide-spread interdisciplinary appeal, the concept of 'aesthetics' has lost much of its initial significance and been imbued with a number of separate projects and interests depending on the discipline and place in which it emerges. The inherent difficulty in 'controlling' or 'taming down' this plurality of meanings as well as in attaching yet another unique meaning to the term, often puts disciplinary dependent scholars off making the concept of 'aesthetics' central to their work. It is not surprising that the intellectuals who feel most at ease using the term often come from academic/intellectual environments that have rich traditions of inter-disciplinarity and a direct connection to the philosophical traditions that gave birth to the modern use of the concept in the first place.

Yet unlike concepts such as 'materialism', 'popular culture', 'the sublime', the 'everyday' or even 'art', the concept of 'aesthetics' affords much richer possibilities for analysis, precisely because of its multiple historical/philosophical/political connotations: it allows, first and foremost, for an inter-disciplinary opening that is not afraid of examining the political implications of 'aesthetics' beyond the traditional sites of international politics – wars, borders, armies, governments – as well as for a re-conceptualisation of practices of political representation which have been so central to our disciplinary understanding of both politics as well as methodology and methods. By bringing the 'senses' back into the discussion, and along with them the inherent subjectivity of all forms of perception and representation – and of course analysis, the concept of 'aesthetics' seems particularly relevant now, in a hyper-mediated world where interactions with the 'international' are increasingly 'virtual' and where most forms of representation are filtered through technologies that in one way or another manipulate the senses.

Engaging with the concept of 'aesthetics' does not necessarily require a wider theory of international/political aesthetics or a single justification for new objects of study, and the relationship between aesthetic theory and the aesthetisation of politics. Nor does it require the development of a single methodology or a single systematic explanation of its impact. Aesthetics is a way of knowing, that can be systematically applied, although not necessarily in the same shape or form, and certainly not in a prescriptive way. As Wechsler explains in her seminal book *On Aesthetics in Science*, aesthetic considerations necessarily affect the form, development and efficacy of models, with aesthetic considerations often acting 'as a kind of intuition in the sciences' (Wechsler 1978: 3). She goes on to argue that 'viewed as a way of knowing, aesthetics in science is concerned with the metaphorical and analogical relationship between reality and concepts, theories and models' (Wechsler 1978: 6). As such, while an analysis that takes into account aesthetic considerations can certainly be systematic in form, the concept of 'aesthetics' in itself cannot prescribe precisely what that form should be. It will however, in most likelihood, include some engagement with practices of representation, the limits of perception and the politics of (en)framing.

The concept of aesthetics, like very few others, encapsulates both ends of the representation process – the subject and the object of representation, as well as the wider processes of (en)framing perception which have significant implications for our understanding of (the politics of) knowledge. It offers a creative avenue for thinking about political ideologies (Buck-Morss 2000), the passing of mass utopia and the future of nostalgia (Boym 2001), the politics of knowledge and class (Rancière 1989, 2004, 2009), the creation of stereotypes and prejudice (Wechsler 1982), art and power (Groys 2013) to name just a few. Each of these interventions constructs its own framework through which to employ the concept of aesthetics and understand its political implications. This book follows in this tradition, seeking to build a unique framework through which to understand the experience of the post-communist transition and some of the playful, creative, but also painful interventions that allowed for the emergence of critical reflective spaces, temporarily pausing the rush of change in order to question both its 'origin' and 'destination'.

While ultimately a book about a particular experience of change, as the title suggests, it is also a defence of the relevance and importance of the concept of 'aesthetics' in (international) politics. As our discipline appears to have quickly shied away from the concept shortly after finding/recovering it, this is an attempt to bring it back in. At a time when other disciplines are increasingly engaged with exploring the contemporary political angle of aesthetics, from philosophy (Carter 2007), art history (Cascardi 2007) and design (Hekkert 2006) to sociology (de la Fuente 2000), communications (Kang 2010) and cultural studies (Perniola 2007), sparking a series of interesting cross-disciplinary and methodological debates, perhaps it is time that we jump back in without fearing the use of the concept of 'aesthetics'.

As a majority of these interdisciplinary debates suggest, aesthetics and aesthetic theory no longer narrowly refer to a classic understanding of art, but rather to an increased politicisation of aesthetics and art. This politicisation occurs on a number of different terrains, from the use of images and art for political mobilisation and ideological purposes, to the inevitable political effects of increased mediatisation and the creative use of different forms of media to engage with both highly charged 'political'/historical moments as well as the seemingly less pressing politics of the 'everyday'. With forms of political participation and engagement increasingly shifting towards the creative domain – online movements, activism based concerts, art gatherings and sit-ins, street performances and pop-up demonstrations, to name a few – it is perhaps time we shift our attention as well.

The discipline has come a long way in recognising that 'the international' does not only reside in the classically acknowledged sites of the state, borders, security, war and international organisations. As such, aesthetic interventions within IR need to also go beyond these sites. Kyle Grayson voiced a similar frustration when it comes to the relatively narrow use of culture within popular culture interventions in IR and urged authors to 'ask very different questions about what politics is, what it does, and where it is located', to 'identify the particularities of politics' instead of relying on de-historicised assumptions about what concepts such as popular culture mean, to go beyond the most popularly examined ways of (en)framing – photography and film (Kyle 2015). I could not have put it better myself, except that I would add that all this applies to aesthetic interventions in IR as well.

Aesthetics here, should not be understood as a subset of (popular) culture, but rather as an important complement to it. While culture refers to the processes of forming a collective bond and the practices that both maintain and erode it, aesthetics is generally concerned with questions of (mis)perception, how 'reality' gets translated into different forms of 'knowledge', and what are some of the different mechanisms of (en)framing that directly affect perception – from class, to technology, to limits of the senses, to processes of normalisation, or repression. The two are certainly connected, but tend to prioritise different things: (popular) culture presumably prioritises the idea of the 'collective' and its 'bond', while aesthetics prioritises questions of 'perception' and its implications. Together, they offer a series of creative opportunities for analysing collective politics today.

This book prioritises a particular form of perception – seeing – and as such makes a particular aesthetic intervention. Within the act of seeing, the subject–object relationship in perception is not as clearly set as some may believe. Seeing is infinitely more complicated than its physical/biological explanation. 'Seeing is metamorphosis not mechanism' (Elkins 1996: 12). The study of perception then cannot rely on any prescriptive formula of the study of the subject/object relationship, but rather needs to focus on precisely this 'metamorphosis': when, how, why does it occur, and how does it become relevant to international collectives and processes? As Elkins' title suggests, the 'seer' is not always human: objects are also imbued with a sense of humanity, an ability to stare back, they 'speak' by invoking certain times, spaces, events or personalities.

The blurriness of the subject–object relationship need not necessarily affect the clarity of sites, processes and techniques through which one can 'see things differently'. These generally mark points of radical turn, transition or transformation in perception that have a significant impact on our ability to understand the world: such as the invention of the novel, the poster and publicity, photography, film, the rise in surveillance, the emergence of the internet, the rise of social media, the decline of newspapers, the use of embedded journalists, the ability to trace and capture violence and war in images, the juxtaposition of different realities in the same space through cable TV/publicity, the rise of virtually policed borders, and the list goes on.

Methodologically speaking, what this books tries to do is: 1) offer a unique perspective on the relationship between perception, politics and power within a particular historical and spatial context: post-communist Central and Eastern Europe; 2) focus on the sites, processes and techniques that point to changes in perception that lead to significant changes in how we understand the post-communist transition; 3) investigate how these sites, processes and techniques affect a subject/object relationship that is never clear cut; 4) make explicit/visible things that are not otherwise visible in a collective whose perception mechanism has been carefully framed in terms of focus, intensity and interpretation; 5) find creative ways to enact particular experiences of perception that do not necessarily rely on the written text.

I have perhaps said enough about what this book is going to do. It is time to let it speak for itself. Let's turn the page.

Note

1 Gearing compares Husserl's methodology of bracketing to the process of bracketing in mathematics: 'Bracketing, as in a mathematical equation, suspends certain components by placing them outside the brackets, which then facilitates a focusing in on the phenomenon within the brackets' (Gearing 2004: 1430). For Husserl thus the method of bracketing was one by which one was able to suspend all previous knowledge and preconceptions in order to focus in on the 'essences', separating in a way consciousness from the world and helping to create a 'reflective stance' (LeVasseur 2003: 411–413).

Bibliography

Aradau, Claudia and Jef Huysmans. 2014. 'Critical Methods in International Relations: The Politics of Techniques, Devices and Acts'. *European Journal of International Relations* 20(3): 596–619.

Arens, Katherine. 2007. 'Stadtwollen: Benjamin's Arcades Project and the Problem of Method'. *PMLA: Publication of the Modern Languages Association of America* 122(1): 43–60.

Benjamin, Walter. 1968. 'Theses on History'. In *Illuminations*, edited by H. Arendt. New York: Schocken Books.

Benjamin, Walter. 1998. *The Origin of German Tragic Drama*. London, New York: Verso.

Benjamin, Walter. 1999 (1982). *The Arcades Project*. Cambridge, MA: Belknap Press of Harvard University Press.

Bleiker, Roland. 2001a. 'The Aesthetic Turn in International Political Theory'. *Millennium: Journal of International Studies* 30(3): 509–533.

Bleiker, Roland. 2001b. 'The Politics of Visual Art'. *Social Alternatives* 20(4): 3–9.

Boym, Svetlana. 2001. *The Future of Nostalgia*. New York: Basic Books.

Buck-Morss, Susan. 2000. *Dreamworld and Catastrophe: The Passing of Mass Utopia in East and West*. Cambridge: MIT Press.

Carter, Curtis. 2007. 'Aesthetics into the Twenty-first Century'. *Filozofski Verstnik* 28(2): 67–81.

Cascardi, Anthony J. 2007. 'The Implication of Images in the Revival of Aesthetics'. *Filozofski Verstnik* 28(2): 167–182.

Caygill, Howard. 1998. *Walter Benjamin: The Colour of Experience*. London and New York: Routledge.

Davies, Matthew and Michael Niemann. 2008. *International Relations and Everyday Life*. New York and London: Routledge.

Davies, Matt. 2012. 'The Aesthetics of the Financial Crisis: Work, Culture, and Politics'. *Alternatives: Global, Local, Political* 37(4): 317–330.

de la Fuente, Eduardo. 2000. 'Sociology and Aesthetics'. *European Journal of Social Theory* 3(2): 235–247.

Der Derian, James. 2001. *Virtous War: Mapping the Military-Industrial-Media-Entertainment Network*. Boulder, US and Oxford, UK: Westview Press.

Elkins, James. 1996. *The Object Stares Back: On the Nature of Seeing*. New York: Simon and Schuster Inc.

Elsaesser, Thomas. 2009. 'Between Erlebnis and Erfahrung: Cinema Experience with Benjamin'. *Paragraph* 32(3): 292–312.

Foucault, Michel. 1967. 'Of Other Spaces, Heterotopias'. Available online at: http://foucault.info/documents/heteroTopia/foucault.heteroTopia.en.html. Accessed July 2015.

Gearing, Robin E. 2004. 'Bracketing in Research: A Typology'. *Qualitative Health Research* 14(10): 1429–1452.

Grayson, Kyle, MattDavies and Simon Philpott. 2009. 'Pop Goes IR? Researching the Popular Culture – World Politics Continuum'. *Politics* 29(3): 155–163.

Grayson, Kyle. 2015. 'Title'. *The Rise of Popular Culture in IR: Three Issues*, 30 January. http://www.e-ir.info/2015/01/30/the-rise-of-popular-culture-in-ir-three-issues/.

Groys, Boris. 2013. *Art Power*. Cambridge, MA: MIT Press.

Hekkert, Paul. 2006. 'Design Aesthetics: Principles of Pleasure in Design'. *Psychology Science* 2: 157–172.

Holden, Gerard. 2003. 'World Literature and World Politics: In Search of a Research Agenda'. *Global Society* 17(3): 229–252.

Holden, Gerard. 2010. 'World Politics, World Literature, World Cinema'. *Global Society* 24(3): 381–400.

Huggins Balfe, Judith. 1987. 'Artworks as Symbols in International Politics'. *International Journal of Politics, Culture and Society* 1(2): 195–217.

Jackson, Patrick Thaddeus. 2010. *The Conduct of Inquiry in International Relations: Philosophy of Science and Its Implications for the Study of World Politics.* London and New York: Routledge.

Kang, Jaeho. 2010. 'The Media and the Crisis of Democracy: Rethinking Aesthetic Politics'. *Theoria* 57(124): 1–22.

Kangas, Anni. 2009. 'From Interfaces to Interpretants: A Pragmatist Exploration into Popular Culture as International Relations'. *Millennium: Journal of International Studies* 38(2): 317–343.

Lee, Christopher. 2014. 'Globality and Aesthetics'. *Third Text* 28(1): 32–45.

LeVasseur, Jeanne J. 2003. 'The Problem of Bracketing in Phenomenology'. *Qualitative Health Research* 13(3): 408–420.

Lisle, Debbie. 2011. 'The Surprising Detritus of Leisure: Encountering the Late Photography of War'. *Environment and Planning D: Society and Space* 29(5): 873–890.

Marx, Ursula, GudrunSchwartz, MichaelSchwartz and Erdmut Wizisla. (eds) 2007. *Walter Benjamin's Archive: Images, Texts, Signs.* Trans. E. Leslie. London and New York: Verso.

Moore, Cerwyn. 2006. 'Reading the Hermeneutics of Violence: The Literary Turn and Chechnya'. *Global Society* 20(2): 179–198.

Moore, Cerwyn and Laura J. Shepherd. 2010. 'Aesthetics and International Relations: Towards a Global Politics'. *Global Society* 24(3): 299–309.

Perniola, Mario. 2007. 'Cultural Turns in Aesthetics and Anti-Aesthetics'. *Filozofski Vestnik* 28(2): 39–51.

Petts, Jeffrey. 2012. 'Review Article: The Necessity of Art'. *Historical Materialism* 20(2): 195–209.

Pusca, Anca. 2009. 'Walter Benjamin: A Methodological Contribution'. *International Political Sociology* 3(2): 238–254.

Rancière, Jacques. 1989. *The Nights of Labor: The Worker's Dream in 19th Century France.* Philadelphia: Temple University Press.

Rancière, Jacques. 2004. *The Politics of Aesthetics: The Distribution of the Sensible.* London and New York: Continuum.

Rancière, Jacques. 2009. 'The Aesthetic Dimension: Aesthetics, Politics, Knowledge'. *Critical Inquiry* 36(1): 1–19.

Salter, Mark. 2015. *Making Things International 1: Circuits and Motion.* Minneapolis: University of Minnesota Press.

Schwartz, Vanessa R. 2000. 'Walter Benjamin for Historians'. *The American Historical Review* 106(5): 1721–1743.

Seal, Bobby. 2013. 'Title'. *Baudelaire, Benjamin and the Birth of the Flâneur*, 31 March. Available online at: http://psychogeographicreview.com/baudelaire-benjamin-and-the-birth-of-the-flaneur/. Accessed July 2015.

Shapiro, Michael J. 2006. 'The Sublime Today: Re-partitioning the Global Sensible'. *Millennium: Journal of International Studies* 34(3): 657–681.

Wechsler, Judith. 1978. *On Aesthetics in Science.* Cambridge, MA and London, UK: MIT Press.

Wechsler, Judith. 1982. *A Human Comedy: Physiognomy and Caricature in 19th Century Paris*. Chicago and London: University of Chicago Press.

Weigel, Sigrid. 1996. *Body and Image Space: Re-reading Walter Benjamin*. London: Routledge.

Weigel, Sigrid. 2009. 'On the "Topographical Turn": Concepts of Space in Cultural Studies and Kulturwissenschaften. A Cartographic Feud'. *European Review* 17(1): 187–201.

Wise, J. Macgregor 2004. 'An Immense and Unexpected Field of Action: Webcams, Surveillance and Everyday Life'. *Cultural Studies* 18(2–3): 424–442.

2 Restaging the 1989 revolution

Television, film, and public spaces

Introduction

This chapter looks at how the 1989 Romanian revolution has been re-staged in a number of different spaces: from the television screen, to the cinema screen, the street – through monuments and street performances, as well as the theatre stage, and the extent to which these different re-stagings have managed to open up new spaces of reflection, reposition participants in the revolution, and engage the wider public, in particular the so-called millenial generation for whom communism appears as a distant memory. By examining each of these different spaces, the technologies behind them, and the key timing of these re-stagings, the chapter seeks to offer an alternative view of the 1989 revolution as much more than a single 'violent' moment that clearly marks the end of communism and the beginning of the transition to capitalism: instead, the chapter suggests that the revolution continues in many ways to unfold through its ongoing re-stagings, each of which opens up new opportunities for reflection on the past, present and future, and creates important 'heteropic' spaces through which the moment(s) of change can be interogated.

The re-stagings are organised both temporally as well as spatially: starting with a discussion of the first 'Televised Revolution' as a unique example of a revolutionary moment where the live televised footage of the revolution, a re-staging in effect, becomes the 'revolution' itself – the 'authenticity' of the re-staging being sealed by the live capturing of the Ceausescu's trial and execution; this is followed by an engagement with the first post-revolutionary re-stagings in the shape of street performances by local artists and alternative documentaries which seek to create alternatives to the official footage of the revolution, all taking place in the early 1990s; next comes a detailed examination of a more recent set of re-stagings through popular films and the rise of the Romanian New Wave, which offer a much more critical engagement with the revolutionary moment and the kind of political, social and economic realities that it created; last but not least comes an examination of the rise of a Theatre New Wave which offers new avenues for engaging with the communist past, the moment of change and post-revolutionary realities, particularly for younger audiences who increasingly only witness the past through uncritical mediatic re-stagings, as well as the rise of a new 'monumental' culture which serves not so much to commemorate and celebrate the revolutionary moment as to use its powerful symbolic appeal for political purposes.

The contested spaces of the 'first televised revolution': the screen versus the street

Romania's televised revolution created an interesting precedent to the way in which revolutions are increasingly experienced today: live, on television and more recently, online. 'Live-streamed' revolutions have a distinct character in that they bring together very different audiences and spaces at once: the pro- testers in the square, the public behind the television or other live-streaming devices, and the (citizen) journalists who mediate the transmission. They also create a unique recording on the revolution that often sets the tone for a particular kind of historical narrative and timeline. Televised revolutions, like the Romanian revolution, become important historical agents, with the power to 'affect change, translate or distort mediated acts or meanings' (Latour cited in Mustata 2011: 77). The 'televised' revolution becomes the first 'staging' of the revolution: the camera directs our attention to specific spaces and people, zooms in and out at key moments in time, captures sound, while the studios or people behind it decide how to edit the footage, which characters to introduce next to which images, and which 'revolutionaries' to emphasise.

Dana Mustata argues that the Romanian televised revolution was a unique historical agent because of its localisation, naturalisation and figuration: 1) at the time of the revolution, Romanian TV was strategically located to negotiate rising tensions between Ceausescu, the people and Securitatea throughout the 1980s, representing the 'climax of a decade-long process in which television audiences rebelled against Ceausescu' (Mustata 2011: 78); 2) television was naturalised as the main medium of the revolution by the failed broadcast which marked the beginning of the revolution and 'inscribed a myth of liveness into the subsequent televising of the Romanian revolution' (Mustata 2011: 86); and 3) while live television appeared as the visible embodiment of the revolution and in many instances was equated with the revolution itself, it was in fact 'merely a figuration of change' (Mustata 2011: 90). The first 'staging' of the Romanian revolution on television has thus often been confused with 'revolution itself'.

While all revolutions suffer to a certain extent from misrepresentation(s), the first staging of the Romanian revolution was so effective that it instantly transformed audiences into revolutionaries, creating the illusion that all those sitting in front of their television sets were active participants in the process of change, whether they joined the crowds in main public squares or not. The television in fact afforded better 'views' for those sitting in their living rooms: they could follow the events unfold across the country, they could be intro- duced to close-ups of the new revolutionary leaders, they could see the crowd from vantage points that would not be possible while sitting in the crowd, and more importantly, they could take part in key events, such as the Ceausescu trial, as if sitting in front row seats. After a decade of limited television access, with only two hours of television per day during the week and four to five hours during the weekend, the constant live broadcast of the Romanian revolution was soaked up by thirsty audiences.

Bombarded with information and shocked by the rate at which change was occurring, Romanians watched incredulously how shots were fired into the protesting crowds, the tanks rolled into the main cities, the images of the dead collected in hospital morgues, the Ceausescus' trial, the firing squad and the close-ups of the dead leaders, the rise of new leaders and the first discussions of the transition to 'democracy' and what that would entail. Unsure whether to trust what they were seeing on the television, they reached out to family and friends, often equally confused. Trying to confirm whether what they saw on the television was real or not, some people joined the crowds in the street. The street became the complement to the television set. One city however experienced things differently: Timisoara was the first city to experience street protests days before the televised revolution began.

Here the revolution unfolded differently: a small protest in front of the house of a known Hungarian priest recently placed under house arrest for inciting change, ballooned into a larger protest joined by workers from local industrial platforms and students demanding reform. Their march across the city towards the offices of local representatives and then the main city square, in front of the national theatre, drew in more participants. The cameras, aside from individual photo cameras, were largely absent from these protests, and the nature of the event was highly localised: the main 'stage' was the open balcony in the national theatre facing the square. The main actors emerged organically from the crowd, forming an initial leadership group that gathered in the national theatre, addressed the crowd from the balcony asking for ideas for reform to bring to local party representatives for negotiation, and managed a creative system of idea notes which were passed on from the crowd, organised and selected for the creation of an official demands document. In its early form, this document was simply asking for the restauration of earlier rights and an ease of the strict travel restrictions along the lines of what locals knew was happening in nearby Yugoslavia and Hungary.

The Timisoara revolution marks an alternative space to the 'televised revolution' that started in Bucharest: if 'the Live Romanian Revolution served to transform televised representations into social realities, concealing the actors that determined the political change and the nature of their agencies' (Mustata 2011: 94), the Timisoara revolution had no preconceived agenda and leaders and relied on the physical space of the main square and the national theatre balcony to bring about change. Unable to see the Timisoara revolution on their screens, people had to join the crowds to know what was happening. The leaders of the Timisoara revolution were able to negotiate with the local party representatives envisioning a much less radical sense of change: they were asking for a reform of the current system as opposed to a change in the system, focusing much more on the individualised, local needs of the workers, students and intellectuals who were part of the movement.

With Timisoara located at the opposite end of the country, about as far away from the official locus of power in Bucharest, and much closer to the border with Yugoslavia and Hungary, the revolution there had a very unique local character. While the two revolutions are often seen as inherently connected, with the Bucharest revolution building on the Timisoara revolution – what many call the 'stolen revolution' or the 'aborted revolution', the two could not be more distinct: Romania experienced in fact at least two revolutions – one may argue that each of the major cities experienced its own version of the revolution – only one of which captured the imaginary of the entire country and led to a significant power shift. Despite its much more humble reform character, the Timisoara revolution was in many respects the only 'democratic' revolution that Romania experienced. The 'televised revolution' however, through its expanded reach, managed to capture the imagination of the entire country and helped normalise not only the new power actors that were introduced, but also, and perhaps more importantly, a specific idea of 'change'.

If the Timisoara revolutionaries were asking for a much softer version of change, the televised revolution normalised radical, often violent change: by exaggerating the regime's violent response to the revolution and the role of the special Securitate forces in shooting at the demonstrators, the leaders of the televised revolution justified the ultimate act upon which change was supposedly predicated: the violent killing of Nicolae and Elena Ceausescu after a short televised trial, the legitimacy of which was later questioned by most of those who saw it. The 'televised trial' was the necessary precursor to the act that would ultimately not only justify change but also set the country on a very specific path to change: one in which the figure of the ultimately oppressive leader(s) was out of the picture forever, making room for new (old) power forces that would not have to fear repercussions and who could pick and choose amongst the old communist *nomenklatura* in order to set up the new government.

The 'televised trial': the staging of Ceausescu's televised death

Like the symbolic cutting of the king's head, the death of Nicolae and Elena Ceausescu by firing squad was captured live on television, after a short staged trial the purpose of which was not so much to dispense justice but rather to legitimate a decision, a death that had already been decided. Visualising the leader's death was essential for clearly marking the moment when a new regime would take over and a new law would be installed: for showing that change was about to happen. Ionut Tudor argues that this carefully staged move was an effective way of masking 'non-change' as 'change', 'normal' as a 'state of exception' and 'old law' as 'new law'. For him, 'the trial plays the role of a "fictitious gap" interposed between the old regime and the new regime' (Ionut Tudor in Acostioaei 2012: 42). Building on Benjamin's essay on violence,

Tudor sees the televised killing as an act of pure violence, necessary for the establishment of new law.

Meant to abruptly erase the Ceausescus from our collective imagination, the trial however managed to do just the opposite: the shocking close-ups of the two dead leaders, the timing of the trial and killing on Christmas day, all served to insure that the images would haunt an entire generation. The 'transition' started under a 'bad omen'. The gesture was violent, and the trial too staged to appear legitimate. Even those present were left shaken: the official judge, Gica Popa, committed suicide shortly after, unable to bear what he had done. The soldiers from the firing squad suffered nightmares and post-traumatic stress which led to many of them losing their families and jobs (Costi Rogozanu in Acostioaei 2012: 50). The trial was ultimately a failed performance introducing a strong element of scepticism in the future of the revolution: from that point onwards, citizens became mere spectators of their own 'transition'. All sense of agency was lost.

Iulia Popovici argues that this failure played an important role in exacerbating the feeling of helplessness that immediately followed the revolution, as well as the frustration associated with old wounds left unhealed. Although filmed live, the trial was effectively a closed door trial because it lacked an engaged public: a little less than an hour long, the trial offered no real opportunity to discuss the crimes of which the two were accused, to examine their motivations, or to hear their confessions. The public could not ask questions, observe remorse or examine evidence. As Popovici well points out:

> The trials with closed doors practically annihilate the performative effect of the trial: it is not the condemnation itself which offers the feeling of exercise of justice, of accomplished revenge, of restauration of order and good things, or on the contrary, of injustice, social hypocrisy etc., but the actual pursuit of the trial, passing through its specific phases […] and the corporalization of the sentence.
>
> (Iulia Popovici in Acostioaei 2012: 52)

At the end of the summary trial, once the sentence had been given, Ceausescu declares: 'We could have been shot without this mascarade' (Cartianu 2009). With a few words, Ceausescu quickly reminds everyone what it was that they were in effect looking at. The interlude of the trial added to the overall sense of confusion amongst television audiences: the cries of Ceausescu is dead, the celebrations in the street, the chorus of new leaders constantly on the screen discussing the set-up of the new government, wanted to quickly erase the moment of death and move on. This swift act of erasure, facilitated by the medium of television which allowed the new regime the opportunity to focus the entire country's attention onto one screen, one main studio, only worked in the immediate short term, largely because of the element of shock. Long-term, the image of the trial, which could be replayed, coupled with the slow realisation that the new regime was largely formed by former communist party members, confirmed Ceausescu's accusations of an unfair trial and political betrayal in the form of a coup.

Years later, an entire generation would declare themselves to have been duped and conclude that they were much better off during Ceausescu's time: 'Did we have flats? – Yes, we did. Did we have cars? – Look, Dacia is good even now. We also had food, because each of us had relatives in the country-side...a chicken, an egg, a pig...' (Bogdan Teodorescu in Acostioaei 2012: 54). The threshold level of satisfaction and well-being is low, but denotes the extreme sense of insecurity that was to follow: unemployment, inflation and overall collapse of social services. Many would go back to the image of the trial and lament what they have helped do: the ghost of Ceausescu would forever haunt them, a constant reminder of what they had done.

The staged televised revolution, with its staged trial and carefully choreo-graphed legitimation of new power leaders was without doubt facilitated by the medium of television and the unique thirst for the TV image in late 1980s Romania. The upstaging of the Timisoara revolution by its televised counter-part, meant that the unique space of street, the square and the National Theatre balcony was quickly lost to the television screen. Attempts to recover some of those spaces and narratives years later led to a series of interesting practices of re-staging through live street performances, documentary and feature films, as well as the building of monuments and museums in memory of the revolution. The remainder of this chapter will look at some of these practices of re-staging and the impact that they have had on sifting through the past and re-negotiating the meaning of the 1989 revolution(s).

Re-staging the 1989 revolution I: early performances of the moment of 'change'

The 1990s were years of great change, dominated by a constant struggle to survive and keep up with the promise for a better future that failed to mate-rialise for most. The year 1989, the revolution, the death of the Ceausescus seemed far behind: remembrance was largely targeted at those who had lost family members during the revolution, and yearly marches through town to commemorate the revolution did not necessarily make room for critical reflection on what had happened. Artists were for the most part reluctant to engage the public head on with critical pieces, knowing that they would not be emotionally ready to accept a portrayal of the revolution as anything other than 'heroic'. The few attempts to do so, such as Ion Grigorescu's perfor-mance piece in one of Timisoara's public squares: *The Country does not belong to the Militia, the Securitate or the Communists* in 1991, Constantin Flondor's *The Blind Man's Sunday*, and Dan Perjovski's performance in the collective act entitled *The State without a Name*, all of which criticised the newly formed 'democratic' state, the violent nature of the transition, and a cold 'West', faced a reluctant public. Public square performances became too dangerous due to the unpredictability of the wider public, and many had to be moved to smaller art gallery spaces where targeted audiences could be reached (Pintilie 2000).

Two early attempts to re-stage the 'televised revolution' through alternative footage carefully juxtaposed to the official, familiar one, were met with equal initial reluctance and criticism: Harun Farocki and Andrei Ujica's *Videograms of a Revolution* and Ovidiu Bose Pastina's *Timisoara December 1989* which appeared in 1993 and 1991 respectively, both sought to question the uncritical eye through which the 1989 revolution was first captured and presented, and provide an alternative, less 'heroic', view. As Parvulescu explains, by using a creative montage of images from the revolution:

> *Videograms* follows a dual process of interpellation. It traces, dialecti-cally, the way images both turn revolted bodies into audiences and create revolutionary subjects [...] It aims to reveal how, in days of unrest, an independent revolutionary gaze emerges, and how it is rendered irrelevant once the revolution has 'triumphed'.
>
> (Parvulescu 2013: 355)

Reporting from an individual perspective, *Videograms* acknowledges the sub-jective nature of the footage, and the limitations of the camera which can only record a marginal aspect of what is happening: the totality of the 'event' is inaccessible not only to the camera eye, but also to any and all individual eyes. Criticising the revolution as a staged event, *Videograms* seeks to depict instead the 'spectacle of power' and re-empower the passive spectator. Unfortunately, the wider public was not yet ready at the initial time of release to be re-empowered. The traumatic experience of the revolution was too raw, with the present and future dominated by too many question marks already to introduce yet another fundamental one.

Ovidiu Bose Pastina's *Timisoara December 1989* was met with a similar fate: criticised for being too impressionistic, blurry, unclear, almost to the point of appearing unprofessional – the film made use largely of crude visuals and sounds by amateurs taken during the revolution and staged blurred imagery to evoke particular states of being. More of an art film, it was seen as belonging to art gallery, art theatre spaces, where counter-discourses could be targeted to self-selected audiences. The prominent role played by sound in Pastina's film, meant to re-create the confusion of December 1989, coupled with images that initially do not seem to correspond, was too abstract for the wider public to absorb at the time. The anonymity of those depicted in both films, along with the seemingly unprofessional footage, did not fit the expectation of Revolu-tionary Film as necessary testimony to a traumatic yet heroic event. It did not serve to justify the legitimacy of what had happened.

It was not until 2000 that the public space became more open to criticism, the distance in time allowing old wounds to heal, a critical young mass to mature, and new generations to be born. A new wave of artists and film makers along with critically engaged academics, journalists and intellectuals, offer a series of new engagements with the moment of 1989. The move coincides with one of the most macabre moments in the early 2000s: the unearthing of the Ceausescu's bodies for DNA testing to confirm to the wider public that they were indeed dead, following speculations that not only the trial, but also their public execution had in fact been staged, and that the two were happily living in Cuba. The DNA test confirmed they were indeed dead, with the unearthing offering another chance for the public to relive the summary execution of 1989: images of the two taken post-execution were presented side-by-side with images of their recently exhumed bodies. Arrows and commentary focused on strange details of what was preserved and to what extent, with the images parading once more their decomposed bodies across the public sphere (Lamasanu 2010).

The decomposed past in front of the public's eyes served as a strange reminder of how quickly everything crumbled in the post-Ceausescu era: the sudden fall of his regime before disbelieving eyes, the spectacle of the revolution, the violence of their death, the exaggerated lies concerning the number of those killed, coupled with an increased public disillusionment with the new regime made room for a much needed critical space of engagement which exploded with a number of creative interventions. Dumitru Gorzo led perhaps the way with his now famous stencils depicting Ceausescu's face sitting on two wings with the text 'Back in 5 minutes' which first appeared in early 2003 (Bardulete 2012). The stencils quickly took over public spaces in Bucharest and became the talk of the town. Ceausescu's re-emergence in public, everyday spaces, the quirky text which suggested he was just around the corner, the wings which brought him back from his violent death in a very serene way, all served to poke the public conscience, to incite even a passing thought on what seemed now like a long-gone time. Coupled with his stencils of an image of increasingly unpopular Basescu, the president at the time, with the inscription 'Will leave in 5 minutes', which appeared a few years later, the stencils offered a quick juxtaposition of the past and the present, suggesting a nostalgic yearning for Ceausescu, who only a few years earlier had in fact been publicly lynched.

Gorzo continued on to create a series of engaging, interactive street art, including: the pink cocoons in 2003, an ambiguous sign of rebirth at a stage when the transformation into the final embodiment had not yet occurred; the murals of portraits of people from his native village of Ieud, an enclave in scenic Maramures that has preserved some of country's oldest traditions until today – meant to perhaps juxtapose old traditions with fast changing, 'West' embracing Bucharest; and the more abstract murals of 'The world seen through the eyes of an old lady sitting on her balcony' which evoked the fast pace of change and the 'outsider'/reflective position of those who were left behind: the old, the unemployed, peering from behind windows and balconies – a familiar image for most urban dwellers in Romania. Gorzo, along with a number of other artists, contributed to the creative re-training of the public eye, so easily duped by the 'televised revolution'. The 2000s marked a

Photo 2.1 Image of Ceausescu with note 'Back in 5 minutes'
Dumitru Gorzo, Romanian Artist, stencil on wall

significant creative jump associated with a critical re-awakening of the Romanian public and a significant new openness to critical public engagements with the moment of the revolution.

Restaging the 1989 revolutions II: re-enactments for the 'trained' eye through the Romanian New Wave

Almost 20 years after the 1989 Romanian revolution, the subject is experiencing a powerful comeback in a number of cinematic reflections that are at the forefront of the so-called Romanian New Wave, including Corneliu Porumboiu's *12:08 East of Bucharest*, Radu Muntean's *The Paper Will be Blue* and Catalin Mitulescu's *How I Spent the End of the World*. Alongside the revolutionary

Photo 2.2 Image of Romanian President Basescu with note 'Will leave in 5 minutes' Dumitru Gorzo, Romanian Artist, stencil on wall

theme lie a number of other important contributions to the New Wave, focusing on both the 'before' and 'after' the revolution, thus neatly bracketing, both spatially and temporally, the period of communism as opposed to, but also in direct relationship to, the period of transition: Cristian Nemescu's *California Dreamin'*, Cristian Mungiu's *4 Months 3 Weeks 2 Days*, Cristi Puiu's *The Death of Mr. Lazarescu* and Corneliu Porumboiu's *Police, Adjective* are just a few examples. Appearing at a time when the revolutionary (and even transition) theme seems almost entirely exhausted by incessant TV talk shows, investigative commissions into communism, the revolution and the Securitate, disgruntled intellectuals, politicians and revolutionaries, these films are surprisingly refreshing. Although they have gained most of their acclaim at film festivals abroad, they are clearly targeting a local public, seeking to reopen, albeit on different grounds, a debate that many considered lost.

Focusing in particular on Corneliu Porumboiu, Radu Muntean and Catalin Mitulescu's films, the remainder of this chapter seeks to establish some of the contributions that the New Wave is making to the re-staging of the 1989 revolutionary moment, and the renegotiation of Romania's present role in the local and global imaginary. The technology of film – by this I literally mean the use of a film camera as opposed to, for example photography – is treated as unique only to the extent that: 1) it has played a key role in the initial representation of the Romanian revolution – with most Romanians experiencing the revolution live on television, as opposed to out in the streets, along with the rest of the world; and 2) it has served as a tool to enhance both the memory and consciousness of the so-called 'moment' of the revolution (what happened during the 16–22 December 1989) by recording, reproducing and re-staging images that could perhaps only now gain legibility.

As such, this examination does not seek to argue that there is something inherent in the technology of film per se, that makes it necessarily relevant or unique, but rather that in particular contexts, at particular points in time, constellations of ideas, techniques, times and spaces can come together in the expression of a film. And when this happens, this unique moment, what Benjamin calls the 'now-time', becomes a door through which the past, present and future can merge in a unique understanding. This is not a 'sublime' moment of transcendence (Shapiro 2006) that puts us 'beyond the bounds of [the] natural or sensory world' but rather, as Hozic argues, the sublime as grounding experience, where we 'understand [our] place in the natural world, and by accepting [our] limitations [find] the way to live [our] li[ves] as a moral person' (Hozic 2006: 964).

The New Wave label recently placed on a series of films produced by Romanian directors, can and has certainly been challenged (Scott 2008). The films, although offering some thematic similarities, are quite different both in their scope and production. Most of the directors, although familiar with each other, would not consider themselves part of the same school (Calinescu 2006; Mezincescu and Dinca 2006; Blaga 2008). The label is very much a product of the unexpected success that many of these films have had on the international film festival circuit, which exposed them to an unintended global audience. The New Wave is an artificial creation that places many of these films clearly outside of their initial intentionality: targeting small local/national audiences. Instead, the idea of a 'new' 'wave' insinuates both that there is something radically different about these films and also, that they form part of a moving whole that deserves not only an international recognition but also a historical classification. It is in this particular context that the Romanian New Wave enters the global imaginary – how Romania, and its communist/post-communist experience is imagined/perceived from abroad: the movies, although shown individually, are inevitably presented as part of a larger whole, a body of work that together, seeks to present a coherent story about Romania's transition from communism to post-communism.

This coherence is justified not only on the basis of a shared international success, but also a perceived similarity in methodology imposed perhaps much more so by the limited financial resources available to young directors in Romania and Eastern Europe in general (Iordanova 1999, 2002), than by a deliberate choice to abide by certain stylistic rules. The methodology is often described as following a deeply minimalist/realist style, enforced by long shots, limited editing, a documentary like atmosphere and a focus on a familiar everyday environment such as unremarkable cityscapes and interiors (Hofman 2007; Kaufman 2007). The scene is formed by familiar characters in recognisable circumstances (Livizeanu 2007). These characters tell the story of the average Romanian, navigating the events in the years right before, during, and after the revolution. Perhaps what binds the films together, more so than a coherent style, is their point of reference: 1989 becomes the ultimate framing mechanism for understanding Romania's past, present and future.

Audiences abroad, from film festivals to film openings, have offered the Romanian New Wave unexpected opportunities: financial ones, but also opportunities to redefine the context in which their films would be interpreted. With a clear majority of their audience abroad – *12:08 East of Bucharest* had an audience of about 15,000 at home compared to over 40,000 in France alone (Stojanova and Duma 2007) – these films are slowly expanding their interpretative horizon to address not only a local but rather a global audience. Although the films focus on 1989 mostly as a local experience, their international audiences are experiencing them as either a complement or alternative to what they saw as the first revolution to be televised live. The ability of international audiences to relate to these films, took many of the directors by surprise, hinting that for them, 1989 was seen as a unique, and private experience of the Romanian people, and not so much as an international event.

This has helped redefine the original intentionality of these films: aimed mainly at disgruntled local audiences for whom the moment of the revolution has become a painful reminder of abuse, corruption and private interest led appropriation – with the intent of rescuing 1989 from this current negative context – the films have instead mainly been addressing international audiences who are now better able to locate the perceived 'exceptionality' of December 1989 in a more fluid historical context, and better able to assess the different and sometimes similar ways in which the televised revolution was experienced 'at home' and abroad. The technology of film plays a key investigative role here, in which its abilities are both mocked (particularly in *12:08 East of Bucharest*) and relished. In this sense, these films help to emphasise the extent to which representations of the revolution through the technology of film have played a key role in shaping both the local and global imaginary surrounding Romania.

The technology of film is crucial not only for marking December 1989 as one of the pivotal moments in which Romania entered the global (contemporary) imaginary, but also, as the moment in which a crucial local imaginary was formed, one that was going to continue to rely on the technology of film to represent Romania's collective historical and contemporary experience. 1989 marked the beginning of Romania's obsession with television: with one of the highest rates of cable television access in the Balkans, at 79 per cent (*Ziarul Financiar* 2007), Romanians have developed a love–hate relationship with the medium: while television is constantly present in most Romanian households – many of the interior scenes in the Romanian New Wave feature a live TV set in the background – the reliability of the information it transmits is almost inevitably challenged, creating a sense of constant frustration and indignation. It is interesting that the potential rescue should come from a series of films that are not afraid to mock the abuses which the medium that they themselves use, has been subject to, particularly when it comes to representing the Romanian transition.

While each of the three films that I focus on here deals specifically with the topic of the Romanian revolution, all three directors identify the present rather than the past as their main concern. They are part of a new generation of film makers whose point of departure is not the communist part but rather post-communist capitalism, making 'their art [...] subject to a different set of cultural and economic conditions [that] they and we view [...] from a new global vantage point' (Livizeanu 2007). Their films blur the edge between documentary and fiction, 'using the cinema as a tool to investigate reality with documentary-like specificity and moral depth' (Gorzo in Livizeanu 2007). Their minimalist model, 'recurrent use of long shots; lateral framing of tableaux-like compositions [...]; minute scrutiny of everyday, often non-spectacular details; a consistent refusal to use any score except some additional musical citations at key moments' along with theatrical mises-en-scène, extreme close-ups and symmetrical openings and closings (Nasta 2007), serve to blend 'story time, historical time [...] and the audiences' suspended reception time [...] into one single, strong emotional state' (Nasta 2007).

Corneliu Porumboiu's *12:08 East of Bucharest* takes place on the 16th anniversary of the 1989 revolution and is centred around a local TV show that seeks to determine whether there was or not a revolution in Vaslui, a small town east of Bucharest. The criteria for determining the answer is based on whether the demonstrators of Vaslui went into the street before or after 12:08pm, the time when Ceausescu left the Communist Party building in Bucharest after being booed by protesters. The film is inspired by an actual TV show that the director watched in his home town of Vaslui. The action centres around the three main characters, Jderescu – the talk show host and owner of the local TV station, Mr Piscoci, his first interviewee – a retiree who has been playing Santa Claus at Christmas time for all the kids in Vaslui, and Mr Manescu, his second interviewee – a high-school history teacher and notorious drunk.

It is Christmas time, and the concern with the revolution in Vaslui ranks about as high as Jderescu's worry over securing the two interviewees he promised to have, Mr Piscoci's search for an appropriate Santa Claus costume, and Mr Manescu's need to borrow some money to pay off his drinking debt and calm down his wife who expects him to bring his full salary home. Jderescu, a former engineer turned journalist, begins the show with an introduction inspired by his last minute search for inspiration in his dictionary of myths:

> Many of you are probably wondering why we are putting together this show, with this theme, after such a long time. Well, I think, that just like people mistook the fire for the sun in Plato's myth, it is my duty as a journalist, to make sure that as we came out of one cave, we didn't enter another one, a bigger one, in which we again mistook a great straw fire for the sun. I say that there is no present without a past, no future without a present. That is why, the clearer the past, the clearer the present and

future. On the other hand, Heraclitus used to say that we people cannot swim in the same waters twice. I say, my dears, let's try to dive back into the same river that was 16 years ago, for the sake of the truth, for a brighter future.

(Porumboiu 2006)

Despite his stutter, Jderescu, just like the other interviewees and people calling into the show, appears to stumble upon something that is being increasingly challenged in the transitology literature: the 'exceptionality' of the revolutionary moment itself. Jderescu urges his guests to remember what they were doing around 12:08 the day of the revolution, and while their responses are constantly challenged by those who call into the show, another story emerges: a story that underlines both the seemingly mundane nature of that day in December, 16 years ago, as well as the later need to turn it into something exceptional. The 22nd of December 1989 marks a key moment of change in Romania's history, and the day itself became invested with a significance tied to specific actions – demonstrating, being out in the streets, being on television – that, if and when missing, dilute not only someone's claim to have participated in the revolution, but also their claim to a post-revolutionary identity.

And yet the narrative of the film unfolds unperturbed by the perceived radical change brought about by December 1989: the symmetrical long shots of Vaslui at the beginning and end of the movie that are meant to portray the city before and after the revolution, reveal no change, just the same poverty stricken environment lit up by the same street lamps that turn on and off in orderly sequence from one end of the city to the other. The television studio, in which most of the film is shot, is reminiscent of the television studios in which the 1989 revolution itself unfolded: improvised, disorganised, with a shaky camera work that breaks the visual field at the most inopportune moments. The comedic irony of the set-up and the characters that inhabit it inevitably leave a different tint on what is otherwise portrayed as a very serious topic: the 1989 revolution and the questions surrounding it appear almost as a joke, an opportunity to distract oneself from the otherwise obvious lack of change.

Porumboiu describes his film as not really being about the revolutionary moment itself, but rather how that moment still percolates in people's minds today (Chirilov 2007). In that sense, Porumboiu is much less concerned with the past itself, than he is with the present. For him, the danger lies not in failing to find out the 'truth' about what happened during the revolution – an obsession that has informed much of the academic work on post 1989 Romania, which Porumboiu seeks to effectively erase by erasing the very word revolution from the Romanian film title, *Was there or was there not* [a revolution in Vaslui]? – but in the self-manipulation of our own unique memories in order to fit a particular narrative. It is these personal experiences, this calm that sits upon Vaslui even at a moment of great unrest, that he is trying to recover, and along with it, give people a much needed peace of mind, a sense that they need not necessarily have been out in the streets before 12:08 on December 1989 in order to have stepped into the future.

Radu Muntean's *The Paper Will be Blue* is also inspired by the director's personal experience of being a young army recruit at the time of the revolution. The film seemingly engages with perhaps one of the most disputed subjects surrounding the Romanian revolution: the role of the Romanian army during the revolution, and the source of the violence that left thousands of demonstrators and by-standers dead. The film focuses on the main character, Costi, a young army recruit who is caught by the revolution three months before his release. He deserts his platoon in order to go defend the Television Tower[1] and, in the process, is caught in a number of different tragic–comic situations, while his Lieutenant and the rest of the crew spend the night of the revolution looking for him. Costi gets confused for a terrorist after being caught in a fire exchange and is taken in to be interrogated along with a gypsy, accused of being a foreign spy. After being released, Costi finally rejoins his platoon in the morning only to be killed while taking a cigarette break outside of his tank.

The film is shot in a similar minimalist/realist style as Porumboiu's, featuring also a symmetrical opening and closing that suggests we are traversing a similar temporal loop, except that this time the film's action is revealed at the end to have been a flashback. We literally end where we begin, with the past, present and future, once again blurring into a mélange that forces us to reconsider their boundaries. Filmed mainly in the dark, the action, sound, camera work appear all murky. The hand-held camera shots force us to experience the action as if we were there, watching, engaged in the action ourselves, guarding our heads from the bullets, sneaking between buildings and cars, trying to make sense of the overlapping sounds of the radio, walkie-talkie, telephone. We are almost forced to follow Costi as an accomplice, whether we agree with him or not. We are always one step behind him, but unlike him, appear to survive the final blow. His enthusiastic attempt to protect the Television Tower ends in a useless death. His defence of liberty, while heroic, appears ridiculous, just like his death.

Muntean explains the purpose of his film as restoring 'the balance between the authenticity of those moments and how ridiculous they seem today, 15 years later' (Paun 2006). He argues that it is important to somehow allow people to relive those moments, those emotions:

> If I manage to teleport people back in a flash-back that's convincing enough to draw out their emotions and to make them think about those moments and what they felt back then, but not like you do when you think of a crazy subject that was explained very poorly both by the newspapers as well as Romanian TV in the last 16 years, then that means I did my job and created a film worth seeing.
>
> (Muntean in Paun 2006)

Restoring the sense of authenticity has little to do with discovering the 'truth' about the revolution for Muntean. Instead, it refers to the need to trust one's own memories and feelings at the time, not as naïve or unreliable, but rather as legitimate and truthful to oneself. Rescuing the moment of the revolution from its current negativity is a task that Muntean deems essential, and film for him is the ideal medium for the renegotiation of those moments, despite its previous abuse of the subject of the revolution:

> I'm perfectly aware of the fact that, in principle, the Romanian spectator is tired of movies that deal with, either directly or indirectly, the 1989 December revolution. My intention is not to discover the truth about the revolution or the terrorists but to tell the story of those people. It is a crazy night in which the army receives orders from poets and actors through the TV, people are called upon to defend the TV tower with their bare hands, the military receive mixed signals, the civilians are distributed guns on the basis of their ID, and the gypsies are arrested as arab terrorists. The film will be, like the revolution itself, a tragicomedy.
>
> (Muntean in *Cinemagia* 2006)

Catalin Mitulescu, a Romanian director living abroad, is also exploring the dangerous effect of the negativity and hatred that surrounds the moment of the revolution. Being stuck in this hatred for him means never really being able to move on, a permanent return to a particularly bleak interpretation of a period that he, at least, is able to recover as still full of charm and family warmth. The film, *How I Spent the End of the World*, is shot through the eyes of two children, Eva and her brother Lalalilu, and how they experienced the last year of Ceausescu's dictatorship. When Eva and her boyfriend accidentally break a bust of Ceausescu in their school, a series of events unfold that see Eva transferred to a reformatory school where she meets Andrei, the son of two dissidents – together they begin to train for their escape to the West across the Danube, and Lalalilu, a seven year old boy, prepares revenge by planning to kill Ceausescu during a planned visit to his school.

The film acts as a nostalgic retelling of a time that although challenging, was also full of positive moments, high expectations, and ambitious dreams. Mitulescu describes his intentions as:

> I wanted very much to see a film about the Ceausescu era. I really wanted to see this film, to see the era, because we're different, we lived in that time and have those memories. At one point the revolution came over us, everything was very agitated and we got lost. All going backs now are followed by hatred, by things unresolved, by conflicts unresolved. I wanted a film that would tell the story of my childhood, my adolescence, that would tell of those times and the happiness and sadness that came with them.
>
> (Mitulescu in Mezincescu and Dinca 2006)

Shot mainly outside, in a rural-like setting and a much warmer natural light, reminiscent of sunny and hot Romanian summers, Mitulescu's film anchors itself much more clearly in a pre-revolutionary past, that, although frustrating, is also full of love and familiarity, the excitement of planning and dreaming an escape to a 'West' that could hardly be imagined. The transition from the past to the future is metaphorically symbolised through the element of water: the crossing of the Danube onto the 'other' side, the intense cold-water training in the abandoned bathtub to survive a winter crossing, and finally, Eva onboard a giant cruiseship on a foreign sea. Unlike Porumboiu and Muntean, the revolution, although also confusing and unexpected, is marked not by a temporal loop that suggests nothing has changed, but by a temporal memory loop – this time marked through Eva's memory – that suggests that although things have changed, perhaps for the better, the past need not necessarily be full of regrets.

His film again, is not really about the revolution, but rather 'a nostalgic kind of recovery therapy' (Chirilov 2007). All three directors are careful to point out that none of their films is really about the revolution. So why this reluctance to engage with the revolution? As Chirilov asks, 'What is wrong with making a film about the revolution?' He suggests that taking on such a subject is perhaps too much of a burden, particularly at a time when people are simply tired of talking about the revolution (Chirilov 2007). And yet, these films are particularly successful at what they set out to do: engage with the revolution, but not really. Perhaps the reason for their success is that they manage to move the question of the revolution onto a much more familiar terrain: that of the everyday, the familiar. Adina Bradean, a researcher of Romanian film practices, argues that 'As lived by the film community, post-socialism was a puzzling time when imagined futures were directly dependent on remembered pasts, and particularly on the actions taken in response to those pasts' (Bradean 2007). Perhaps what these movies teach us is that it is not just the film community that experienced post-socialism as dependent on a particular way of remembering the past, but rather an entire society.

Both academic discussions as well as popular culture have committed the revolutionary year of 1989 to a series of emblematic times and spaces, two of which have perhaps been most prominent: the fall of the Berlin Wall in November of 1989 and the (first) televised Romanian revolution in late December 1989. It is these particular times and spaces that later provided a most fertile ground for academic explorations as well as political campaigns that searched for 'the truth' of the revolution: 'the truth' was to be uncovered by re-discovering and re-playing exactly what happened within these spaces and narrow timeframes – who was present and who was not, what were they doing at critical times during the uprising, what kind of evidence do they have to prove their claims.

The revolution thus emerged as: 1) a historical event that seemed clearly bounded by a specific spatial and temporal frame: in the case of Romania, the Timisoara main square and Opera House, the Bucharest main square, Communist Party Headquarters and the Television Tower, during the period of 16–22 December; 2) an event that was captured, represented, investigated and remembered through the technology of film, the medium thus playing an essential role in how the revolution and memories of the revolution continue to be experienced; and 3) an exceptional turning point that was imbued with a series of high expectations about what the future would look like. Each of the three films addressed here seeks to challenge both the spatial and temporal assumptions about what constitutes the revolution, the role of the technology of film and images of the revolution as less of an 'investigative' tool, and more of a 'recovery' tool, and the expectations embedded in the moment of the revolution itself as a necessary turning point towards something better. They do so by presenting a view of history that is in many ways similar to Walter Benjamin's reading of history.

Walter Benjamin and the 1989 revolution (I know, he died long before, but please indulge)

The idea of change often hinges on a series of clearly identifiable moments and spaces – whether it be revolutionary spaces, or the spaces of dissidence – that become imbued with the promise of a hidden meaning to be later uncovered. This assumption lies at the basis of much of the studies on transitology, where 'critical moments' and 'critical spaces' emerge as key sites of examination. Part of this is perhaps a result of how research is conducted – one needs to begin somewhere and focus on something – but also, a result of the methodological constriction imposed by a rigid understanding of concepts such as 'communism', 'democracy/democratisation', 'transition' and 'revolution.' Calls for widening the meaning of such concepts are certainly not new (see Wydra 2007) yet new methodological innovations to fit these more fluid understandings are few and far between. If communism and democratisation do not correspond to neatly divided temporal spaces (before and after the revolution) then how is one to address them without focusing on a set temporal and spatial arena?

Philosophical explorations of the experience of 'shock' (Pusca 2007), 'rupture' (Moore 2009) and 'a breach in understanding' (Bleiker 2006) offer a potential alternative by turning to psychology, literature and art in order to address change more as a rhythmic back and forth that, while influenced by particular events, derives its driving force from a much wider field of life experience – whether it be a non-exalted, normalised 'everyday', or the unique excitement of literature and art. Yet, even such explorations continue to rely on the assumption of some kind of linear progression and division between the past, present and future, thus placing change, even this new 'rhythmical' change as I call it, in one of these three temporal (and spatial) domains. By doing so, they invariably limit not only the possibility of interpreting 'past' change but also the possibility of continuing to have an impact on it. One theorist who has managed to break our philosophical dependency on the neat division of the past, present and future, has been Walter Benjamin.

Walter Benjamin's reading of history is best reflected in his dialectical understanding of the relationship between the past, present and future. For

Benjamin, the past acts, if one is to use a Heideggerian term, almost as a standing-reserve for both the present and the future. The past however does not emerge as a linear progression of events that culminate into a present, but rather as an accumulation of images, acts and memories that can be called upon to justify and inspire particular actions within the present. Benjamin describes revolutionary moments – key moments to which revolutions are generally ascribed, such as the storming of the Communist Party building in Romania – as key invocations of particular images and memories of the past which are used to imagine and inspire a different future. Thus, for Benjamin, unlike most scholars of revolutions, revolutionary change is not a moment of culmination of a series of incremental changes, but rather a key moment of remembrance, a 'full-moment' (Lowy 2005: 95).

It is within these moments that history comes alive for Benjamin. When talking about the French revolution, he remarks both on its ability to draw from the past – in 'view[ing] itself as Rome reincarnate' (Benjamin 1968: 261) – but also on its ability to introduce a new way of living the present and looking at the future – through the introduction of the modern calendar which 'presents history in time-lapse mode. […] basically, it is the same day that keeps recurring in the guise of holidays' (Benjamin 1968: 261). The moment of the revolution thus is the ultimate 'full moment', 'concentrate of historical totality', 'constellation linking the present and the past' (Lowy 2005: 95). As Lowy remarks, revolutions are in this case, not the locomotive of world history, but rather quite the opposite, the emergency break, the moment of arrest, the moment of invocation of the past and reflection (Lowy 2005: 66).

Just like revolutions emerge as invocations of the past, Lowy argues that the memory of the revolution is itself, in turn, also invoked 'in a moment of supreme danger, [when] a saving constellation presents itself linking the present to the past' (Lowy 2005: 45). The memory of the revolution is thus also in itself a potentially revolutionary moment at a time of great danger in the present. It is within this context that the three films addressed here are read as critical to rescuing the 1989 revolutionary moment from its current negativity, and along with it, the spirit and image of an entire country. By re-staging the moment of the 1989 revolution in a much more forgiving and familiar everyday context, the films manage to diffuse a series of unrealistic expectations about how the revolution came about, who were its main initiators and what the revolution was supposed to bring in terms of change.

Just like Benjamin, the films question the idea that historical time should necessarily follow a political time directed towards happiness – progress (Hamacher 2005: 38), or that revolutions should necessarily bring about only positive change. In the films, the re-staging of the 1989 revolutionary moment is not meant to re-create a missed moment of opportunity that would explain the unfulfilled present, but rather, quite the opposite: to represent an opportunity fulfilled to the best of people's abilities at the time. As such, the films clearly suggest that current invocations of 1989 should no longer appear as opportunities to somehow 'correct the miss, to do the undone, to regain the wasted and actualize the has-been-possible' (Hamacher 2005: 39). In this light, the Romanian obsession with recovering the 'truth' about the 1989 revolution – particularly through a recovery of the exact times, spaces, actors and acts of the revolution – appears as nothing but a futile attempt to correct something that perhaps was never really mistaken.

Porumboiu, Muntean and Mitulescu each reject the possibility of locating the revolution in a clear and exact past. They suggest that the revolution is not bounded by a set timeframe and space, but rather by a much looser framework in which the pre-revolutionary past and the post-revolutionary present come together. The present plays an essential role in their movies, for although exploring the topic of the revolution, each of their movies seems ultimately more concerned with the present, as the current moment of danger: their worry is the negative aura that surrounds the memory of the revolution, an aura that threatens to deny particular memories of the past and with them the possibility of being at ease in the present. By invoking the moment of the revolution and reaching back into the past in order to explore the source of this negativity, Porumboiu, Muntean and Mitulescu recover a series of everyday events that repaint the revolutionary past in a broader spatial and temporal timeframe thus taking some of the pressure off the revolutionary moment as exceptional.

By suggesting that this 'exceptional' label has forced us to significantly narrow down the spatial and temporal terrain of our investigation of the revolutionary moment, they propose instead that we turn to a series of 'unremembered' personal pasts to understand the extent to which the revolution was imagined and experienced differently. These unremembered pasts, explored as slices of everyday life that depict moments before, during and after the revolution, are meant to introduce the present as the real moment of choice, the true 'revolutionary' moment. For the three directors, the present is once again catastrophe bound, and it is only by invoking, and rescuing the revolutionary past from its negativity, that the present can turn to a different future. In this sense, the revolutionary moment that these films deal with, is perhaps not so much the moment of 1989, but rather an inhibited present that finds it easier to blame the 'transition' on the faults of 1989 than on itself.

The time and space of the revolution is challenged on at least two different terrains: 1) the terrain of the past, whereby the global imaginary of the revolution as attached to very specific times and places is undermined by a different imaginary that revives forgotten everyday spaces and moments; and 2) the terrain of the present, whereby the 'revolutionary' moment is reinterpreted to address a current moment of danger and the need for an interruption and reassessment 'now' as opposed to 'then'. Placing these two past and present revolutionary moments side by side, the films create an interesting constellation that places the burden of 'change' on the present as opposed to the past: the current moment of danger cannot be solved by attempting to discover 'the truth' about the 1989 revolution through a minute examination of exactly what happened, when and where, in order to understand what went wrong at the 'original moment of change'. The 'derailment' did not occur at the 'origin', but rather throughout the transition, and as such, the present is at least equally responsible as the past. If, as Benjamin suggests, a revolutionary moment should not be understood merely as an uprising but rather as a moment of pause and reassessment, then these films both beg for and seek to instigate a present revolution in themselves.

The frustration over the missed opportunities of December 1989 appears to have spilled over into an obsession with clearly identifying the source of change: who is responsible for the 1989 revolution? Who were the doers? The need to question the identity of the doer has more often than not been read as a practical need to weed out the 'non-doers' who claim to be 'doers' and celebrate instead the 'real' doers. Perhaps the wider fear is the possibility that a majority of Romanians were in effect, 'non-doers', and as such, a historical disappointment that cannot really be restored or re-written. The hatred of the 'non-doer' who claims to be a 'doer' – conveniently read mainly as the current political elite – has also, or so the films seem to suggest, turned into a hatred of oneself.

The trap of the 'doer' versus the 'non-doer' is set on the one hand by what constitutes 'doing' or 'non-doing', and on the other, by attributing 'change' to a very specific set of actions. For Porumboiu, the 'doer' versus 'non-doer' dichotomy is defined by whether someone was out in the streets demonstrating on 22 December or not, as well as whether they happened to be out before 12:08 or after. For Muntean, the dichotomy was explored on the one hand by whether the soldiers had joined the popular demonstrations, thus disobeying state orders, or not, and on the other, by whether they had contributed to the critical defence of the Television Tower. For Mitulescu, the dichotomy served to emphasise who had the nerve to oppose the Ceausescu regime before it fell, and how they reacted to their political (re)positioning after the fall.

Unlike the established Institute for Totalitarian Studies, Institute of the Romanian Revolution, the National Council for the Study of the Securitate Archives, or Institute for the Investigation of Communist Crimes, all designed and funded by the Romanian state as investigative tools into the communist past and the revolutionary moment, the films explore the 'doer'/'non-doer' dichotomy in a more flexible context, in which the 'non-doers' are also accepted as credible participants, and the 'doers' are questioned as the necessary origin of 'change'. For the three film directors, this is essential in order to recover a sense of identity that is not necessarily linked to December 1989, but rather what came before and after. For Porumboiu, the before and after are not necessarily so radically different, at least not in the case of his home town of Vaslui. In an interview with Andrei Cretulescu, Porumboiu explains why, in his film, the characters cannot find the answer to the question of whether there was a revolution in Vaslui or not:

> [the answer] doesn't exist because I don't believe in history with [a] capital H, just in personal/individual histories. Which is exactly what interested me in this film. After the revolution, the history books will only show two

or three heroes, two or three villains, but never will it show the view from below where the grass grows... I rather think that there was no transition.

(Porumboiu in Cretulescu 2007)

If there is anything that Porumboiu teaches us, it is that there is no 'moment' (singular) or 'space' (singular) of the 1989 revolution, but rather a multitude of moments and spaces; that the celebration of change need not necessarily be dependent on an ability to clearly anchor that change in a particular moment in time and space; and that the ultimate public/collective event of the revolution is also a very private and emotional one that continues to deeply affect the individual as well as the collective sense of self-worth. It is perhaps precisely this present loss of self-worth that Porumboiu, as well as Muntean and Mitulescu seek to recover through a different invocation of the past.

The 1989 revolution and the technology of film

Film has always closely accompanied both the events of the Romanian revolution as well as how we remember and analyse the revolution. While it was the technology of film and live television that made the revolution possible in the first place, this same technology has been blamed for turning the moment of the revolution into an event forever suspect (Baudrillard 1994). It is then perhaps surprising that the attempt to rescue the memory of the revolution, and more importantly, what came before and after it, should also make use of the technology of film. This section of the chapter will try to examine the relationship between the technology of film and history in light of the ability of film to negotiate change, rescue and reveal historical memory, bracket and enframe unusual spaces and temporalities.

In his 1935 essay on 'The Work of Art in the Age of Mechanical Reproduction', Walter Benjamin argued that 'the mode of human sense perception changes with humanity's entire mode of existence' (Benjamin 1968: 222). As the ultimate modern form of human perception, the technology of film has accompanied and helped capture the transition towards a new mode of existence, one in which we have become both distant, distracted and curious spectators to our own existence. Benjamin is particularly fascinated by film's ability to guide us as a collectivity into an unconscious – and perhaps now increasingly conscious – examination of ourselves. As he sees it:

a different nature opens itself to the camera than opens to the naked eye – if only because an unconsciously penetrated space is substituted for a space consciously explored by man [...] The camera introduces us to unconscious optics as does psychoanalysis to unconscious impulses.

(Benjamin 1968: 237)

According to Benjamin, the camera's ability to introduce new fields of vision and as such new views on familiar spaces, to slow or speed up movement, allows us to experience both space and time differently from unmediated human perception. The camera captures history in the making, at its key moments of arrest when decisions are taken that change what Werner Hamacher calls the continuum of time and intentions (Hamacher 2005: 53). The camera and technology of film itself does not serve to decipher the events that it captures, but merely to reproduce them at a point in the future when the images captured attain a new legibility. The camera thus functions as an enhanced memory and consciousness through which the past and the future come together in the present. The film's ability to capture both 'reality' as well as 're-stagings of that reality', allows it to play with the meanings that historical moments have acquired, but also, perhaps more importantly, the recreate important moments in the past that have been, for one reason or another, ignored or forgotten.

If, as Benjamin argues, history does decay into images, then the possibility of recreating historical images is an essential tool for recovering what was lost or denied in the memories of many. The restaging of the Romanian revolution through the three films discussed here, forces a reassessment of past and the suspicion that surrounds it, and through it, a reassessment of the present. Perhaps what is most important about these re-stagings is their ability to re-assess and re-direct the origin of change away from the streets and main squares where demonstrators gathered, away from the Television Tower, and into people's living rooms. Change is in this sense celebrated less as an opportunity created by those out in the streets and more as an opportunity realised through a shift in perception. The films do not so much seek to rewrite the past, but perhaps to point out that the past does not have legibility at the time of its occurrence – and as such, seeking to reexamine it through the eyes of the past makes little sense – but rather only in the present or future. As Hamacher explains:

> This turning to the past, which gives the past a belated direction, a turning that directs and judges the past, has though, a double meaning. First, the present, if it is one, does not make claims of the future, but is present along as that upon which the past makes demands: present is always present *out of* the past and present *for* the past. And second, the past not only has in this present its intentional object but its intention comes in it to a standstill: what has been shines in the present, if it is one, and unites with the Now of its cognition.
>
> (Hamacher 2005: 52)

The technology of film, through its ability to depict a particular past in front of a present audience, emerges as the ultimate tool for revealing or questioning the intentionality of past events. The three films present 1989 not as a moment of 'great' change, but rather as one of confused intentionality, in which the demands on the future attain a highly personal nature: from a desire to escape to the West, to a desire to share the enthusiasm of the demonstrating crowd and achieve a sense of self-worth. The films clearly suggest that the social and political significance of 1989 that was acquired during the event itself was for the most part sustained through a particular depiction of the moment but also through the presence of a global audience that located the event in a global context, for the most part foreign to Romanian audiences.

The three films try to imagine how this significance could be read differently by creating an imaginary recording of what the private, everyday environments must have been experiencing at the time. This imaginary recording seeks to counterbalance the excessive images filmed on the streets and in the TV Tower during the revolution, in order to first rebuild a sense of trust in the medium of film itself, and second, to suggest a different reading of the intentionality of the revolutionary moment, one that perhaps would sit much less comfortably with the global imaginary at the time.

While Baudrillard sees the excessiveness of the Romanian revolution – as a staged event and ultimate simulacrum – as inevitably leading to the 'demystification of the news and its guiding principle' (Baudrillard 1994: 60), and through this, the possible demystification of the technology of film and other virtual technologies, the Romanian New Wave suggests quite the opposite: that this excessiveness has led to a love–hate relationship with the technology of television and film, a relationship that needs to be salvaged from directing the public in an increasingly gloomy addiction to a 'search for truth' that is doomed to failure. The solution for them is however – perhaps not surprisingly for film directors who make a living by exploiting the technology of film – not a rejection of television and film as simulacrum, but rather a celebration of television and film as providing the cure for the problem they created in the first place.

This faith in the technology of film for the Romanian New Wave is however not based on the film's ability to capture and enframe any kind of ultimate truth, but rather, quite the opposite, the film's ability to capture a healthy diversity of experience that could restore a much needed sense of ease to a public that has concentrated so much of their collective angst on a very specific idea/image of the revolution as captured during the week of 16–24 December. By diffusing this collective angst, the Romanian New Wave hopes to restore a new sense of collective optimism as well as perhaps a healthier relationship to the media of film. As one of the most 'wired' countries in Europe when it comes to cable television, the Romanian public needs to learn to trust this technology not only to entertain it but also to allow it to better negotiate change. By playing on humour, nostalgia and a more relaxed time frame of events surrounding the Romanian revolution, the Romanian New Wave may just be the antidote that recovers the revolutionary moment from its current gloom and gives the collective a new sense of purpose.

The revolution between the 'exceptional' and the 'everyday'

By locating the revolution in the realm of the everyday, Porumboiu, Muntean and Mitulescu, seek to dispel its exceptional status, and as such, the need for its exceptional treatment. The revolution, for them, was equally an individual affair as it was public, and by focusing on these individual experiences they could reveal a familiar environment that the average individual could relate to. By dispelling the idea that the revolution was an event that occurred purely in the public realm, the films help to not only legitimate a series of private experiences of the revolution, but also accord them equal significance, thus encouraging audiences to perform their own personal archaeology of how they experienced the revolution, without dismissing the familiar and non-exceptional experiences they had at the time as irrelevant.

This attempt to recover the everyday is a trend that has also gained significant ground in the social sciences. Inspired by earlier phenomenologists such as Heidegger, Levinas, Patocka and Schutz, as well as Marxists such as Lefebre and Debord, the movement to rehabilitate the everyday has been thriving in contemporary French philosophy, through people such as Lyotard, Foucault, Derrida, Deleuze and Jean Luc-Nancy (Mihali 2007).

A student of Nancy, Ciprian Mihali seeks to apply this re-discovery of the 'everyday' to communist and post-communist Romania, by arguing, in many ways along similar lines as Porumboiu, Muntean and Mitulescu, for the importance of an 'archeology of communist daily life' in order to uncover the everyday as an essential realm of resistance not just during communism, but also post-communism:

> everydayness was the place where communism has left the deepest traces also because it was the last refuge for the unprotected in his public, political or professional life. And the fall of communism hasn't led to the disappearance of these traces but to their keeping as routines and inertia to protect individuals and communities from daily convulsions, or to show them off as open wounds whenever exhibiting them as weaknesses, insufficiencies or prejudices could bring the smallest profit by stirring up the westerners' compassion.
>
> (Mihali 2007: 2)

Mihali is highly sceptical of the extent to which such an archaeology can be conducted by government appointed institutions, since they are almost entirely focused on condemnation and finding guilty parties. For him, a different archaeology of everydayness is needed, one that would focus on the continuities, and gaps, created post 1989, continuities and gaps that sustain to a large extent the social (in)stability of Romanian society today.

Mihali identifies sovereignty and precariousness as the two extremes under which 'everydayness' is suspended either though encroachment of the state or through encroachment of nature, and is quick to point out that our celebration of the post-revolutionary recovery of the everyday is perhaps premature, for:

> if sovereignty and precariousness invest excessively today [in] the life of millions it is because life itself is looking for everydayness with meaning

and is constantly mobilized – by the illusion of sovereignty to be found again and the fear of precariousness to be avoided.

(Mihali 2007: 4)

The post-revolutionary liberatory potential of the everyday, for Mihali, is lost in the illusion of sovereignty as well as the continuation of precariousness. This is perhaps precisely the source of the post-revolutionary angst that Porumboiu, Muntean and Mitulescu identify, although unlike Mihali, they seem to believe in the authenticity of the pre-revolutionary everyday, an authenticity that has perhaps been lost after the revolution, but can potentially be recovered through a re-staging of both the revolutionary moment and what came before it.

Mihali seems much more sceptical of such a possibility, as for him, there is no authenticity to recover: instead, we merely see a continuation of oppression of the everyday in different forms, perhaps more dangerous ones for they are less visible. He gives the example of the crucial role that television has been playing in the lives of Romanians since 1989, giving a false sense of refuge in an imaginary world of soap operas and celebrations of material good life, as well as the example of health care 'reform' that has left an entire older generation begging for their right to continue to live by denying them access to easy health care and medicine. The recovery of the 'everyday' for Mihali does not lie in any kind of return to a previous, more nostalgic 'everyday' of the pre-revolutionary or revolutionary period, but rather in an awakening to the realisation that the 'exceptional' moment of 1989 was perhaps not quite so exceptional. In either case though, a return to the 'exceptional' moment of 1989 is required, for different purposes: if Porumboiu, Muntean and Mitulescu seem convinced that the recovery of the 'authentic' and positive emotions that surrounded December 1989 at the time is crucial for instilling a new sense of positive thinking, Mihali believes that a return is perhaps warranted by the possibility of seeing essential – and problematic – continuities between communism and post-communism. In both instances however, a re-staging of the revolution seems key to uncovering both the revolutionary as well as the potentially oppressive character of the everyday.

Re-staging the 1989 revolution III: memory, theatre, monuments

In addition to film, some of the latest attempts to re-stage the 1989 revolution and its aftermath have taken place in the theatre as well as on the street through the erection of a series of commemorative monuments. The theatre world has been rather slow to create, perform and reflect upon contemporary events, relying for the most part on an existing repertorium. It was not until the rise of new independent theatre groups, such as DramAcum, that things began to change. A new generation of theatre makers, largely students, has been looking for ways to engage with socially and politically relevant issues, and reflect upon both the communist past as well as the period of 'transition'. Cristina Modreanu describes this new theatre-making as relying on:

socially relevant themes [...]; professional documentation, the use of techniques inspired from journalistic practice [...] the collective work process, based on inputs in which hierarchies disappear and the limits between creative departments blur; methods of involving the spectators and provoking the audience's immersion, either by directly addressing it, or by placing it in the performing space.

(Modreanu 2013: 387)

Among the main representatives of this New Wave in Theatre, Gianina Carbunariu has perhaps been the most prominent, writing and directing a series of critical plays, including *Stop the Tempo* – a manifesto of the millennial generation in Romania and their experience of the 'free' world; *20/20* – a reflection on the ethnic clashes that took place in March 1990 between Romanians and Hungarians in Targu-Mures; *Sold Out* – about the 'selling' of German citizens of Romania to the German state in the 1970s and 1980s; *Red Mountain/Politically and Physically* – an engagement with the controversy surrounding the exploitation of Rosia Montana mine; and most recently *Xmm from Ykm* – a creative re-staging of the discussion between Romanian dissident Dorin Tudoran and the Romanian Secret Police based on documents from the recently opened Secret Police Archives.

Each of these engagements skirt the question of the revolution as a critical passage from one era to another, yet one that is hardly remembered by the millennial generation. Dealing with the consequences of a past that was not experienced first hand, leaves a large part of this generation in the dark, having to rely on informal re-tellings as well as official documents and recordings. As a generation that is generally much more sceptical of the possibility of a single 'truthful' version of the past, the most creative amongst them, have sought to re-imagine alternative scenarios according to which the past could have played out: less concerned with 'what actually happened', representatives of this generation, such as Carbunariu, are more interested in creating opportunities for discussion around the past and through it, around the present.

With her latest play, *Xmm from Ykm*, Carbunariu seeks to imagine a series of different 'realities'/possible scenarios for the discussion between Tudoran and the Secret Security representatives, which she builds from the fragments of text found in the Secret Security Archive. Playing with the fact that official recordings of secret service discussions were often edited to target different audiences – thus several slightly altered copies of the same recording would be filed in each folder – she uses the stage to play out how the very meaning of the discussion changes along with these subtle edits. Intending this to be a point of departure for further discussion, Carbunariu's work functions as an inherent criticism of the multitude of attempts to 'settle' the past, place final verdicts on actions and people and (ab)use the media to secure political capital. She accepts the possibility of 'multiple realities', multiple points of view, and a past that has been edited and re-edited to a point where the only relevant message can only come through the re-playing of the different edits and their possible meaning. That is precisely what the actors in her plays attempt to do. According to her, what Dorin Tudoran had the courage to say in 1985 is something that can also be said about what is happening today: the attitude of most politicians, the opportunism of many intellectuals in terms of their relationship with the powers that be, the arrogance of those in power (Carbunariu 2012).

Carbunariu's plays, along with those of others from her generation, such as David Schwartz's plays focusing on marginal mining communities in Romania and their decreasing political capital, offer an interesting complement to the Romanian New Wave in film. Although their public exposure is perhaps significantly smaller, their unique ability to engage with the public as much more than a spectator and to speak to a generation that for the most part is completely disconnected from the communist past, offers yet another critical space of engagement and reflection. For now, Schwartz and Carbunariu have intentionally placed themselves on the fringes of the Romanian stage, but from those fringes, they have been able to

> explor[e] the intersections of theatre and late capitalism with its human collateral damage in a society like Romania – awoken from the Communist dream to face the reality of the cost of capitalism [where] Romanians have spent the last two decades of 'freedom' chasing the capitalist illusion which the western world is already questioning.
>
> (Modreanu 2013: 394)

As a space that has always been key to re-staging the past as a way to reflect on the present and future, the theatre stage is a uniquely suited place to explore the meaning of 1989 today.

If the theatre can erect temporary 'monuments' to the past as props through which to peer backwards and forwards in time, the street has the potential to do the same, with more semi-permanent interventions. Street monuments dedicated to 1989 abound, yet few are as controversial as the latest 'erection', the Re-birth Memorial in Bucharest. Built in 2005, yet inaugurated as a site in late 2004 – at a key moment of the passing of power from Romania's first post-revolutionary president, Ion Iliescu, to Traian Basescu – the monument looks like a stick with a potato on top – nicknamed 'Teapa Nationala' (roughly translated as: they stuck it to us). While the designer, Alexandru Ghildus argued that it was meant to be an obelisk in the shape of a pyramid with a crown on top – a symbol of the passing of time, the message was entirely lost on the wider public who saw it as oddly imposing, dwarfing the rest of the monuments in the square, without a clear aesthetic sense, combining every material possible, and perhaps more strangely, including a little hut for a monument guard (Bercea 2005).

Mihai Oroveanu, the director of the National Contemporary Art Museum in Bucharest, sees it as yet another monument erected largely for political purposes and the need to create an artificial inauguration moment whereby the significance of 1989 could be positively associated with key political figures. He tells the story of several such monuments erected and later destroyed or removed, testimonies of fickle times and political interests. The monument speaks perhaps most eloquently of the problematic re-appropriation of the 1989 moment to elicit an emotional response and to confer an aura of heroism and respect to those presiding over the inauguration. Mihaela Grancea addresses the monumentary cult of 1989 as having legitimating functions. Unlike written testimonies of 1989, which for the most part remained the domain of intellectuals willing to go into the archives, the 1989 commemorative monuments are meant to act as strong public reminders of the communist oppression and the sacrifice of those who died. They have become real 'memory sites' that are meant to both preserve and promote a particular image of 'sacrifice' and 'heroism' – key to how many want to remember close family members who died, but also, 'elements of a festive scenography' of yearly pilgrimages and inaugurations that are less concerned with the memory itself and more with the status it confers (Grancea 2012: 28).

She goes on to explain that

> there is a certain waiting period during which the image of the hero is formed and spread. In the process of mythical transfiguration of the individual, his real biography is lost in time, becomes an 'accident', and his individuality is remodelled after the archetypical cannon [...] Around this image [of the mythical hero] one sees the crystalization of a collective ensemble of hopes, nostalgia and utopias, a new horizon of expectations.
> (Grancea 2012: 38)

Revolutionary memorials are thus also sites of power, capable of invoking and shaping strong collective emotions. Unfortunately, very few manage to act as sites of critical reflection and to incite a more meaningful connection to the past. This, partially has to do with the spaces in which most of them have been placed, highly impersonal, often busy and noisy public squares, as well as the 'official' character of many of them, which often means that they have been erected without a meaningful consultation with the local community or a real public/community effort. Although located in central places, the monuments often remain invisible until key commemorative moments. Utilising often abstract symbolism, they do not necessarily speak to the wider public, which prefers more informally erected '*troite*' – often just a cross where people can bring flowers and candles and say prayers.

Unlike Gorzo's creative street performances, the 1989 monuments fail for the most part to engage the public in their everyday interactions and as such constitute problematic re-stagings of the moment of 1989 which are easy prey for politicians and power players. As key sites of memory, the monuments favour a selective approach to remembrance which is, for the most part, only designed to celebrate as opposed to question. Caterina Preda argues that the failure to open a museum dedicated to the memory of communism and the moment of 1989 in Romania – a space that is generally designed as a reflective space – is largely a result of a political environment where memories are still disputed and where competing institutions devoted to the study of communism seem more interested in establishing their version of the 'truth' as opposed to engaging the wider public with the key materials they hold in their possession.

While 'the official gaze onto the past does not use on a large scale artistic means to express its version of memory (except for the monument raised for the martyrs of the December revolution)' (Preda 2010: 149), the unofficial gaze has experienced an interesting revival that relies more on temporary performances and engagements with less heroic aspects of the communist past and 1989: street performances, small theatre and art film performances, as well as some increasingly popular film performances.

Conclusion

This chapter has offered an alternative exploration of the 1989 Romanian revolution as a contested event that takes place on several different temporal and spatial planes, increasingly multiplied by a renewed critical interest in the communist past, the moment of 'transition' and its effects. The different re-stagings of the 1989 revolution serve as creative entry points into explorations of the past, that unlike other intellectual/academic endeavours that seek to uncover the 'truth', present alternative possibilities and points of view, and perhaps more importantly, satisfy the nostalgic needs of a post-revolutionary era that has seen all of its grand illusions collapse and continues to struggle to find its place within the wider historical legacy of the region and the world. The different re-stagings mark a continued fascination with the role of the technology of film – both on the television screens as well as cinema screens – in capturing not only key historical moments but also wider social moods and individual struggles that easily translate into wider collective struggles; as well as a perhaps newer fascination with how public, everyday, spaces can become key performance spaces for engaging with the past as a way of reflecting on the present.

As the initial 'moment' of the 1989 revolution becomes more distant in time, new spaces open up through which it can be interrogated: if initially, street performances and the erection of the first revolutionary monuments were seen as sacrilegious spaces where only a heroic representation of the Revolution was possible, lately, these same spaces have made room for much more critical engagements that can question not only the actors of the revolution but also its political re-appropriation as a symbolic space. If initially, these re-stagings were met with violent criticism that largely silenced them and pushed them into a marginal, relatively elite existence, newer re-stagings are met with much wider public acclaim and interest, particularly from the so-called millennial generation which is increasingly keen to understand its historical legacy and re-enact the past as a way of re-creating a unique loca-lised self in an era of globalisation. For them, the past becomes politicised not through attempts to uncover the 'correct' version – a sense of collective truth on which history can be built, but rather through individualised explorations that bring the past alive in the collective 'everyday', a much less threatening space in which one can more playfully engage with painful historical moments: the role of the Secret Security, the brutal killing of the Ceausescus, the violent revolution, or the painful transition to capitalism.

Note

1 The tower was one of the first official buildings to have been taken over by the demonstrators and was being fired upon as the revolutionaries gathered there were trying to address both a local and international audience via a free medium.

Bibliography

Acostioaei, Dan. 2012. *Trial/Proces*. Iasi: Universitatea de Arte 'George Enescu'.

Bardulete, Miruna. 2012. 'Ceausescu – vin in 5 minute' – de ce a facut un celebru artist Roman stencilurire din Bucuresti. *B365: Bucurestiul Zi de Zi*.

Barker, Adele Marie. 1999. *Consuming Russia: Popular Culture, Sex, and Society since Gorbachev*. Durham, NC, and London: Duke University Press.

Baudrillard, Jean. 1994. *The Illusion of the End*. Trans. Chris Turner. Stanford, CA: Stanford University Press.

Benjamin, Walter. 1968. 'Theses on the Philosophy of History'. In Hannah Arendt (ed.) *Illuminations*. New York: Schocken Books.

Benjamin, Walter. 1968. 'The Work of Art in the Age of Mechanical Reproduction'. In Hannah Arendt (ed.), Trans. Harry Zohn, *Illuminations*. New York: Schocken Books.

Bercea, Maria. 2005. 'An Offense: the Revolutionary Monument'. *Revista 22*.

Blaga, Iulia. 2008. 'Noi Facem Film Pentru Romani, Iar Romanii Nu Mai Merg La Cinema' (We Make Films for a Romanian Audience, but Romanians Have Stopped Going to the Movies)'. Available online at: http://agenda.liternet.ro/articol/7675/Iulia-Blaga-Radu-Muntean/Noi-facem-film-pentru-romani-iar-romanii-nu-mai-merg-la-cinema-Boogie.html. Accessed 20 March 2010.

Bleiker, Roland. 2001. 'The Aesthetic Turn in International Political Theory', *Millennium: Journal of International Studies* 30(3): 509–533.

Bleiker, Roland. 2006. 'Art After 9/11'. *Alternatives* 31: 77–99.

Bleiker, Roland. 2009. *Aesthetics and World Politics*. London and New York: Palgrave Macmillan.

Blum, Martin. 2000. 'Remaking the East German Past: Ostalgie, Identity, and Material Culture'. *Journal of Popular Culture* 34(3): 229–253.

Bradean, Adina. 2007. 'Death and Documentary: Memory and Film Practice in Post-Communist Romania'. Available online at: http://www.kinokultura.com/specials/6/bradeanu.shtml. Accessed 20 March 2010.

Calinescu, Roxana. 2006. 'Filmul Nu E Manualul De Functionare a Unei Masini De Spalat' (Film is not like a user manual for a washing machine). *Atelier LiterNet*. Available online at: http://atelier.liternet.ro/articol/3541/Roxana-Calinescu-Corneliu-

Porumboiu/Corneliu-Porumboiu-Filmul-nu-e-manualul-de-functionare-a-unei-masini-de-spalat.html. Accessed 20 March 2010.

Carbunariu, Gianina. 2012. '*X MM From Y KM* – About a Possible Performative Archive'. *Scena.ro.*

Cartianu, Grigore. 2009. 'Nicolae si Elena Ceausescu: "Impreuna am luptam, sa murim impreuna"'. *Adevarul.*

Carver, Terrell. 2010. 'Cinematic Ontologies and Viewer Epistemologies: Knowing International Politics as Moving Images'. *Global Society* 24(3): 421–431.

Chirilov, Mihai. 2007. 'You Can Run but You Cannot Hide: New Romanian Cinema'. *Kinokultura*. Available online at: http://www.kinokultura.com/specials/6/chirilov. shtml. Accessed 20 March 2010.

Cinemagia. 2006. 'Reconstruirea Atmosferei Capitalei Din Decembrie 1989' (Reconstituting the Atmosphere of the Capital in December 1989). Available online at: http://www.cinemagia.ro/filme/hartia-va-fi-albastra-14838/articol/14508/.   Accessed 20 March 2010.

Cretulescu, Andrei. 2007. 'Corneliu Porumboiu: Nu Cred Istorie Cu Majuscule, Ci Doar in Istorii Personale'. Available online at: http://atelier.liternet.ro/articol/4206/ Andrei-Cretulescu-Corneliu-Porumboiu/Corneliu-Porumboiu-Nu-cred-in-istorie-cu-majuscule-ci-doar-in-istorii-personale.html. Accessed 8 February 2010.

Doucet, Marc. 2005. 'Child's Play: The Political Imaginary of International Relations and Contemporary Popular Children's Films'. *Global Society* 19(3): 289–306.

Frost, Lola. 2010. 'Aesthetics and Politics'. *Global Society* 24(3): 433–443.

Grancea, Mihaela. 2012. 'The Myths of December 1989. "Places of Memory": Statues, Graveyards, Testimonies'. *Interstitio: East European Review of Historical and Cultural Anthropology* 4(1–2): 19–40.

Hamacher, Werner. 2005. 'Now: Walter Benjamin on Historical Time'. In Andrew Benjamin (ed.) *Walter Benjamin and History.* London, New York: Continuum.

Hofman, Katja. 2007. 'Romanian Cinema on the Rise'. *Variety.* Available online at: http://www.variety.com/article/VR1117967521.html?categoryid=13&cs=1. Accessed 20 March 2010.

Holden, Gerard. 2006. 'Cinematic IR, the Sublime, and the Indistinctness of Art'. *Millennium: Journal of International Studies* 34(3): 793–818.

Hozic, Aida. 2006. 'Book Review of Vincent Mosco's the Digital Sublime and Jean-Michel Valentin's Hollywood, the Pentagon and Washington'. *Millennium: Journal of International Studies* 34: 967–970.

Iordanova, Dina. (1999) 'East Europe's Cinema Industries since 1989: Financing Structure and Studios'. *The Public* 6(2): 45–60.

Iordanova, Dina. 2002. 'Feature Filmmaking within the New Europe: Moving Funds and Images across the East-West Divide'. *Media, Culture, Society* 24(4): 517–536.

Jackson, Patrick Thaddeus. 2010. *The Conduct of Inquiry in International Relations: Philosophy of Science and Its Implications for the Study of World Politics.* London and New York: Routledge.

Kaufman, Anthony. 2007. 'Romanian's Cinematic Revolution: Struggling against the Past'. *IndieWire*, Available online at: http://www.indiewire.com/article/romanias_ cinematic_revolution_struggling_against_the_past/. Accessed 20 March 2010.

Lacy, Marc. 2008. 'Designer Security: MoMA's SAFE: Design Takes on Risk and Control Society'. *Security Dialogue: Special Issue on 'Security, Technologies of Risk and the Political'* 39(2–3): 333–357.

Lamasanu, Stefana. 2010. *Capturing the Romanian Revolution: Violent Imagery, Affect and the Televisual Event*. PhD, Department of Art History and Communication Studies, McGill University.

Livizeanu, Irina. 2007. 'Romanian Cinema on the Edge'. Available online at: http://www.filmstudies.pitt.edu/romanianfilmseries/index.html. Accessed 20 March 2010.

Lowy, Michael. 2005. *Fire Alarm: Reading Walter Benjamin's 'On the Concept of History'*. London, New York: Verso.

Mezincescu, Carmen, and Oana Dinca. 2006. 'Catalin Mitulescu: Asta Este Meseria Mea, Sunt Regizor, Sunt Povestitor'. *Revista HBO*. Available online at: http://atelier.liternet.ro/articol/3771/Redactia-HBO-Catalin-Mitulescu/Catalin-Mitulescu-Asta-este-meseria-mea-sunt-regizor-sunt-povestitor.html. Accessed 9 February 2010.

Mihali, Ciprian. 2007. 'Between Sovereignty and Precariousness: Post-Communist Daily Life Condition'. Institut Francophone Régional d'Etudes Stratégiques: Europe centrale et orientale. Available online at: http://www.ifres.info/europe-centrale-orientale/Rubriques/equipe-ifres-eco/Direction-de-l-IFRES-ECO/ciprian-mihali-directeur-de-l/article/textes. Accessed 6 February 2010.

Mitulescu, Catalin. 2006. *Cum Mi-Am Petrecut Sfarsitul Lumii*. Les Films Pelleas Strada Film, released 15 September 2006.

Modreanu, Cristina. 2013. 'Elements of Ethics and Aesthetics in New Romanian Theatre'. *New Theater Quarterly* 29(4): 385–393.

Moore, Cerwyn. 2009. 'Heretical Conversations with Continental Philosophy: Jan Patocka, Central Europe and Global Politics'. *The British Journal of Politics and International Relations* 11: 315–331.

Moore, Cerwyn. 2010. 'On Cruelty: Literature, Aesthetics and Global Politics'. *Global Society* 24(3): 311–329.

Moore, Cerwyn and Laura Shepherd. 2010. 'Aesthetics and International Relations: Towards a Global Politics'. *Global Society* 24(3): 299–309.

Mungiu, Cristian. 2006. *4 Luni, 3 Saptamani Si 2 Zile*. Mobra Films, released 14 September 2007.

Muntean, Radu. 2006. *Hartia Va Fi Albastra*. Antena 1 Multimedia Est, released 13 October 2006.

Mustata, Dana. 2011. '"The Revolution Has Been Televised…" Television as Historical Agent in the Romanian Revolution'. *Journal of Modern European History* 10(1): 76–97.

Nasta, Dominique. 2007. 'The Tough Road to Minimalism: Contemporary Romanian Film Aesthetics' Available online at: http://www.kinocultura.com/specials/6/nasta.shtml. Accessed 9 February 2010.

Nemescu, Cristian. 2007. *California Dreamin'*. Nesfarsit MediaPro Pictures, released 1 June 2007.

Parvulescu, Constantin. 2013. 'Embodied Histories. Harun Farocki and Andrei Ujica's Videograms of a Revolution and Ovidiu Bose Pastina's Timisoara-December 1989 and the Uses of the Independent Camera'. *Rethinking History: The Journal of Theory and Practice* 17(3): 354–382.

Paun, Alexandra. 2006. 'Radu Muntean: Interviu Exclusiv Cu Cinemagia'. Available online at: http://www.cinemagia.ro/filme/hartia-va-fi-albastra-14838/articol/14777/. Accessed 9 February 2010.

Pintilie, Ileana. 2000. 'Problems in Transit: Performance in Romania'. *ArtMargins*. Available online at: http://www.artmargins.com/index.php/archive/424–problems-in-transit-performance-in-romania. Accessed 16 February 2015.

Porumboiu, Corneliu. 2006. *A Fost Sau N-a Fost?* 42 km Film, released 29 September 2006.

Preda, Catalina. 2010. 'Looking at the Past through an Artistic Lens: Art of Memorialization'. In *History of Communism in Europe, Vol I – Politics of Memory in Post-communist Europe*, edited by Mihail Neamtu. Bucharest: Zeta Books.

Puiu, Cristi. 2005. *Moartea D-Lui Lazarescu*. Mandragora Movies, released 23 September 2005.

Pusca, Anca. 2007. 'Shock, Therapy and Postcommunist Transitions'. *Alternatives* 32: 341–360.

Roman, Denise. 2003. *Fragmented Identities: Popular Culture, Sex, and Everyday Life in Postcommunist Romania*. Lanham, Boulder, New York, Toronto and Plymouth: Lexington Books.

Scott, A.O. 2008. 'In Film, the Romanian New Wave Has Arrived'. *The New York Times*, 19 January. Available online at: http://www.nytimes.com/2008/01/19/arts/19iht-fromanian.1.9340722.html?pagewanted=all&_r=0. Accessed July 2015.

Scott, A.O. 2008. 'New Wave on the Black Sea'. *New York Times*, 20 January 2008. Available online at: http://www.nytimes.com/2008/01/20/magazine/20Romanian-t.html?scp=1&sq=New+Wave+on+the+Black+Sea&st=nyt. Accessed July 2015.

Shapiro, Michael. 1999*Cinematic Political Thought: Narrating Race, Nation and Gender (Taking on the Political)*. Edinburgh: Edinburgh University Press.

Shapiro, Michael. 2006. 'The Sublime Today: Re-partitioning the Global Sensible'. *Millennium: Journal of International Studies* 34(3): 657–681.

Shapiro, Michael. 2008. *Cinematic Geopolitics*. New York: Routledge.

Stojanova, Christina and Dana Duma. 2007. 'The New Romanian Cinema: Editorial Remarks'. *Kinokultura*. Available online at: http://www.kinokultura.com/specials/6/introduction.shtml. Accessed 20 March 2010.

Sylvester, Christine. 2008. *Art/Museums: International Relations Where We Least Expect It*. London: Paradigm.

Weber, Cynthia. 2006. *Imagining America at War: Morality, Politics and Film*. London and New York: Routledge.

Weldes, Jutta. 2003. *Science Fiction and World Politics*. London and New York: Palgrave Macmillan.

Wydra, Harald. 2007. *Communism and the Emergence of Democracy*. Cambridge: Cambridge University Press.

*Ziarul Financiar*2007. 'Romania Are Cea Mai Mare Rate De Penetrare a Televiziunii Prin Cablu Din Balcani' (Romania Has the Highest User Rate of Cable TV in the Balkans). Available online at: http://www.zf.ro/zf-24/romania-are-cea-mai-mare-rata-de-penetrare-a-televiziunii-prin-cablu-din-balcani-3029542/. Accessed 20 March 2010.

3 Erasing communism

Industrial and human ruins of post-communist Europe

The past cannot just be erased, it cannot disappear without trace into the immediate unknown; at most it can be neutralised or rendered invisible. In the immediate rush to separate itself from its communist past, much of former communist Europe was keen to bury or destroy monuments, portraits, signs, party memorabilia, and strip former sites of their previous meaning, as if communism could simply be removed through the removal of key objects and symbols. What remained was something that people would later call 'the communist mentality', 'the culture of corruption', the 'relics of communism', all of which recognised that communism did not just seep into the material (buildings, monuments) but also into the mind, body and logic of society.

With much of the newly born civil society institutions that emerged after 1989 focusing on 'changing attitudes' – fighting the culture of corruption, backward mentalities or fearful approaches – building confidence and developing democratic engagement, there was little recognition of the complete dependency of certain key sites – particularly large industrial sites and cities – on the logic of the past. No amount of 'reform', political or economic, could ever revive these sites to their former, perhaps inflated and foolish 'glory', but more importantly, nothing could make them sustainable as the mammoth entities that they once were: places where work, collegiality, leisure, housing, services, were all dependent upon an entire working-class community existing as its own separate self-sufficient pod.

The industrial communist city was often a unique space, unlike capital cities or cities with a long historical legacy that stretched well beyond communism: they were built from scratch and designed to create a community whose entire existence could only be justified while the plant continued to exist (Rauta 2013). The working classes of these industrial cities were in that respect unique as well: their skills were not necessarily transferable as they were often trained on-site with the specific equipment and functioning of the plant in mind, while their existence and their needs were organised and catered to in light of the needs of the plant – from timetable scheduling, to health needs. The city made sense as long as the plant continued to exist, with the working class of these cities completely dependent on the functioning of the plant. The subsequent plant closures and privatisations resulted not only in unmanageable levels of unemployment but also in the complete disruption of the social fabric of these cities.

The destruction of these plants is not equivalent to the removal of communist symbols or neutralisation of communist architecture – although these industrial cities were the ultimate living embodiments of communism – as a reconfiguration of life beyond the plant is often unimaginable (Bartmanski 2011). While sheer survival might be possible, like it is even in a post-apocalyptic scenario, the rebuilding of a sustainable social fabric oftentimes is not. Along with the material relics of the plant lie the human relics: those who cannot be retrained, re-employed, re-located. Like the ruins of the plants themselves, they become slowly invisible, ghost like characters roaming the city, purposeless, carrying within them the memory of a different time, decaying in silence to a point of non-*recognition*. Unlike some of the machinery left in the plants, which can often be sold, re-fitted and re-used, they often carry no value: their being as worthless now as the ideology that shaped them.

This chapter looks at a series of attempts to reclaim former industrial spaces and bring them into a new kind of visibility, giving them a second life and purpose: the photographing of the Hunedoara Ironworks, the Vitkovice Ironworks, the Petrila Mines Project and the recent launch of *Of People and Snails*, a film engaging with the industrial decay of small town Romania, each in their own way, seek to shed light on often forgotten territories and spaces, and more importantly, on often forgotten people.

These are not 'regeneration' projects per se: they do not seek to permanently stop the decay and rebuild. Instead, they merely seek to temporarily arrest and capture this ruination process before it erases all that is left. The timing of these attempts is crucial: capture the ruins while people can still relate to them, while they can still translate their previous meaning and purpose, and scratch the consciousness and memory of those who would like to pretend that they are already part of a distant past, irrelevant to today's ambitions. The photographing of the ruins, the use of film to imagine continuing life amongst the ruins, constitute what Dragos Dascalu calls a form of contestational architecture, whereby otherwise marginal, forgotten spaces, take centre stage, are reimbued with purpose, power and a sense of community, at a point when otherwise they would simply become invisible (Bors and Dascalu 2012). They are 'aesthetic' interventions in the sense that seek to reposition, spatially and politically, forgotten decaying industrial spaces and the people that inhabit them, and through that repositioning, capture their 'actuality' by allowing them to reclaim a space in the 'here and now' of the present, as opposed to the 'there and then' of the past.

Neither here nor there: post-industrialism and the disappearance of the 'worker'

Krishan Kumar describes the transition to post-industrialism as the transition from 'the co-ordination of machines and men for the production of goods' to a 'post-industrial society [...] organized around knowledge, for the purpose of social control and the directing of innovation and change' (Kumar 1976: 455). Thomas Hutton pushes this definition further and interprets post-industrialism as

> not only a phase of urban development characterised by the contraction of basic manufacturing and the supplanting of traditional industry and labour by service industries and the centrality of theoretical knowledge, but also as an expression denoting political acceptance of the implications of industrial restructuring.
>
> (Hutton 2004: 1955)

Margaret Kohn adds that post-industrial transformations in city architecture and the tendency towards the transformation of former urban industrial spaces into upscale leisure destinations: 'illustrates many of the forces that are reconfiguring cities: commodification, gentrification, the city as theme park and spectacle [...] and the consumer preferences of the creative class' (Kohn 2010: 359). The themes are clear: knowledge versus force/labour, political adjustment to and acceptance of the decline of labour and the rise of the creative class – along with their consumer preferences.

While often invoked in the context of re-building, or commodifying spaces that previously belonged to the 'industrial' era, what post-industrialism often does not capture is what the decline of traditional industry and labour actually means in terms of its human costs: what is lost within the tacit acceptance of industrialism as a ruin of the past, is the very category of the 'worker' and along with it, the continuous existence of those who once carried this label. The 'workers' in post-industrial societies are effectively erased from the picture, even while still inhabiting ruinous industrial spaces. They are erased on an economic level – by effectively being rendered redundant/irrelevant; on a political level – through the dissipation of the unions (Ost 1993, 2005); and on a social level – by the removal of all sense of collectivity and collective protections.

Charity Scribner argues that Europe's post-industrial turn is also a cultural turn, in that it does not just signify a change in economic system and a prioritisation of new 'spaces of capital', but also a radical change in how people 'reflect on'/ 'think about' their society. She notes a clear move away from the written medium to a visual one, and a radical change in how people relate to one another: increasingly through antagonisms and oppositions, such as rich/poor, majority/minority, male/female (Scribner 2003: 159). It is on this cultural level though that we have noticed some of the most interesting attempts to reclaim the value of the 'industrial', the 'worker' and the 'collective'. Her work focuses on a number of authors and artists who seek to salvage 'not the mechanical function of managed labor, but rather the collective sites of resistance that also occupied that historical moment' (Scribner 2003: 6).

While Scribner focuses on processes of collective nostalgia, mourning, melancholia and disavowal that characterise the post-communist period and often focus on practices of collecting 'now dead' objects for the purpose of memorialisation, or 're-enacting' traditions that have now disappeared, this chapter is more interested in practices that seek to confirm the continued use and relevance of 'industrial patrimony' as well as the continuation of life amongst 'industrial ruins'. Like a species that is about to go extinct, the former communist 'workers' still rummage through their old habitat trying to make some sense of everything that hit them. While their ruinous bodies physically betray them (Kideckel 2008) insuring their most-definite destruction, their faces speak of many stories left to tell before they go. A handful of artists have taken it upon themselves to stop, listen and record. In the process, they have uncovered an often invisible world, repackaged it according to 'post-industrial' conventions and preferences of a creative class that is increasingly drawn to industrial chic, and planted it smack in the middle of a post-communist society that seems to have long forgotten how to be a 'collective'.

Kombinat, a collective work, features a series of photographs that focus on the decaying 'industrial patrimony' of Romania, including the famous Hunedoara Steelwork. The first publication of its kind in Romania, it started an important tradition within Igloo Press to feature artists and work that engaged directly with the legacy of communism and its continuous impact on contemporary life. It helped spur a rising movement of young architects, photographers and intellectuals to think not only about how these spaces could be brought into visibility, but also, how decaying ones could be reclaimed for their aesthetic rather than financial value. The Start-up Petrila is one such movement that this chapter will touch upon, along with the dual photography project – *Post-Industrial Stories*, of Ioana Carlig and Marin Raica, two Romanian photographers who have been on an impressive two year journey through the main industrial sites of Romania, sites that they themselves inhabit for months at a time in order to build a stronger connection to their subjects.

As a complement to the collective work of *Kombinat*, StartUp Petrila and *Post-Industrial Stories*, the chapter will also look at Vaclav Jirasek's photography, in particular his Vitkovice Ironwork photographs and their ability to engage with a landscape that lies at the heart of an important debate on the re-appropriation of industrial patrimony either as a museum or as a new form of capital. The film *Of Men and Snails* takes this important debate on the ability to 'capitalise' on former industrial resources further, through an 'imaginary' yet entirely plausible scenario that would see an old car factory transformed into a snail packaging plant. Each of these interventions serves to engage both our literal eye as well as our intellectual eye in a joint effort to understand how the material, visual and human artifacts of an ideology – communism – continue to co-exist with a more newly built environment that prioritises new sources of capital.

A journey through the wasteland of communism

Perhaps the sorest sight for the traveller through the Eastern European countryside is that of industrial ruins, surrounded by cities and communities that now lie in equal ruination. Industrial ruins are certainly not your usual entry point into the study of post-communist transitions, although there is a long intellectual and artistic tradition of engaging with ruins as an important source of historical understanding: the fascination with modern/industrial ruins dates back to Eugene Atget, Andrieu and the photographers of the Franco-Prussian war and the Paris Commune, Georg Simmel and Walter Benjamin (Jemison 2009). They have inspired contemporary writers such as Tim Edensor to consider the relationship between materiality and human emotionality in the context of industrial ruins, which, as he argues, are particularly imbued with ghosts, memories and spatial practices of resistance that serve not only as a reminder of the damaging effects of change, but also of the continuing capacity of these spaces to challenge the spatial and emotional forms of organisation that have followed them (Edensor 2005a; Edensor 2005b; Edensor 2005c).

Industrial ruins in Eastern Europe are seen to represent, perhaps more so than anything else, the hard shell of communism: the last remains of a now past era that are littered around the post-communist landscapes, often empty and abandoned, stripped of any recyclable material to a point where their previous role becomes unrecognisable even to those who used to work there. Attempts to revive these sites through privatisation have more often than not failed, the success stories having only been able to salvage a very small part of the industrial plants that once stood there. As the debate around these former industrial sites is moving ahead with the recognition that many of them are not salvageable and will remain nothing but empty and decaying shells, attempts to aestheticise and museumise them are opening up new ways of engaging with these spaces by tapping into their emotional and redemptive potential.

Space, and the built environment in general, has always been connected to certain notions of human utopia, whether social, economical or political. Decayed spaces such as industrial ruins, can thus, by correspondence, be connected to a certain notion of dystopia. If, as Susan Buck-Morss eloquently explains, spaces and buildings were used to visually inscribe the communist utopia into people's minds, the ruination of these same spaces can be directly connected to the dismantling of that utopia. Along with the buildings, it was not just an ideology – mass-utopia or dreamworld as Buck-Morss calls it – that went crumbling, but also a particular collective and individual identity, a social order that sustained life both physically – through the industrial platforms and the cities surrounding them – as well as emotionally – through the communities and solidarity that emerged within them.

This collapse has often been examined under the concept of disillusionment – understood as the loss and destruction of particular collective illusions – a concept however that has been rarely connected and explored through the prism of space and spatial destruction. Academics were quick to investigate post-communist disillusionment through interviews and polling techniques and attempt to theorise it in light of notions of social disruption and economic need, yet most ignored its spatial representations in post-communist cities: the sudden (physical) collapse of all industries, the destruction of local government buildings, monuments and stores, and the emergence of so-called temporary architectures – open markets, make-shift bars and kiosks – that resembled partial ruins more than construction.

Dystopia – and the collective disillusionment that went along with it – was clearly marked in the physical collapse of cities, especially industrial cities, whose infrastructure relied almost exclusively on the industries that created them in the first place. Thus, heating, water, gas and electricity distribution began to collapse, resulting not only in further infrastructure decay, but also in a continuous decay of the bodies inhabiting the cities. Accidents such as gas explosions – as a result of replacing water heating with gas heating using make-shift second-hand boilers – became more and more common in industrial cities throughout Romania, while suicide rates in industrial towns skyrocketed along with unemployment.

The ruination of the human body – both physical and psychological – went hand in hand with the ruination of space. As industrial spaces were slowly emptied out – through the theft of all recyclable materials – so were the industrial cities connected to them: this was marked by mass migration towards other cities and sometimes the countryside – which provided at least a means of subsistence through agriculture – as well as migration towards Western Europe – rings of trafficking as well as illegal workers can often be traced back directly to such failed industrial towns (Iancu 2006; Iancu 2007a; Iancu 2007b; Ioan 2006).The rate of decay was quick: within two to three years industrial horizons became unrecognisable, collapsed in a pool of dust, regrets, corruption and more importantly a sense of self-destruction and futility that directly challenged discourses of progress and positive change.

Just like the utopia of communist industries was built both on the physical space itself as well as on a certain discourse of worker emancipation, the dystopia emerged not only through the physical destruction of these spaces but also through the replacement of their symbolism: the revolutionary symbolism, imbued both by communist propaganda as well as the 1989 revolutions – the majority of which originated on industrial platforms – was quickly replaced with a symbolism of disruption and threat – as industrial cities collapsed and workers rebelled, often disrupting the fragile order of the years immediately following 1989. Ruined industrial spaces thus became a testimony of change, as well as a testimony of the human ruination that followed.

Yet many of these ruins lay, often conveniently, outside of major capital cities, and could thus be easily disregarded as non-representative of the general experience of the post-communist transition: they were the 'minority' losers of the transition, while everybody else stood to win. This kind of discourse erased not only the agonising pain of millions of people but also the extent to which post-communist change was at least equally founded on destruction and ruins as it was on construction and images of positive change. The erasure of ruins, both physically as well as metaphorically, denied former workers the possibility of positive engagements with their former work-spaces, and the rest of the population the ability to identify with their plight.

As Richard Sennett argues in *Flesh and Stone,* the body and the built environment have always lived in close symbiosis throughout history, with notions and understandings of space and construction often being directly derived from knowledge of the body, organs and blood circulation. The traditional, Roman city, according to Sennett, was designed to function very much like the body: with a centre that pumped 'blood' into the city and peripheries that served to feed the centre. Community life was created through particular designs of the city that brought individuals together in central squares during the day, and dispersed them in individual and family accommodations during the night. If the central squares, the heart of the traditional city, generally housed churches and parliaments, modern cities and communist industrial cities in particular, replaced these with industrial platforms: the latter becoming the productive heart of the city, the place where the community gathered under the watchful eye of the state (Sennett 1994).

Like most modern cities, communist industrial cities were often artificially created from scratch: people, construction and production materials were uprooted and brought in from different parts of the country, appeased by the promise of an urban lifestyle – family flats, cinemas, schools, medical centres – and the security of a stable job for each member of the family. Although artificially created, the sense of collectivity developed in such cities was not easily replicated in non-industrial cities. Trained together, living and working together in traits and jobs that rarely rotated, inhabitants of industrial cities learned to depend on each other, both on the line of production as well as outside. Their bodies inhabited the industrial spaces in a mutual symbiosis that extended much beyond the workplace itself, towards the entire city. The city was the workers and the workers were the city. This symbiosis was certainly not unique to communist industrial cities. Industrial cities in the West experienced a similar collective ethos, as John Kirk explains was the case in the UK 'the working community is not merely a material reality but a collectivist imaginary, in which the sense of purpose and endeavor is a shared one' (Kirk 2003: 180). Unlike in the West though, the collective imaginary of the communist industrial city was carefully designed and controlled by the state, and thus in many ways dependent on the continuing existence of the state.

With the collapse of the communist state and the process of centralised economics, it was not just the economy that unravelled but also this collective imaginary that depended on an ingrained respect for the worker as a human being and a social category, as well as for his/her work. The worker and the physical space they inhabited – the industrial platform – formed the belly button (umbilicus) of the communist industrial city. The destruction of the umbilicus meant the destruction of the city, for with the umbilicus lay the purpose and logic of the city. As Sennett argues was the case with historical cities, a city could only be rebuilt from the old umbilicus outward, often requiring either the reconstruction of the 'temple' – in this case the industrial platform – or at least the symbolic recognition of the old temple – either through a religious symbol or a square. If the logic still applies, then the reconstruction and revival of communist industrial cities also depends on the ability to physically and materially acknowledge the former industrial platform as the centre, either through preservation and restoration/museumisation efforts or through representation practices that serve to memorialise the workers, their community and the spaces they once inhabited (Czaplicka, Gelazis, and Ruble 2009).

Each of these practices serves to recreate the illusion of a particular space and interaction that is now missed: either by preserving actual parts of the former space, by recreating similar spaces, or by symbolically enacting a particular memory. They are key to proving not only an important sense of belonging to a community but also of self-worth. With many post-communist industrial towns often capitalising – usually rhetorically – on their former 'glory' as a means of attracting new investments, tourism and state or regional funding – such as, more recently, EU funding – memory clearly plays an important role in their self-image and future image.

The closure of former industrial plants pushed not only workers, but entire communities, permanently outside of these spaces, denying them the physical and emotional comfort of coming into contact with them again. Within a matter of months, after the collapse of the industry sector in 1990, factories closed their gates, built new fences or simply started tearing through old structures looking for scrap to resell. The workers and local communities could only look in from outside as their former offices, workspaces, assembly lines were torn apart, leaving behind complete destruction and desolation. Machinery they once serviced lay abandoned, taken apart or rusting in the rain, a constant reminder to the futility of years of service and hope for potential reinvestments. Forced to look in from outside, the worker became seer: the gaze and not the body leading the interaction with space. In this shift, memory and reflection replaces action, leading to melancholy and a certain amount of disengagement. As Walter Benjamin explains, the panoramic gaze imposes both a physical as well as a mental and emotional distance that forces the mind to reflect upon the 'object' in sight (Benjamin 1970).

The ruination of these industrial complexes frees them of the utopian communist rhetoric embedded in them, but at the same time also burdens them with new questions about the possibility of creating non-utopian spaces/ reflections/representations that do however still capture the pride, self-worth and sacrifice of the worker in history. If Benjamin is correct in arguing that '.in the ruin history has physically merged into the setting' (Benjamin 1998: 177), then erasing the ruin is equivalent to the erasure of irrecoverable history. The physicality/materiality of the ruin is thus essential to the possibility of reflection. Practices of representation, such as photography, according to Benjamin, serve only as a second best mediator, an illusionary pause in the destruction process. Philosophers such as Jacques Rancière, however, revived the potential of these (aesthetic) practices by arguing that they have an unrivaled emancipatory ability. By defining aesthetic experience as 'a specific sphere of experience which invalidates the ordinary hierarchies incorporated in everyday sensory experience' (Rancière 2005: 15) Rancière suggests that aesthetic representations have the physical potential to bring about radical change (Rancière 1989).

As the gaze of Rancière's workers shifts from machinery to the written text, so does their position of subordination through the imagination of new possibilities. The workers re-imagine themselves through a simple shift of the gaze. The 'shock' of discovering new possibilities is not the 'coup de foudre' of the Kantian 'sublime' but rather the slow shifting of routines that eventually lead to an attempt to clearly redefine their positioning – in Rancière's analysis, the French Revolution. The aesthetics of change for Rancière is thus not contemplative alone, but rather active, carrying a powerful potential in itself. Aesthetics – often viewed as representation – is not separated from action. New forms of seeing create new possibilities for action, as Rancière explains.

The redemptive character of the aesthetics of change, as pointed out by Rancière, is however challenged by the privileging of the gaze of 'outsiders'. Aestheticising practices such as photography, film and museumisation, aimed at the industrial ruins of post-communist Europe, have mainly been led by 'outsiders', people whose gaze is not part of the 'everyday' of the communities involved. With workers often lying outside of the picture – literally speaking, the photographs depicting industrial ruins – it is easy to decouple the scenery from a particular historical context and admire it for its physical/geometrical lines alone. The human traces serve only as temporary reminders of a population that must have been there sometime. The worker disappears physically as a material fragment, and the image of the world no longer contains him/her: as such, the worker disappears as an ideational category.

While some artists and photographers purposefully attempt to bring the worker back into the scenery, they often blend them into the space itself, creating the visual illusion of the human and the ruin physically merged into one: the spectre of colours swallows the workers into the form of the whole, their matter seemingly no longer organic, alive, causing them to become just a material fragment, just like the tools that they hold or the chair on which they sit. Vaclav Jirasek's portraits of workers, as we will see later, capture the merging of the two: a beautiful metaphor of symbiotic ruination, material and physical decay into one. The possibility of salvation is literally out of the 'picture' as the tired or covered eyes of the workers reveal complete passivity and acceptance of their ruined 'fate'. Despite its destruction, the space around them remains comfortable for as long as they can inhabit it. The moment of spatial exclusion is the moment of death.

Photographic representations of ruins and the workers inhabiting them also carry the potential of creating reflective counter-sites, by symbolically emptying space out of its former utility and human content and refilling it with new meaning. Foucault captures this process through his notion of heterotopias: defined as 'counter-sites, a kind of effectively enacted utopia in which the real sites [...] are simultaneously represented, contested and inverted' (Foucault 1967). Assigning a particular mood to the past through practices of representation such as photography and museumisation, does put us, in a way, in control of history, as Schönle (2006) and Lahusen (2006) argue, and any such form of control is potentially dangerous. It is only through the unmediated gaze alone, they argue, that the natural, organic decay can be captured. Any attempts to aestheticise it through the eyes of the artist, photographer or preservationist, ruins its reflective potential.

Yet the industrial ruins of post-communist Europe are most often sealed off, erased from the gaze of outsiders and allowing only limited peaks for the gaze of local communities. The grief and pain associated with the ruination of these sites is not only triggered by their decay but also by the inability to interact with them. Aestheticising practices such as photography or museumisation, from this perspective, do not necessarily appear as negative. While they run the risk of feeding the already rampant communist nostalgia, as Lahusen suggests, he also points out that this is unlikely to happen to 'those who still live in its ruins, because they are home' (Lahusen 2006: 736). One can however only assess the positive versus negative effects of different representation practices, such as photography and museumisation, in context alone.

Kombinat: *photographing the Hunedoara Ironworks*

The steel and metal processing plant at Hunedoara – also known as the Fire Fortress – employed over 20,000 workers as of the late 1980s and sprawled over 250,000 square meters, not including the funicular and rail connections to exploratory sites, or the water dam that redirected water for the cooling process. The gigantic stature was supported by hundreds of constructions on site, from four blast furnaces to several cooling towers, to tens of industrial halls, private rail system and locomotives, roads and over the surface piping. Built originally in 1881 on a historical metal extraction and processing site that goes back to Roman times, the Hunedoara processing plant continued to grow both in size and production capacity until 1990, when the collapse of the communist systems throughout Central and Eastern Europe brought much of the production process to a halt, resulting in large layoffs in 1998 – over 7,000 people lost their job – and continuous layoffs since then as the plant fell into disarray and was sectioned and sold to different private enterprises under the privatisation scheme. In 2004, there were only 3,000 workers left at the plant, now employed by Mittal Steel, one of the largest steel processing companies in the world that acquired the Hunedoara plant as part of a larger buy-out of several other metal and steel processing plants throughout the country.[1] By November 2008, the plant announced that it was getting ready to file for bankruptcy and was shutting down production for the following two months as a result of the economic crisis. This is the first time since 1930 that the plant has been completely closed.

The plant lies at the heart of the city of Hunedoara – home to about 68,000 people – a grey, industrial town that once attracted people with the promise of secure jobs and now fights to support its diminishing population. With unemployment reaching a high of 17 per cent in 2000, the city managed to bounce back towards late 2005 by attracting a number of private companies through tax-free policies and the opening of an industrial park. With large parts of the former 'Fire Fortress' in ruins, and most of the construction material stolen – from bricks to train tracks to knobs and anything else that could be reused – the land on which it once sat remains one of the main valuable assets of the city, apart from the two electrical furnaces that Mittal Steel now threatens to dismantle and sell for scrap. A number of ongoing trials over property rights however keep a large part of the land unused, as different owners dispute their right over the parcelled terrain – mainly a result of a faulty privatisation process and corrupt mechanism of land and property registration. Despite the local administration now challenging the so-called 'management of theft' that took place since the beginning of the privatisation and parcelling process in 1997, there is little left to be done in terms of recuperating lost property and equipment, much of which has been stolen or sold (Replica 2007).

For the majority of the workers who were laid off, the Ironworks remain nothing but a shadow of what they once were and what they stood for. The sacking forced most of the workers into early retirement or part-time jobs that keep them just at about floating level. Many have left the city or even the country in search of new opportunities. With the Ironworks unlikely to help sustain the region's economy as they once did, the city seems doomed: over 80 per cent of its high school students leave the city to go to university and most of them never return (Iancu 2007a). The infrastructure continues to decay while investment in the region remains relatively low despite the generous package of tax incentives that it offers.

In several interviews conducted by local newspapers, former workers and administrators expressed being significantly affected by the state of the Iron-works, often getting teary eyed when walking past them. Those who have long left the city are shocked to notice upon return that even the train tracks have been ripped out, leaving old wagons and locomotives stranded and emptied out. Piles of red tainted soil, used to extract iron, now have grass growing on them, adding to the desolation of the place. While environmentally cleaner, the air of the city has already left its imprint on the greying buildings: the soot, although no longer present in the air, has melted into the material: everything still appears dusty, and where fresh layers of paint have not been laid, the city looks the same as it always did: a wavy grey.

Stefan Tripsa, the hero-worker of Hunedoara who came to impersonate the ideal of the communist worker is saddened as well. Glorified by communist propaganda as an example of hard work and efficiency, the engineer could at one point see the soot coming out of the smoke stacks of the industrial plat-form and tell from their colour and consistency which piece of machinery was malfunctioning and which needed adjusting. His naked eye could describe the quality of the iron produced without the need for laboratory results. His skills are now useless. Although he can still see the smoke stacks from his house up

Photo 3.1 Cooling Towers Hunedoara
Tamas Dezso, Romanian–Hungarian Photographer

Photo 3.2 Metal Scrapping Hunedoara
Tamas Dezso, Romanian–Hungarian Photographer

on a hill about two kilometres from the ironworks, the smoke is long gone, and long with it, his sense of purpose.

As part of a larger movement that advocates the preservation of old industrial buildings as part of Romania's industrial patrimony, a group of photographers supported by Igloo Press published a catalogue of photographs focusing on industrial ruins entitled *Kombinat* (2007). The word carries particular connotations, signalling the informal way in which workers addressed the industrial plants where they worked: Combinat. The 'K' is both ironic as well as 'hip', signalling a clear shift in the way in which these industrial spaces are treated. The album contains a combination of photos from the largest industrial plants within Romania – including Hunedoara – as well as a series of essays discussing the symbolism and possible future uses of these spaces. As Bruno Andresoiu explains, the album is clearly critical of communism as an ideology that had a particular impact on Romania's built environment as well as society at large:

> *Kombinat* is not only a different way of spelling the name given to large industrial platforms – combinate – but also the name that we chose to give to this bizarre world of industrial ruins, of concrete and iron monsters in decay, of forbidden sites of the now dead socialist economy. Perhaps the most somber built expression of a criminal ideology, *Kombinat* illustrates the violent destruction of a society in the name of ideology. *Kombinat: Industrial Ruins of a Golden Era* is also a collection of images from some of these industrial sites whose abandonment led not only to an advanced state of ruin of their built components but also of the society surrounding them.
>
> (Andresoiu 2007)

The album however goes beyond a simple critique of communism. In fact, the images speak a different language from the essays: the critique of communism is far less obvious in the pleasing black and white aesthetics of the half built and half ruined. The spaces are not mourned, saddened or even perceived as an environmental threat. Instead, the photographs focus on unexpected symmetries and asymmetries created by the collapse and transformation of different materials, as well as on the refreshing possibility of wide-open vistas that register no human presence. The ruins seem to have a positive emotional and aesthetic appeal, similar perhaps to that of natural landscapes.

The essays accompanying the volume reinforce this optimism by arguing that new uses for these industrial sites are not only possible but can also help regenerate communities culturally, socially, economically and politically. Other successful transitions from former industrial sites to museums and commercial spaces provide important inspiration, such as London's TATE Modern, Manchester's Museum of Science and Industry or Saint-Maurice, Canada's the Forges Du Saint-Maurice. Proposals to preserve entire industrial or historical cities, such as downtown Detroit or Rhyolite, Nevada offer even more ambitious perspectives, suggesting a possible merging of everyday spaces with museumised spaces. These proposals, although perhaps unrealistic as far as the Hunedoara Ironworks are concerned, have opened up new critical spaces of discussion and imagination, with young architecture students working on would-be plans for the Ironworks. Although largely unrealistic, due to lack of funding, these, for now, largely imaginary proposals have spurred an increasingly active movement whose actions have sought to creatively interact with and preserve some of Romania's industrial patrimony. Amongst the most interesting projects spurred by this movement are the StartUp Petrila project and the *Post-Industrial Stories* project, by Ioana Carlig and Marin Raica.

StartUp Petrila

Initiated by a group of young student architects in partnership with the Cultural Foundation Conditia Romania back in 2012, the project focused on saving from demolition a few of the buildings from the larger Petrila mining operation in Romania. The city of Petrila largely owes its existence due to mining, with a long historical tradition of coal mining in the area that began back in 1859. A majority of the local community has in one way or another been involved in mining exploitation for much of their life. With a majority of the mines now closed and mining activity reduced by over 80 per cent, locals are struggling to make sense of what is to come. All Petrila mines have now been closed and the process of demolition of the buildings and installations used in the mining exploitation has been scheduled to take place by December 2015. The process of closing the mines, overseen by the Romanian government and funded by the European Commission and the International Monetary Fund, does not require demolition of all buildings. Instead, it simply requires the securing of buildings from a structural and chemical standpoint and insuring the de-contamination of the soil. Giving that funds have already been allocated for this process, a series of local activist groups along with students have started arguing in support of using the funds for preservation rather than demolition purposes.

Under the aegis of a working group on urban, post-industrial regeneration, architecture, urbanism, sociology and geography students from around the country have researched the mine, the local community and the current use of public spaces in relation to the mines. Based on this, they came up with a series of different solutions for preserving the Petrila buildings, which they presented to the local administration, while at the same time filing for the recognition of several of the buildings as industrial patrimony, which as such, should be protected from demolition. Recognising the value of a nearby urban centre, a series of structures that could be easily rehabilitated given that they are already connected to local utilities, a strong human resource base willing to retrain, a surrounding rural landscape that holds value for tourism, and funds that could be accessed through the European Union, the students proposed that several of the buildings be listed as industrial patrimony, preserved and redeveloped.

The action was partially successful, in that several of the buildings were indeed recognised as industrial patrimony and are in the process of being listed as such. A series of demolitions of buildings deemed 'unsafe' is however scheduled to take place, despite a hands-on proposals that looked at the potential for rehabilitating the site for partial economic use – as a wood processing plant, with interested investors; for cultural use in the shape of a museum that would commemorate the history of the area and local community; and for mixed use, including the possible relocation of the mayor's office in the old administrative building of the mining plant and the extension of the local railway system to include Petrila in order to ease access for tourists.

In order to protest these demolitions, the students, supported by the Plus-Minus group, organised a small participatory project, which included the temporary opening of one of the mine buildings to the public and involved the painting of several of the spaces in order to showcase how they could be used for creative and community purposes. The movement, although it has left only a minimal physical trace since no actual regeneration project has started, has generated an impressive number of materials, conference papers, opinion pieces, interviews with participants, and led to a strong mobilisation of local actors and communities, students, architects, and activist groups. In the process, Petrila was imagined as a different kind of space, one imbued with much more optimism, a sense of local history and community pride, a place where stories could be re-told and preserved and where members of the local community could reengage in new ways with spaces that have long played an important role in their lives.

Perhaps most importantly, this imagined Petrila has sparked a movement amongst young students, and architects in particular, to begin to discuss the future of Romania's industrial patrimony. A series of publications, including Ph.D. theses (Balana 2014), mark an increased interest in imagining these spaces beyond their purely economic purpose, and focusing instead on recovering their 'existential', 'reflective' and 'metaphoric' purpose along phenomenological lines. The most visible publications however have been the posters and pamphlets used by the students to advertise meetings, conferences and working groups, as well as to call for further intervention and public participation. Through the creative use of a series of powerful images, such as the painting of one of the cisterns on the mine site in the shape of a Campbell can – in the style of Andy Warhol – reading 'Conserve the Petrila Mine', and performances such as the opening of the Centre Pompidou on site – which celebrated the wall paintings of several artists on the site buildings, the students managed to create an important temporary space with a lasting virtual presence: the pictures now populate a series of virtual internet sites aimed at helping the preservation process, including a facebook support page.

The creation of these imagined/virtual spaces in direct connection to the physical space of the mining plant has significantly expanded the potential for action beyond the immediacy of the plant and has, perhaps more importantly, managed to involve a series of other actors into actively thinking about Petrila in particular, and industrial ruins in general. Although still a specialised discourse, the increased awareness of the potential of industrial patrimony in Romania and the desire of young people to get involved in different preservation efforts has marked an interesting new cultural turn in a post-communist society that has been accused of excessive apathy and pessimism leading to inaction. StartUp Petrila, along with a series of other more prominent movements such as Protect Rosia Montana, mark perhaps not only an important cultural turn but also an aesthetic move to rethink the importance of ruined spaces and the communities that inhabit them and re-empower them through a wider collective effort, that at the very least, ensures their stories will be heard.

Post-Industrial Stories

Ioana Cirlig (www.ioanacirlig.com) and Marin Raica (www.marinraica.com), two Romanian photojournalists, have recently embarked on a personal journey that seeks to uncover the effects of deindustrialisation in Romania, and in particular, how these changes affect the people and the landscape (http://postindustrialstories.com). Unlike other photographers interested in photographing a declining industrial landscape, Carlig and Raica have decided to actually move to the areas that they will photograph and live among the local communities for extended periods of time. Envisioned as a visual ethnographic project, what they hope to uncover and present to the rest of the world is just how local communities relate to this increasingly ruinous landscape, the everyday role that it continues to play in their lives, and how the continuous process of decay is affecting their ability to function as a community and as individuals. Carlig and Raica address this as the phenomenon of collective depression and its unique manifestation in areas that have lost their central activity and along with it, their main sense of purpose.

They see themselves as storytellers, astute observers of 'characters and gestures borne of generations of hard labour and [...] punctuated by subtle moments of joy and dignity' (Christine 2014). Cirlig's photographs often focus on the impact of the post-industrial transition on different generations, youth on the verge of adulthood, young mothers, and children in particular. Planted amongst an environment whose purpose now seems completely disconnected from their reality, many of these youths have creatively attached new meaning to former industrial spaces and the machinery that still inhabits them. They have become familiar playgrounds, private spaces to steal a kiss or get away from the parents. Old posters and paintings that used to celebrate workers and their work have been removed from the factory buildings and now sit awkwardly in people's homes, masking a crack in the wall or an unused doorway. Everything seems both strangely homely and out of place.

The poverty is pervasive, and acts like a trap. Parents are too poor to move and offer their children a different future, and children are too young to make a life for themselves elsewhere. A new pair of jeans and converse shoes, a tight new dress and some cheap makeup offer the illusion of a different life. As

Cirlig says, coming from Bucharest, where new shopping malls and foreign businesses offering much higher salaries have completely transformed the look and possibilities of the city and its inhabitants, the poverty of this rural post-industrial landscape seems even more shocking. They form two different worlds, each increasingly out of touch with the other.

If Cirlig's photographs often engage head on with their subjects and their desires, Raica's photographs are much more eerie. Focusing more on spaces and machinery, the photographs are saturated with light, appearing almost as if out of this world. The human presence is sparse, and when it appears, it seems almost out of place: the subjects act almost as spectators of their surroundings. Dealing with everyday spaces that, at one time, used to be humming with life, yet now sit abandoned, his photographs recall the aura of a not so distant past. Emptied out of their previous purpose, machine rooms, former leisure spaces, landscapes, appear ghost like. Here and there, an odd figure sits by one of the machines that still works. Their presence is surreal, out of place, like they belong to a different time altogether. They look more like characters in a film than real people. And perhaps that is what Raica is in a way trying to tell us: for those of us sitting in front of our computers at our comfortable desks, they might as well be characters in a film.

The physicality of the ruins and the people inhabiting them is essential to understanding the radical transformation that these communities have undergone. For those inhabiting them, the ruins have now gained a sense of normality. For those exposed to them for the first time, they are striking, shocking, yet, in an odd way, appealing. Tim Edensor argues that ruined industrial spaces offer much beyond pleasing aesthetics: they offer an important alternative/critique to organised public space, for they help underline the extremes of space control we experience today. Left to the whims of natural decaying elements, these spaces gain a life of their own in which human intervention is rare and often minimal, thus allowing the infrequent explorer to enter potentially reflexive spaces (Edensor 2005c).

Like getting into the underbelly of history, walking through ruins reveals the physical traces of time and change left as they would be after a war or an abandoned city, in which the human presence is still felt yet not physically there to rebuild and transform. Edensor seems to suggest that ruins, and perhaps industrial ruins in particular, offer, what would otherwise be a once in a lifetime opportunity to explore such spaces at times other then extreme destruction – such as war or other natural disasters – for they are some of the few spaces preserved unchanged and uncontrolled in their desolate status. He explains the liberating effect of walking through such spaces almost as a unique opportunity to transpose oneself into a different time, as if one could walk into an old photograph or movie:

> Ruins are sensually charged with powerful smells, profuse and intrusive textures, peculiar and delicate soundscapes, as well as perplexing visual objects, juxtapositions, and vistas, all at variance to the sensually ordered

world outside. [...] Movement through the ruin confounds the performative conventions of the sites of memory identified above as well as modes of movement through the city more generally. With nobody to supervise movement, ensure assigned performative roles, or maintain peer-group norms, there is no need for self-consciousness. Released from self-policing, the body may explore the potential for expressive manoeuvres and open up to the multiple sensations present.

(Edensor 2005a: 837–8)

What Cirlig and Raica's photographs do is allow us to take a virtual walk through the ruins that they have encountered, meet the communities that inhabit them, and get a closer sense of what life is like for those who are still trapped in the physical remains of the communist dream. Although distant enough for the new generation to seem almost surreal, the youth inhabiting these ruins have a very different perspective on the past, present and future.

Photographing the Vitkovice Ironworks

Further north from the Hunedoara Ironworks, lie the Vitkovice Ironworks – in what is now the Czech Republic – another large industrial platform built close to the mining area of Ostrava. With a long history, dating back to 1828, the Ironworks helped sustain the iron based construction of bridges, railways, boilers and cylinders in the Austro-Hungarian empire, later to become one of the biggest Ironworks in Europe, featuring over six blast furnaces and a complete production line, from source to finished product. Due to the Ironworks, the region of Ostrava saw the rise of one of the largest industrial cities in the Czech Republic, the city of Ostrawa. As early as 1944 the plant had close to 34,000 employees, with the numbers likely to have increased significantly by the late 1980s.[2] Following the collapse of the communist regime in 1989, the Vitkovice Ironworks struggled along with other industries to follow the privatisation strategy, slowly diminishing its workforce and closing down its last blast furnace in 1998.[3] Only the mechanical and the constructional engineering part of the Ironworks survived in its privatised form, which is now called the Vitkovice Holding Group.

Unlike the Hunedoara Ironworks, the Vitkovice Ironworks has been much more successful, at least since its privatisation in 2003, in building a professional image and reinventing itself. Although the downsizing has been radical as well, with only about 5,138 employees currently working at the plant,[4] the image of destruction is much less prevalent. More importantly, due to the early interest by a local government employee – Milos Matej, a conservator at the Heritage Council of Ostrava – to preserve the closed down parts of the Ironworks, they have now been assigned a Unesco Industrial Patrimony Status[5] and have received significant financial support to help with the preservation efforts from the European Route of Industrial Heritage programme. This has become one of the most substantial industrial preservation projects of its kind in Europe, comparable with Volklingen or Duisburg-Meiderich.

With access to the once closed down sites restored, former workers and their families can easily explore and relive the past through the preserved spaces. In a survey conducted by Charles University, 83 per cent of respondents, all Ostrava residents, 'wanted to see the city remembered as a symbol of industry, while 91 per cent believed that Vitkovice Ironworks is part of Ostrava's image' (Logan 2003). Former miners saw the preservation efforts as paying homage to their work and their colleagues who died there, and reiterated the importance of the local emotional connection to the site itself by calling the buildings 'part of the landscape, region and history of Ostrava' (Logan 2003). Stopping the physical erasure of the Ironworks has thus had a significant impact on the local community, not only by reinforcing a sense of pride, but also by allowing for continued interaction with the site itself. With the umbilicus of the city preserved, life around the Ironworks can build in new directions and once again thrive.

The preservation efforts at the Vitkovice Ironworks are however not emblematic of changes in other industrial spaces throughout the Czech and Slovak Republics. The Czech photographer Vaclav Jirasek[6] has tried to capture another reality through a series of striking portraits of workers as well as a number of exhibits featuring both abandoned as well as half-dead industrial sites across the Czech Republic. In his images, the Czech workers appear equally 'destroyed' and abandoned as the workers of the rest of post-communist Europe. Unlike the photographers of the *Kombinat* photo album in Romania, Jirasek chooses to draw a direct connection between the industrial space and 'ruin' and the worker, showcasing in one of his latest exhibits – *Industria* – a series of striking portraits which seek 'to depict the forgotten people, those tested by harsh reality'.[7]

Just like the spaces themselves, the workers come across as ruined yet enduring elements, hurt yet strong, forgotten yet still present. The few that are left are presented as relics of an industrial world not so far removed, yet completely forgotten and erased from our modern consciousness. In Jirasek's photographs, the workers themselves seem to become part of the industrial patrimony, blending in with the factory space, enriching the colour palette and blurring the line between still 'nature' and human portrait. The photographs focus not only on the workers and the spaces that they inhabit, but also on material attempts to 'tame' the otherwise inhospitable working environment through what Jirasek calls: 'strange home-made or individually adapted pieces of furniture and bizarre decorative "installations"'.

When describing his fascination with industrial ruins, Jirasek writes:

> Frequently, I had the sense that factories are live organisms, functioning outside the awareness of the individuals that work there. Old buildings interweave themselves with new ones; disused pipes and wires are left where they lie, with new ones sprouting on top of them like the lianas of the jungle. Industry's penetration of the landscape, and the following return of nature into industry's remnants, makes it clear that technology is only a peculiar form of nature itself.[8]

Photo 3.3 Workers
Vaclav Jirasek, Czech Photographer

If technology is indeed a peculiar form of nature itself, then should the preservation of old industries take a similar route to environmental preservation campaigns? Are the workers of failing industrial plants nothing but endangered species themselves? And if so, what is the best way to save them? While retraining and employment into new sectors is certainly one road, preservation of former industrial spaces seems to be equally if not more important to preserving the mental and emotional sanity of many of these workers and their families. Where preservation through museumisation is not possible, photography seems to serve at least a limited intermediary purpose, helping to preserve fragments of workers' lives as embedded in the industrial material itself.

The importance of supporting aesthetisation practices such as photography and film making or museumisation lies in the fact that it is mainly through such practices that the link between industrial spaces – such as the largely abandoned industrial platforms of post-communist Europe – and their human inhabitants is clearly drawn. The focus on privatisation and regional development policies often ignores the extent to which the identity of the space itself as well as its inhabitants are reliant on these industrial platforms, thus making decisions such as scrapping entire parts of the 'industrial patrimony' with ease, and justifying them in terms of efficiency and profit making. This act of erasure is both dangerous and harmful. Tudor Giurgiu's 2012 film, *Of Snails and Men*, explores the human effects of such acts of erasure through a painful, yet funny, true story of a dying car factory, its workers, and the two French investors who promise to change their lives.

Of Snails and Men: a tragi-comedy

Tudor Giugiu's 2012 film *Of Snails and Men*, named the most popular Romanian film of the year, follows the story of a group of workers at a declining car factory in Campulung Muscel, Romania and their desperate attempt to save the factory by attempting to sell their sperm at a Bucharest sperm bank. The film is loosely based on a true story where the workers union at the ARO (Auto Romania) factory, faced with imminent closure due to increasing debts and failure to pay salaries over several months, put out a statement that they are willing to sell their sperm for money in order to save the factory. The sperm sale is seen as an alternative to the attempted privatisation of the plant, which would see it transferred – in the film – to a father–son snail canning company, a pretend façade for two French business men who see in this an opportunity to make quick money by selling the plant for scrap.

The film takes issue with what has been a particularly sore point in the history of Romanian car making: the real life bankruptcy of ARO, after a botched privatisation attempt which saw the factory sold to a problematic US based company for less than US $150,000 under an illegal contract that allowed them to sell the factory's equipment for scrap and get away with stealing over $3million (Dnistran 2014). This has been a pattern in the privatisation efforts of most former industrial platforms in Romania, with workers often forced to witness the intentional collapse of profitable factories under problematic deals clearly intended to favour a specific few. Choosing the sperm-selling incident at ARO as a desperate yet funny point of departure, the film captures the tragic–comic aspects of the early transition period and the significant status change in the category of the 'worker' from 'hero of the nation' to an underclass whose sperm is not acceptable at an international sperm bank because its genetic material is seen as inferior.

Taking an incident that was otherwise quickly erased from the collective memory, the film uses the incredulous sperm-selling story as a background for exploring what Kideckel call the 'frustrated agency' of the post-socialist worker caught between their growing social and political irrelevance and their personal struggle to maintain some sense of self (Kideckel 2008). The sexual subtheme of the film, both a source of comedy and tragedy, is explored as a way of pointing to the slow emasculation of the workers, physically, emotionally and politically. Left with nothing but their bodies, the workers are effectively willing to prostitute themselves, sell all that they have, in order to preserve the factory, which lies at the centre of their very existence: the director's secretary, torn between a love affair with the married leader of the workers' union and a potential new life with one of the French investors who promises to take her to France, chooses the latter. Defeated on every front, the workers are left to imagine a future picking up snails from the fields adjacent to the factory.

Met with some criticism for seemingly making fun of an episode in the life of a real community that continues to suffer, the film enjoyed surprisingly large audiences. A sign perhaps that society at large is finally able to shrug off the foolishness of earlier years, the now obvious naïve attitude towards problematic foreign investors and accept that, as sad as it may be, the working class, as imagined during communism, and its last remaining sense of solidarity, is now a thing of the past. A wonderful metaphor for what happened to an entire class of people, the film takes the pain of the ARO factory workers, humanises it, and then gives us the much needed imaginary happy ending that has you walk out of the theatre thinking: well, thank God that's all over now. It is a light touch way of tapping the national consciousness to remind everyone that, after all, 1992 was not quite that long ago, and to bring back the image of the worker, that forgotten figure who seems to have otherwise disappeared from our collective minds, yet continues to survive, even if barely, in the now forgotten fields of Campulung Muscel.

With the wounds of the past now somewhat healed, ruined workers across the post-industrial landscape in Romania have accepted their fate. Somewhere between humiliation and a surreal lightness of being due to the futility of resisting their fate, a whole group of people find themselves trapped: they are trapped in their declining towns and ruinous infrastructure, their slowly decaying bodies, and their irrelevance. Increasingly, they are trapped as objects of our renewed interest in the not so distant past, as visual evidence of a dying species. Entranced by the aesthetic appeal of their leathered faces, old uniforms, and now useless machines, a new generation seeks a sense of purpose and perhaps even delayed justice, in defending the memory of these workers and their factories.

Conclusion

Each of these projects, from the *Kombinat* photo album, the Hunedoara Ironworks, the Petriala StartUp and Cirlig and Raicu's photographic journal, to Jirasek's photographs of the Vitkovice Ironworks and Giurgiu's *Of Snails and Men*, speaks to a renewed interest in the aesthetic potential of former industrial sites. These are not just attempts to memorialise a unique aspect of the communist past, but to reclaim a political space for 'workers' as a dying social class, and for the cities whose life was entirely dependent on now defunct industrial platforms. At the risk of using surviving workers as visual props in works that carry a strong political message, these new artists, photo-graphers and film-makers are trying to carve out a space for sites and people that would otherwise fall into invisibility. By bringing them forth into the collective imaginary, they seek to create new spaces for reflection and crea-tive engagement with the past, to rethink how now defunct spaces could reshape dying communities through creativity rather than capitalisation, and to bring together communities that have grown so separate that one is no longer aware of the existence of the other.

This chapter has tried to show precisely how each of these projects has contributed to the creation of new aesthetic and political spaces, and more importantly, to discuss what this has meant for the ability to 'save' and rethink the role of the worker in today's post-industrial society. The wide exposure of many of these projects and the rising interest that a new generation of youth has shown in them, speaks of an interesting momentum to bring real and imagined spaces together in order to rethink how communities and solidarities can be rebuilt, how decaying spaces could be re-imbued with meaning and how workers can find a renewed sense of self-worth, even when opportunities for re-investment, capitalisation, and economic re-generation are not there. Turning the 'saving' discourse of privatisation on its head, these projects imagine different ways for creating 'opportunities' that are not based on economic profit, but rather on a sense of renewed 'visibility', 'recognition' and acceptance.

Notes

1 For more information see the official website at: http://cetateadefoc.lx.ro/ and http://www.mittalsteel.com/Facilities/Europe/Mittal+Steel+Hunedoara/.
2 For more information see: http://en.erih.net/index.php?pageId=109&anchor=274&cfilter=. Downloaded 23 January 2008.
3 For a short history of the plant, see: http://www.vitkovice.cz/en/firma/history-7-periods.php. Downloaded 23 January 2008.
4 See details in their 2006 annual report: http://www.vitkovice.cz/informace/vyrocni-zpravy/vyber_vz_vitkovice_cz-2006.pdf. Downloaded 23 January 2008.
5 Much of the disused plant, the Hlubina Colliery, the coke ovens and blast furnaces along Mistecka Street and the steel plant and rolling mill on Ruska Street, includ-ing many nineteenth-century buildings, have been declared a National Cultural Monument, and are in process of conservation. For more information see: http://en.erih.net/index.php?pageId=109&anchor=274&cfilter=.
6 For more information on his work, see: http://www.vjirasek.com/index1.htm. Downloaded 28 January 2008.
7 For more information see: http://www.moravska-galerie.cz/en/exhibitions/vaclav-jira sek/. Downloaded 28 January 2008.
8 Quoted on the website of the Moravska Galerie: http://www.moravska-galerie.cz/en/exhibitions/vaclav-jirasek. Downloaded 28 January 2008.

Bibliography

Andresoiu, Bruno. 2007. *Kombinat. Ruine industriale ale epocii de aur* (*Kombinat: Industrial Ruins of the Golden Age*). Bucharest: Igloo Media Press.

Balana, Luciana. 2014. *Situri Industriale in Tonuri Gri*. PhD, Architecture and Urbanism, University of Architecture and Urbanism Ion Mincu.

Bartmanski, Dominik. 2011. 'Successful Icons of Failed Time: Rethinking Post-communist Nostalgia'. *Acta Sociologica* 54(3): 213–231. doi: 10.1177/0001699311412625.

Benjamin, Walter. 1970. 'A Small History of Photography'. In *One-Way Street*, edited by W. Benjamin. Frankfurt: Suhrkamp Verlag.

Benjamin, Walter. 1998. *The Origin of German Tragic Drama*. London, New York: Verso.

Bors, Sabin, and Dragos Dascalu. 2012. 'Notes Towards a Theory of Contestational Architecture'. Available online at: http://www.academia.edu/5596513/Notes_towa rds_a_Theory_of_Contestational_Architecture. Accessed July 2015.

Czaplicka, John, NidaGelazis and Blair A. Ruble. 2009. *Cities After the Fall of Communism: Reshaping Cultural Landscapes and European Identities*. Washington DC: Woodrow Wilson Center Press.

Dnistran, Iulian. 2014. 'Istoria ARO: gloria şi moartea chinuită a unei legende auto româneşti'. *ProMotor*. Available online at: http://www.promotor.ro/masini-noi/dosa r-analize/istoria-aro-gloria-si-moartea-chinuita-a-unei-legende-auto-roma nesti-13502547/comentarii. Accessed 9 February 2015.

Edensor, Tim. 2005a. *Industrial Ruins: Space, Aesthetics, and Materiality*. Oxford: Berg.

Edensor, Tim. 2005b. 'The Ghosts of Industrial Ruins: Ordering and Disordering Memory in Excessive Space'. *Environment and Planning D: Society and Space* 23: 829–849.

Edensor, Tim. 2005c. 'Waste Matter – The Debris of Industrial Ruins and the Disordering of the Material World'. *Journal of Material Culture* 10(3): 311–332.

Foucault, Michel. 1967. 'Of Other Spaces, Heterotopias'. Available online at: http://fouca ult.info/documents/heteroTopia/foucault.heteroTopia.en.html. Accessed July 2015.

Hutton, Thomas. 2004. 'Post-industrialism, Post-modernism and the Reproduction of Vancouver's Central Area: Retheorising the 21st-century City'. *Urban Studies* 41(10): 1953–1982.

Iancu, Bogdan. 2006. 'Marirea si decaderea patrimoniului industrial Romanesc' (The rise and decline of the Romanian industrial patrimony). Available online at: http://www.bloombiz.ro/economie/marirea-si-decaderea-patrimoniului-industrial-romanesc. Accessed February 2015.

Iancu, Ciprian. 2007a. 'Hunedoara, te-am pupat si am plecat!' (Kisses and Good-bye Hunedoara!). *Replica*. Available online at: http://www.replicahd.ro/replica_db/index. php?pagerun=2&p=118&more=1&?jal_no_js=true&poll_id=9. Accessed July 2015.

Iancu, Stefan. 2007b. 'Ruine Industriale ale Epocii de Aur' (Industrial Ruins of the Golden Age). *Romania Libera*. Available online at: http://www.romanialibera.ro/ actualitate/fapt-divers/ruine-industriale-ale-epociide-aur-96496.html. Accessed July 2015.

Ioan, Augustin. 2006. 'Urban Policies and the Politics of Public Space in Bucharest'. In *The Urban Mosaic of Post-Socialist Europe*, edited by S. Tsenkova and Zorica Nedovic Budic, 337–348. Heidelberg, New York: Physica-Verlag.

Jemison, Annette. 2009. 'Representations of British Interwar Urban and Industrial Decline'. *Photography and Culture* 2(1): 7–30.

Kideckel, David A. 2008. *Getting By in Postsocialist Romania*. Bloomington, Indianapolis: Indiana University Press.

Kirk, John. 2003. 'Mapping the Remains of the Postindustrial Landscape'. *Space and Culture* 6: 178–186.

Kohn, Margaret. 2010. 'Toronto's Distillery District: Consumption and Nostalgia in a Post-Industrial Landscape'. *Globalizations* 7(3):359–369.

Kumar, Krishan. 1976. 'Industrialism and Post-Industrialism: Reflections on a Putative Transition'. *The Sociological Review* 24(3): 439–478.

Lahusen, Thomas. 2006. 'Decay or Endurance? The Ruins of Socialism'. *Slavic Review* 65(4): 736–746.

Logan, Steven. 2003. 'Machines as Monuments: Old Industrial Plant Commemorates a Lost Way of Life in Ostrava'. *The Prague Post*, March 19. Available online at: http://www.praguepost.com/archivescontent/36961-machines-as-monuments.html. Accessed July 2015.

Christine, McFetridge. 2014. 'Interview: Ioana Cirlig and Marin Raica'. *Lucida.* Available online at: http://lucidamagazine.com/?p=3184. Accessed February 2015.

Ost, David. 1993. 'The Politics of Interest in Post-Communist East Europe'. *Theory and Society* 22(4): 453–485.

Ost, David. 2005. *The Defeat of Solidarity: Anger and Politics in Postcommunist Europe.* Ithaca and London: Cornell University Press.

Rancière, Jacques. 1989. *The Nights of Labor: The Worker's Dream in 19th Century France.* Philadelphia: Temple University Press.

Rancière, Jacques. 2005. 'From Politics to Aesthetics?' *Paragraph* 28(1): 13–25.

Rauta, Alexander. 2013. 'The State of Ambiguity of the Communist Civic Center in Three Romanian Secondary Cities: Braila, Pitesti, and Sibiu'. *Journal of Urban History* 39(2): 235–254. doi: 10.1177/0096144212465394.

Replica. 2007. 'Hunedoara, de la comunism la capitalism' (Hunedoara: from communism to capitalism). Available online at: http://www.replicahd.ro/images/replica 235/special1.htm. Accessed February 2015.

Schönle, Andreas. 2006. 'Ruins and History: Observations on Russian Approaches to Destruction and Decay'. *Slavic Review* 65(4): 649–669.

Scribner, Charity. 2003. *Requiem for Communism.* Cambridge, MA: MIT Press.

Sennett, Richard. 1994. *Flesh and Stone: The Body and the City in Western Civilization.* London, New York: Norton.

4   Building capitalism
Consuming desires and the architectures that sustain them

It is not coincidental that the rise and fall of different regimes and ideologies is most often marked by the material construction or destruction of symbolic buildings, statues, walls, constitutions or flags. This material does not just stand for marking particular political, economic or historical illusions and disillusions, but represents in itself a reflection of historical time and social change. The idea of change is thus inextricably related to the material world, whereby the material is used to support, confirm, justify and legitimate change. With any process of radical social and political change, there is an expectation that this change will be positively and significantly reflected in the material horizon. The relationship between social change and material change is often mediated through the visual – and the visual horizon of particular communities.

This chapter traces the transition from communism to capitalism by focusing on how new consumption practices radically reshaped the material and architectural environment of the transition economies by effectively replacing old communist symbols of production, enlightenment and community with new symbols of consumption, enrichment and individual growth. It does so by examining the unique thirst for consumption across the post-communist economies of Eastern Europe that were coming out of a long era of shortages, how that thirst was translated into the creation of different spaces of consumption that could satisfy initially cash poor consumers, and later evolved into an increasingly segregated economy – with its own segregated spaces – that could feed the needs of both the incredibly rich and the overwhelmingly poor.

The aesthetic dimension plays a particularly important role here, as the visual transformation of public, private and media space served as the ultimate test for change and progress. In this respect, 'progress' was often confused with increased availability of 'Western' goods and the creation of 'Western-like' spaces – hypermarkets, shopping malls, new office spaces, gated communities, villas – where those goods could be 'accessed'. While the newly rich could consume these newly available goods, the overwhelming majority was left to marvel at the visual spectacle around them and consume cheaper alternatives of what was paraded in front of their eyes on a daily basis. In the process, the spectacle of consumption took over every inch of public and private space, with publicity banners covering buildings in the city centre and beyond, commercial space monopolising television time, and public spaces becoming increasingly commercialised.

There were few, if any, spaces of resistance, at least initially, in a context where the ability to consume itself was held as a Western standard and a sign of progress. In the rush to consume and acquire, radical takeovers of public and community space were accepted and even embraced as desirable. As consumption spaces shifted from initially temporary constructions – such as improvised open markets and the 'garage' architecture of minimarkets that took over the first floors of most apartment buildings – to more permanent and increasingly segregated spaces – such as hypermarkets, shopping malls, and gated communities – the 'Western' dream became a reality for some, and a strangely present yet inaccessible dream for others. In examining the radical effects of these new practices of consumption and the architectures that support them, the chapter also turns to looking at some of these spaces and practices of resistance, including artist interventions criticising excessive consumption, but also alternative uses of hyper commercialised spaces.

Consuming desires: from shortages to overwhelming consumption

Liviu Chelcea, Otto Gecser, David Kitzinger, Michael Serazio and Wanda Szarek (Chelcea 2002; Gecser and Kitzinger 2002; Serazio and Szarek 2012), amongst others, all describe some of the strange practices of consumption created by a culture of shortages during communism. They argue that the unbounded admiration for 'Western' goods which were always perceived as necessarily being of 'higher quality', the use of shopping for 'forbidden' Western goods as a form of rebellion, the odd attachment to Western consumer catalogues and empty containers of Western goods such as cigarettes, chocolate wrappers, alcoholic and beverage bottles – characteristic of the late communist shortage economies, all led to an odd and often unhealthy continued attachment to foreign goods and obsession with the ability to consume them.

Consumption, in this sense, was less about consuming itself and more about the desire for consumption and surrounding oneself with certain goods. This often-unsatisfied desire was fed by glimpses of what life could be like 'on the other side', which were embedded in different forms of consumer promotional materials. 'Western adds' were thus often confused with 'Western life' and consumed as fantasies of well-being 'oriented against the greyness and monotony of everyday life, [often] resulting in innovative practices, and (re)making things' (Svab 2002: 75). Svab goes on to argue that this unique form of consumption, and the practices associated with it, such as shopping tourism, smuggling of goods over the border, cheating and small-scale corruption, became in turn a form of subversiveness against the authority of the state. Chelcea supports this view adding that small-scale traffic and trader tourism were essential mechanisms of survival and resistance, particularly in border towns and villages (Chelcea 2002).

In this sense, Eastern European consumers were produced as such well before the fall of communism: the thirst for consumption was remarkable and created a market that could come to life effectively overnight, and more importantly, a market that was used to consuming without requiring a strong infrastructure of well established shops and brands. The lack of discrimination against 'Western brands', independent of their quality, meant that lower quality 'Western-like' goods could be quickly introduced in the aftermath of communism and sold through make-shift structures such as open markets. The carnivalesque atmosphere of the open markets that dominated the 1990s, littered with colourful second-hand goods, helped sustain the post-revolutionary illusion of freedom marked by a multitude of choices and a lack of shortages, when in reality people were left to consume effectively 'garbage'. But it was a different kind of garbage, and more importantly, it was colourful and lively.

Colour, as Svab also notes, played a very important role in the transition: colour not only helped break the monotony of greys that dominated the communist decades, but also created an immediate sense of change and dynamism. It is not surprising that strikingly vivid colours, such as fluorescent colours, dominated the years of the transition. People walked around in bright blues, yellows, greens and pinks, a cacophony of styles and colours, blissfully unaware of the ridiculous spectacle that they provided to the outside world. The celebration of clothes and goods was coupled with an extreme celebration of the body, which was often left uncovered or clad in tight clothing that would leave nothing to the imagination. It is thus not surprising that some of the most successful businesses in the 1990s were the make-shift clothing stores, beauty parlours and neighbourhood gyms that appeared in the empty garage and laundry rooms on the bottom floors of most buildings – what Dandolova calls 'garage architecture' (Dandolova quoted in Hirt 2006: 477).

Serazio and Szarek argue that the 1990s experienced a radical process of 'aestheticization of everyday life', much of which was guided by commercial messages:

> such commercial messages attempted to conjure a new sense of self for individuals living within an embryonic consumer society. They thrust new demands upon the [...] psyche, seeking to engineer self-consciousness, cast judgments about social differentiation, and nurture elitist exclusivity in contrast to the classlessness and collective solidarity that marked communist propaganda.
>
> (Serazio and Szarek 2012: 763)

While the 'Western adds' that leaked across the border during communism through catalogues and other forms of Western goods created an indiscriminate desire for consumption of 'anything Western', the strong publicity infrastructure that emerged in the aftermath of communism sought to 'train' the indiscriminate consumer and lift those with higher purchasing power above the rest through access to seemingly 'elite' goods. A previous culture of extreme shortages however meant that everything could now be portrayed as an 'elite good': from coffee and tea, to shampoo and detergent. Yet, in time, increased accessibility of 'Western goods' inevitably decreased their appeal: as one of Svab's interviewees in Slovenia remarks 'The Fa shampoo does not smell so fine any more and it is only an ordinary shampoo' (Svab 2002: 77). New Eastern European consumers did not take long to develop increasingly sophisticated tastes, with elitism becoming more and more celebrated as successful individualism.

The transition from sitting in endless lines for the most basic of goods to sipping $5 Starbucks coffees in malls happened surprisingly fast. Yet what few authors note is that this transition largely occurred in urban spaces, leaving much of the countryside and smaller industrial towns behind. Gerald Creed is amongst the few to addresses the effects of this new culture of excessive consumption on rural spaces (Creed 2002). Focusing on how consumption developed in rural spaces in Bulgaria, where most cash-poor villagers could not afford to participate in the consumption fest that took over richer urban spaces, Creed looks at how this new environment significantly altered the identities of the 'peasantry' and the 'working class.' For many of the villagers, Creed argues, the only alternative to engaging in these new consumption practices was to allow themselves to 'be consumed': 'Many rural Bulgarians see their only hope in the commodification of their abject position via the tourist market for folklore and rurality [...] If you can't consume, then you must be consumed' (Creed 2002: 124).

More importantly, Creed points to how new consumption practices served not only to effectively further segregate rural, industrial and urban populations, but also, to significantly change the identity of the 'peasantry' and 'workers' – the traditional pillars of national identity under communism. With the avid consumer increasingly hailed 'as the exemplar of national and global citizenship' (Creed 2002: 122), those involved in any form of manual production were quickly stripped of any sense of pride and increasingly shamed for their inability to compete in a consumption based economy. For them, access to a world of consumer paradise had simply not materialised, creating a disillusioned class that had not only lost access to the new economy but also their only sense of pride. As Creed explains:

> By the late 1990s, however, they [Bulgarian peasants] were doing little production or consumption beyond basic subsistence. Their socialist identity as producers was taken away and their anticipated capitalist identity as consumers was unavailable [...] The inability to consume or acquire goods has greater potential significance than just austerity.
>
> (Creed 2002: 122)

The unique nature of rural consumption in post-communist Bulgaria, and Eastern Europe overall, is, I believe, key to understanding the sometimes not-so-subtle nuances of the uneven transition to capitalism. Villagers and workers who have failed to enter the new consumption based market economy on an even footing, are not necessarily emerging as critics of the new capitalist regime – most of them would love nothing more than to be able to enjoy equal access as their richer, urban based counterparts – but rather as 'victims' of the transition. They emerge as 'sacrificial beings', struggling with basic subsistence in the increasingly marginalised rural and industrial town landscape, now strategically bypassed by new highways. While the local production – and consumption – market became inaccessible to them, many sought their luck abroad, with entire villages relocating to countries that maintain a strong agrarian/ manufacture economy such as Italy, Spain and Portugal, where they effectively took over the low-level manual based jobs. Much of the rural economy across post-communist Central and Eastern Europe largely survives on remittances.

The outside influence shows its head through remarkable new transformations in the rural landscape, with new constructions that imitate the rural architecture experienced abroad, yet often completely alien to the local rural environment, the emergence of surprisingly large villa-like compounds which are often left empty for a large part of the year while their owners work abroad, and a village life that is increasingly punctuated by increased activity around the holidays and major religious celebrations, when those abroad make their way home, and a dead calm the rest of the year when villages lie almost empty. By allowing themselves to 'be consumed' by the 'West' by effectively selling the only thing they had left – their manual labour – Eastern European villagers found a way of maintaining relevance and surviving. In the process, they have sacrificed an important sense of identity and pride and replaced it with a different form of conspicuous consumption that they can often only afford in the limited times that they are 'at home' – and increasingly less so, as the euro's purchasing power has significantly decreased.

The problematic consuming desires of an entire generation of thirsty Eastern Europeans that lived through the worst of the communist era shortages gave birth to a series of different architectures of consumption which marked not only their increased sophistication in time, but also their willingness to 'be consumed'. These architectures of consumption served not only to support and further feed consuming desires, but also to mark progressive change: just like the growth of a child is often marked in pencil on the door frame as a way of visualising change over time, these new architectures of consumption were also used to track the economic growth (or stagnation, in some cases) of Eastern European economies and give the 'transition' a seemingly forward trajectory. While the forward progression was seen as obvious in many large urban spaces where open-markets gave way to increasingly sophisticated malls and hypermarkets, many semi-urban and rural spaces continued to rely on make-shift garage architecture and barter-like open markets for years to come.

Architectures of consumption I: the seeming 'fragility' of garage architecture

The collapse of the communist regimes in Central and Eastern Europe was marked by the literal collapse of structures and bodies previously perceived as indestructible – the Berlin wall, the bringing to trial and shooting of dictators such as Ceausescu, the tearing down of 'communist' statues and the closing down of former industrial giants. Destruction, rather than construction, seemed to prevail, clearing up space for new ways of inscribing the material with fresh colours, new memorials and a different kind of hope. The process of construction, often inhibited by lack of funds, relied mainly on renovation and decorative work as well as a series of temporary structures such as kiosks and open markets. Thus, much of the initial material change that occurred in post-communist Europe focused on superficial change such as the painting of facades, the replacing of old communist slogans with new publicity panels, the appearance of stores at the street level of most buildings as well as new brands and fashion.

The old squares of Prague, Budapest or Warsaw did not incur any major structural change, yet they did look and feel different. The creation of restaurant patios opened up the space for a different kind of gazing, the establishment of large shopping areas, the neon-signs, the memorabilia stands, the casinos, the new memorials, created a colourful, vibrant atmosphere that led journalists, tourists and even locals to conclude that radical social change had indeed occurred. Compared to old images taken during the 1970s or 1980s demonstrations, the Wenceslas square in Prague seems unrecognisable today, and yet the structures are almost identical. Assuming that social change can indeed be read into changes in the material environment, one cannot help but wonder whether the assumed radical social change read in the otherwise superficial material change should not be reconsidered.

The expectation that social change should necessarily be followed by visible and significant material change in the environment surrounding us is quite strong in post-communist Europe. While this should not be surprising, given that, as Susan Buck-Morss argues, the communist social utopia was largely supported through visual and material reminders of progress and well-being (Buck-Morss 2000), what is surprising is the relatively little and often temporary effort that is required to fulfil or appease it. A quick glance away from the main city squares reveals the prevalence of cheap construction materials, fake facades that hide destruction and collapse, unfinished projects and an overwhelming number of temporary structures, such as kiosks and open markets that serve, in turn, to promote different types of temporary facades such as fake brand electronics and fashion, used cars and pirated music. This superficial material change, however, should not necessarily be dismissed as nothing but a transition phase soon to be replaced by more permanent structures.

These temporary facades and structures, such as the kiosk and the open market, do in fact play an essential role in negotiating people's understanding of change. On the one hand, they provide everyone with material proof that things are indeed changing, and on the other, they create an atmosphere of 'dress rehearsal' whereby both spaces and people are covered in temporary facades that mimic and perform change as if the process of change had actually been completed. Much like the transition from communism to capitalism, the transition from temporary facades to an actual change in structures, from fake brands to real brands, from dilapidated buildings to strip malls, marks, according to some, a normal step in a so-called natural progression towards a more 'Westernised' and 'European' post-communist Europe (Kreja 2006). In this progression, the temporary structure appears as a much-needed appeasement, yet one that everyone wishes away as soon as it is no longer necessary.

Architects such as Srdjan Jovanovic Weiss would disagree. He describes temporary architecture as 'an exception to the stable and obedient arrangement of space' one that also implies an inherent 'accepting [of] a deadline of its own expiration, the end of its own incapability to be stable' (Jovanovic Weiss 2007: 333) He notes, however, an important characteristic of temporary architecture in post-communist Europe, in his case, the city of Belgrade, is that it fails to accept its expiration and thus creates an environment that is based on a series of 'temporary evasions'. The superficial facades, the improvised bars, the party streets that only look good at night under colourful lights, thus become a permanent fixture of the city, one that it does not necessarily seek to change (Jovanovic Weiss 2007: 334). These temporary 'permanent' structures serve not only to question the idea of change as following a gradual progression from the unstable to the stable (with its material implications included) but also act as a claim to a unique identity that captures the 'transition experience' in its very look and celebrates the ability to 'normalise' otherwise shocking conditions through the acceptance of the temporary as permanent.[1]

This process of normalisation of the temporary is mediated by particular routines and the association of temporary spaces – such as improvised neighbourhood bars or kiosks – with the struggle for survival. In these instances, the temporary space itself becomes a witness to the economic struggle of transition – inflation, unemployment, poverty – as well as a faithful friend that does not boast, but remains simple, unsophisticated, cheap and to the point. The night shift worker who stops to drink a quick shot of vodka or buy some bread at the neighbourhood kiosk finds comfort in this space, perhaps because, in its very makeshift, rusty way, it stays true to the larger social transformation taking place and does not seek to hide behind a mask of pretence.[2] Through their very presence at the kiosk, and its inclusion in their daily routine, the workers make a powerful statement about the way in which they experience the transition. This statement, however, becomes quickly invisible when one tends to look for written or verbal confirmation, and is often confused with a state of apathy or even worse, a state of idleness. The impulse to erase this idleness through an act of spatial erasure through the destruction of these make-shift constructions and kiosks, also erases along with it the very public presence of the individuals who populate these spaces, for they can no longer afford to be anywhere other than their homes, and sometimes not even there.[3]

Architectures of consumption II: the seeming 'permanence' of shopping malls and hypermarkets

It has been 20 years since the fall of the Berlin Wall, and a new generation, untouched by the previous communist regimes, has come to adulthood throughout the post-communist world. The Iulius Group's[4] logo – 'Born to shop!' – suggests that these are born shoppers: the capitalist babies of Central and Eastern Europe who are sustaining the largest growth in retail and shopping malls in Europe. With no living memory of shortages, queuing, or government restrictions, they know only the limit of their own – or their parents' – pocket/credit. Their world could not be more different from the one that their parents and grandparents experienced: both the abundance of goods and services, as well as the opulent settings under which they are now sold, offer striking visual contrasts to the not-so-distant past. In addition, the very experience of consumption is directly connected to the way in which the current social fabric – and new social divisions within it – is interwoven with the physical and architectural changes taking place in the urban setting.

It is this generation that has supported the growth of mall empires such as the Iulius Group in Romania, which now controls the largest chain of shopping malls in the country and is an important player in the property market, helping to develop futuristic visions of shopping/living cities.[5] The Group owns four of the biggest malls in the country – in Iasi, Timisoara, Cluj, and Suceava – and is constantly expanding its terrain. The Timisoara Mall is doubling its current space to close to 180,000 square metres, now that it has won a licence to open the first Auchan supermarket in the country. This growth promises to potentially double its current figure of over 10 million visitors/year (Wall-Street Online 2007).[6] Two other large mall projects are being developed in Timisoara, one funded by Plaza Centers and the other by Romanian businessman Ion Tiriac – each worth over 100 million euros (Jinaru 2008). Surprisingly, this city of less then half a million people (320,000), can sustain three major malls and still promise profitable returns to all. This level of consumption would have been unheard of even four years ago, when the Iulius Mall in Timisoara was inaugurated. Yet consumption and marketing alone cannot explain the mall phenomenon in Timisoara and throughout Central and Eastern Europe.

Shopping malls represent the 'dream-world' of capitalism, to use Walter Benjamin's words (Benjamin 1999) – the unbounded optimism on which capitalism is sustained, using striking architecture and futuristic visions of what cities will one day look like. Just like the original arcades, the shopping malls of today have generally maintained the iron/glass architecture, the suspended double or triple galleries, the long corridors framed by shops, and an openness of space that still offers protection from outer elements. They are idealised cities, where streets are always lit, clean, and air-conditioned, where everything is readily available, where everyone looks happy and no one is poor. The dirt, pollution, poverty, noise, traffic and physical danger are kept outside this magic city's doors, creating a sealed bubble of joy and happiness. The mall is in every way the material expression of capitalism: from its architecture to the fashion and services that it sells, the mall is capitalism incarnate, the undeniable physical proof that capital works. It is thus not surprising that the Central and East European transition to capitalism would be most clearly marked through the emergence of the mall.

A more in-depth examination of Iulius Mall Timisoara reveals the nature of these 'dream-worlds.' Susan Buck-Morss describes Benjamin's notion of dream-worlds as: 'expressions of a utopian desire for social arrangements that transcend existing forms' (Buck-Morss 2000: x), suggesting that they are as much a socio-political project as they are an economic one. In fact, most forms of social engineering require the creation and manipulation of a dream-world, generally through the implementation of specific physical, architectural and visual structures to support it. In this sense, malls are not only the new town squares (Staeheli and Mitchell 2006) but also the new Houses of the People.[7] They have very effectively replaced the communist dream-world of an equal community with the capitalist dream-world of a wealthy and individually glamorous community. Just like the former House of the People, the mall is first and foremost an assembly, a communal space. The mall provides a different kind of 'collective dream', one that connects the idea of happiness and community to that of material consumption: from storefronts, posters and enticing cafes, everything points to fashion, food and relaxation as the ultimate source of both individual and collective happiness.

Despite its appeal to modernity, progress and the optimist future, the mall is ultimately a stagnant place: it signifies security through the creation of a sealed space, one that is not affected by unpredictable change. It is a controlled space, although playful (Maclaran and Brown 2005) and theatrical (Backes 2004). Within it, '[t]he dreaming collective knows no history. Events pass before it as always identical and always new. The sensation of the newest and most modern is, in fact, just as much a dream formation of events as "the eternal return of the same"' (Hugo von Hofmannsthal cited in Benjamin 1999: 546). The modernity of the space itself thus corresponds to a false idea of temporal progression/change: isolated from the world 'out there', the mall is a reflection of the future only to the extent that we desire our future to be as such. It is a 'wish-world' as much as it is a 'dream-world'. Outside the mall lie charity shops, failed industries and collapsing infrastructure.

The wish-world is sustained by visible and material proof that 'better' is possible: the mall as wish-world is physically accessible to everyone, whether they can afford to shop there or not. In fact, just like the Parisian Arcades of the nineteenth century, the mall is a promenade space, a place of visual enjoyment and entertainment. Informal discussions with friends, family and regular shoppers at Iulius Mall revealed that their presence in the space is not only about consumption but also about the ability to enjoy a 'Westernised' space: clean, cool, problem-free.[8] Consumption is directly related to the need to preserve and actively participate in this wish-world: high prices that often exceed the cost for similar products in Western Europe are not a deterrent even for the more modest buyers. It is in fact quite common for consumers to spend more than half of their monthly salary on a luxury item. Clothes and accessories, just like the mall itself, become material and visual proof that one is a part of this particular wish-world.

The illusion of wealth and well-being, even for the more modest consumer, is created through the easy access to goods: one can at least try them on if not buy them. It is also created through the theatrical role of the mall's entertainment spaces – which include not only the bars, cafes and restaurants, but also the lounge areas and the promenades themselves. To be seen at the mall, to be dressed well at the mall, to consume and entertain at the mall, is a sign of prosperity and wealth, whether real or theatrical. Out of the 210 shops at Iulius Mall in Timisoara (*before* its major expansion), 84 are for clothing, 29 for entertainment and food and 51 for services. Each section of the mall, whether a clothes shop, a cafe or a bank, provides an opportunity to act a part, whether real or imaginary: everyone can fake belonging by posing as a businessman/woman, browsing through stores one could not normally afford, or sipping expensive coffee. Despite its large open spaces, this theatrical 'scene' is protected by the material and visual illusion of intimacy: furnishings and bars in the open spaces that suggest a kitchen or a living room, and music and sounds that create distinctively different atmospheres in different corners of the mall.

Fashion, as the ultimate decorum, also adds to the mall's theatrical aspect. Everyone dresses the part: along with architecture, fashion has become one of the most important pillars of 'Westernisation'. Quickly evolving from the 'jeans' and 'Adidas' obsession of the early 1990s, to the laid-back classics of the early 2000s – Gap, Calvin Klein, Zara – to the high-class labels of today – Prada, Louis Vuitton, Channel – fashion spells out one's connections, travel itineraries and social status. As an immediate visual sign of 'development', fashion has been used throughout the Central and East European transition to capitalism to mark both a desire to follow the 'West' and a desire to prove success. Fashion and accessories are often as important to Romanian businessmen and women as their bank accounts. Visually marking success and material well-being, whether one has it or not, ensures a way to step up in the newly established hierarchies of wealth. Writers such as Manrai argue that there is a direct relationship between fashion and economic development/ Westernisation. Comparing Hungarian, Bulgarian and Romanian consumers, she argues that one can compose an accurate economic hierarchy based on the type and quality of fashion goods consumed (Manrai *et al.* 2001).

While fashion is similarly used in 'developed' economies, the surprise element in 'transition' economies such as Romania is the extreme to which modest shoppers go in order to mark their belonging to a higher class and to act a part that they do not easily fit – that of a Westerner as opposed to a 'transitioner'. Young adults spend as much as 80 per cent of their salaries on clothes and accessories, often buying products that clearly exceed their buying capacity. Without easy access to credit cards, they resort to informal forms of borrowing from family and friends, buying knock-off brands, and shopping sprees to outlets abroad. As being poorly dressed is becoming more and more of a social stigma, the notions of what it means to be 'well-dressed' are also changing. In Timisoara in particular, the strong presence of Italian immigrants is clearly reflected in the popularity of Italian fashion and design as well as the success of Italian restaurants and lounges. Style and class is thus often defined according to Italian standards. With an increasing international presence, this is likely to change in the future, shifting perhaps more towards the Western 'exotic': Japanese style and cuisine are now slowly rising to the top of what is considered to be 'high-class'.

The theatrical performability of fashion is, however, easily broken by those who cannot help but act their real part: the 'poor' of the transition. They are also present at the mall, and they do not always have the means to act differently. By positioning a number of important government services in the mall, such as the passport office, the driver's licence and car registration office, and the marriage licence office, the Timis local government has achieved its goal to move these offices to a more central location, in a more 'civilised' setting. Yet, through the 'universal' access to these services, it has also disrupted the underlying logic of the mall through the physical and visual presence of non-consumers. Forced to queue and wait sometimes hours at a time, these non-consumers attach a particular stigma to certain parts of the mall: the passport office is often surrounded by a large gypsy/Roma population, clearly marked by its colourful fashion and hats, while the driver's licence and car registration office is often surrounded by frustrated drivers. They provide a striking contrast to everyone else, making, at least a portion of the mall, in many ways not much different from other spaces often associated with transitions, such as 'outdoor markets'.

The proof of non-belonging is once again physically marked, either through fashion, attitude, or both. While much of the gypsy/Roma population willingly resists blending in by choosing more traditional forms of dressing – much of which resembles the traditional dress style of Romanian peasants, albeit often with more colourful accents – the nouveau riche amongst this population find alternative means of showcasing wealth: cars, jewellery, and houses. The lower class, which finds itself both attracted to and trapped in the mall – by the necessity of using some of the government offices located there – shies away from the most visible parts of the mall. Rather than frequenting the cafes, restaurants and main stores, they find refuge in the few discount stores and larger supermarkets that allow them to lose themselves in the crowd.

The dream-world of capitalism is thus sustained as much by 'real' development as it is by an ardent desire to reach some kind of an 'end' goal. Fashion, goods and the architectures that house them serve as visible marks of both the actual as well as the wishful progression towards 'the West'. The unexpected expansion of the malls' 'empires' throughout Central and Eastern Europe is thus more than just a sign of a successful strategy of foreign direct investment – it is also a sign of the need to materialise at least part of the Westernisation dream. Because of its rushed nature, however, much of this process of materialising is focused on transitory architectures – basic structures that are effectively 'adorned' through signs and marketing to suggest a more radical change – and transitory goods, such as brands and fashions, that change radically from year to year.

Despite their seemingly 'permanent' structures, malls are often built on very simple skeletons of iron and glass. In fact, a closer look at Iulius Mall will reveal its simple structure. It is one large hall, divided by suspended promenades and glass walls that are as easy to disassemble as they were to assemble. Malls are often seen (and used) as a natural progression from the outdoor markets of the 1990s – which are still very popular, particularly with the larger part of the population who cannot afford to shop in malls. However, their permanence, as a sign of stability, is questionable, as Srdjan Jovanovic Weiss argues. Improvised structures, such as corner bars and kiosks or open markets, are often more honest in terms of their acceptance of their own temporary nature than are permanent structures (Jovanovic Weiss 2007). Without a pretence of permanence and stability, they still manage to offer an important comfort to the 'transition' consumer: prices that he/she can afford and spaces that are not afraid to accept the slow rate of 'change'.

Seemingly permanent structures such as malls risk to offer a visual and physical comfort that is less stable than it might appear, particularly in the current context of the latest economic crisis, which risks a shutting down of all sources of international credit and significantly slowing domestic ones as well. The shock of closed-down malls could equal that of closed-down factories, both for the consumers as well as for the employees, managers and owners of these malls. With not only financial capital but also a large amount of human and hope capital invested in them, these malls now represent an important part of the Eastern European self-image.

Architectures of consumption III: the emergence of gated communities and the transformation of public space

One of the latest transformations in the visual urban horizon of post-communist Central and Eastern European has been the emergence of gated communities, the culmination of the ultimate privatisation of space and a new form of elite consumption which seeks to openly isolate the poor from the rich to a point where their interactions can be almost completely avoided in everyday life. Gated communities extend the bubble of still somewhat inclusive spaces like shopping malls to include private parks and playgrounds, pools and tennis courts, living spaces and parking, shopping spaces and kindergartens. Exclusive mini-cities in themselves, gated communities are an expression of excessive elitism that seek not only to turn fairy-tales of exclusive wealth, security and well-being into reality, but also to completely bypass the stubborn poverty that 'tarnishes' an otherwise already Westernised post-communist Europe.

They symbolise a peak of excessive consumption, the successful creation of an elite class that can not only afford to live in an alternate universe but also increasingly desires to completely detach itself from all that is seemingly not developed. The luxuries afforded by this elite class often go well beyond the luxury afforded by most 'Westerners': this new class is now part of an exclusive club of wealthy global citizens that set their own standards of well-being far removed from the constraints of local economies, transitioning or not. They are the successful entrepreneurs of the 'transition', many self-employed, who have amassed enough wealth to make all their dreams come true without having to leave their home countries.

Sonia Hirt describes these gated communities as mini sovereign states in themselves: with barriers, guards and borders that demand legitimation, entry permits, face control policies, they are often more difficult to pass than crossing an actual border (Hirt 2014). As carefully guarded and controlled private spaces, they are purposefully devoid of any 'politics': their purpose is to preserve an exclusive status quo and keep all possible disturbing elements out. By precluding any form of political mobilisation, they create a constant illusion of calm that ignores all that happens beyond the sometimes not so narrow confines of the gated community. Hirt sees them as the peak of the fast erosion of public space taking place across post-communist Europe, a symbol of what she calls the 'post-public city'. She argues that the on-going encroachment on public spaces through aggressive privatisation and commercialisation of everyday life is happening at a much faster rate in post-communist Europe than the rest of the Western world, permanently distorting local identities and, perhaps more importantly slowly removing possibilities for democratic political participation that are often so closely connected to critical public spaces, such as the street or the square (Hirt 2014: 124).

This is certainly not unique to gated communities in post-communist Europe, yet, the radical changes in the commodification of public spaces, the speed at which they occurred as well as the relative complacency, if not out-right excitement, these changes have been met with, signal a worrisome uncritical stance towards transformations that are likely to be very difficult to undo. Lured by their Western allure, even those who cannot afford to live in such communities, are excited to be allowed to stroll through the grounds at set times of the day (Smigiel 2013). Their mere existence excites, offering a strange sense of pride, a celebration of the achievement of the few that can be at least aesthetically enjoyed from afar by the rest of the population.

Just like malls, these communities offer a false sense of progress in the city, one that ignores the reality of the majority, which continues to live in slowly decaying communist flats, with failing infrastructure. The privatisation of most apartment buildings, and along with it, all infrastructure connected with them – from heating to water and sewage, has pushed low income and many lower middle class families out of desirable neighbourhoods. Imitating their 'Western' counterparts, apartment co-ops are increasingly pushing for expensive invest-ments that will increase the value of the apartments, without regard for families who simply cannot afford to pay for them. With decisions left in the hands of majorities, poorer families find themselves sometimes forcefully cut off from the public 'infrastructure' grid, yet unable to pay for the installation of self-owned heating and gas systems.

The massive decay of infrastructure coupled with the sometimes almost complete lack of control by city planning offices over the chaotic development of many cities, is often hidden behind a deceiving façade of fresh paint and colourful ads. With control over the city infrastructure left to poorly funded bureaucracies that are easily susceptible to bribes and outside influence, effective and coherent public planning is non-existent in many places. As Smigiel explains: 'urban development is predominantly organised and directed by a few powerful private stakeholders imbedded in a neo-liberal state regime (with weak public stakeholders and missing urban policy guidelines). Within this environment arrangements function as the main instrument of policy-making' (Smigiel 2013: 131).

While this may be somewhat sustainable in the short-run, it could be disastrous in the long-run, as no private stakeholder can manage the necessary basic public infrastructure that makes most cities possible. The slow emergence of urban slums across post-communist Europe, many of which are now inhabited by some of the most vulnerable parts of the population, such as Roma minorities, are perhaps a worrisome sign of the increasing discrepancies in the social and infrastructure base of many of these societies. The continued decline of public space at the expense of a consumer culture that indiscriminately celebrates anything 'Western looking' leaves little room for meaningful forms of public critical reflection on fast changes that are experienced on a daily basis.

A few cities and artist collectives have however taken it upon themselves to find creative ways to engage the wider public in such forms of critical reflection, even if only on a temporary, fleeting basis. By engaging the wider community in their everyday activities such as walking or shopping, they seek to draw attention to the radical nature of change within the 'transition' and actively stimulate and awaken dulled senses through shocking juxtapositions. Creatively employing the same visual strategies that have lured communities into excessive consumption and commodification of public space, they seek to literally slow down the walking pace of the average citizen in order to allow them to take in all that is happening around them. By turning average citizens into twenty-first-century 'flâneurs', they hope to create alternative spaces of reflection and public engagement.

Bringing the nineteenth-century flâneur into the twenty-first century

The concept of the flâneur can be traced back to Baudelaire's poetics (Baudelaire 1985) where it is associated with a particular way of experiencing the city, whereby one strolls aimlessly in order to observe otherwise insignificant details and draw upon them for inspiration and insights into the nature of society at that particular moment. Walter Benjamin was particularly inspired by the concept as well as the technique of strolling, using them as a way to explore nineteenth-century Naples, Berlin, Paris, Marseilles and Moscow and develop a new understanding of history as directly related to images and the material (Buck-Morss 1977). For Benjamin, the flâneur was associated with those who lay at the margins of society – the homeless, the whore, the sandwich-man, the collector (Benjamin 1970). What they all shared was a privileged way of seeing the city from angles that would not be accessible to anyone else – the city at night, the back alleys, the abandoned buildings, the antiques that could only be seen as interesting by collectors. The flâneur thus marked a way of seeing as well as a particular way of framing what one sees.

The flâneur's association with the act of walking is equally important to the act of seeing. Modern theorists of visuality, such as Aumont argue that 'the idea of space is fundamentally linked to the body and its movement' (Aumont 1997: 20). The bodily movement combines both elements of space and time. It is through the body in movement that we are exposed to different frames of seeing, as well as the passing of time. The latter is directly marked by synchronies and asynchronies in the material and spatial change as noted by our sight. The notion of change, and the passing of time, is thus directly connected to our ability to see change marked in space and our material surroundings.[9] Our patterns of walking are thus essential determinants of what we see as well as the way in which we interpret what we see. Walking, as an everyday practice – as opposed to marching or a street gathering and demonstrating – can also be seen as a political practice that determines our frames of seeing as well as our conceptualisation and interpretation of space.

Social theorists such as De Certeau (1984), Lefebvre (1984) and Guy Debord (1994) developed a particular interest in analysing the practice of walking as essential to our social and political awareness. To the extent that all politics and historical transformation is marked directly into space, the practice of walking is essential to uncovering those markings. In his writings, and more importantly his political practice, Guy Debord – as the leader of the Situationalist movement and the main inspiration for today's psychogeographers[10] – continued to emphasise something that Benjamin had noted before, namely that maintaining certain patterns of walking served to normalise change, by masking the shock of change through the maintenance of similar frames of seeing. This is why the literal breaking of walking patterns was an essential practice of the Situationalists, not as an act of rebellion, but rather an act of re-framing that would allow otherwise marginal or different frames to be adopted as well.

The more recent work of Iain Sinclair (1997, 1995a, 1995b) shows how this breaking of walking patterns can serve as a way to break down not only visual frames but also temporal frames. In his explorations of London, Sinclair writes about his own experience of seeing as much more than the physical act of seeing and framing, but rather as an imaginative, creative process whereby the images recorded are immediately associated with other images, emotions, thoughts and recollections. By tracing changes in the meaning of different objects, buildings and sites throughout time – from churches, to statues, to neighbourhoods, shops and pubs – Sinclair uncovers a universe in which the 'real' and 'representation', objects and images, past and present have similar qualities, to a point where they become interchangeable (Watson 2007). Physical space then becomes much more than what one can see. It becomes also something that one can recall or imagine. Walking thus exposes us to a series of different visual as well as temporal frames, breaking down space into a montage of material, visual as well as imaginary representations of that material.

New technologies of seeing, such as photography, film and 'new media' have also played with this relationship between the representation and imagination of space. As Benjamin predicted, they have indeed changed our modes of perception (Benjamin 1968a: 222), and at the same time the way in which we perceive or read the material environment surrounding us. Beyond providing new frames of seeing, many of these technologies have removed the need for the act of walking in the representation of space, serving to silence the continuing role that this act has on perceptions of change and expressions of the political in the physical environment. From media studies to the so-called 'aesthetic turn', the fascination now lies with the question of 'representation' as related to film, photography, images, and no longer with the direct act of seeing, unmediated by particular technologies.

Representation is, however, often not completely removed from the material environment. In fact, a majority of representational images – such as posters, publicity, paintings, photo exhibits – maintain a material quality, and thus remain an important part of the surrounding material environment. Given the increase in reproduction mechanisms and techniques (Benjamin 1968b), these visual representations have the ability to radically alter the material environment with little financial effort as well as within a short period of time. They serve to manipulate easily experiences of change, both by normalising the temporary and questioning the permanent, as the two short explorations of Tirana and Prague will attempt to show.

Walking and seeing are thus intrinsically connected, particularly when it comes to experiencing social change as inscribed in the material environment. The concept of the flâneur brings our attention to the impact of following or breaking particular patterns of walking and seeing. New technologies of seeing, when examined in relation to the practice of flânerie, show the extent to which different forms of representation have come significantly to alter the material environment, by confusing the temporary and the permanent, and thus blurring expectations that radical social change can only be read in radical material change.

By taking the notion of the flâneur seriously and engaging with the relation-ship between walking and seeing as a new possible methodology for examining the so-called aesthetics of change, the two case studies examined below seek to offer one possible way of employing such a methodology. Acknowledging the subjectivity of the flâneur experience and the impossibility of recognising every-one's field of vision and internalisation of change through the act of walking and seeing, these two case studies seek to offer nonetheless a possible entry point into a different kind of empirical work that openly acknowledges not just what is being seen, but also who sees, what and how. Relying on Benjamin's conviction that images are not only material fragments but also thought-fragments that capture within themselves a miniaturised image or idea of the world, the case studies will seek to offer an alternative view of the politicisation of the transition experience that seeks not so much to refute but rather to complement the already rich, albeit rather homogeneous, literature on post-communist transitions.

The Painting Tirana Project and the *Czech Dream* documentary thus serve to showcase different ways in which visual representations have radically altered the material environment, triggering an increasing awareness of space, and its role as a potential political mediator. Following Jacques Rancière's argument that politics lies within the (re)configuration of space as the framing of a specific sphere of experience (Rancière 2005), the two case studies suggest that it is precisely within such gestures of manipulation that possibilities of political action are created or reconfigured. The manipulation of space and the visual experience itself thus serve to challenge previous expectations and, in some cases, act as a form of critical engagement with both the material motivations underpinning spatial change as well as the visual technologies that sustain it.

Painting Tirana: a town of post-communist flâneurs

Initiated by its artist mayor, Edi Rama, almost immediately after his election to City Hall in 2000, the Painting Tirana Project involved the revamping of the old communist flats of the capital of Albania through bright colourings that would change both the look of the city as well as inspire its citizens with vivacity, a fresh new start and a brighter horizon. The project was part of a larger movement towards the 'city's renaissance' that also involved the refurbishment of abandoned parks and river banks turned into refuse dumps, the repairing of roads and a lighting project that sought to revive the city at night. The results are showcased on the main website of the municipality of Tirana in a before and after photo gallery with the new facades, the lighting project, the refurbished parks and the newly paved streets bringing a ravaged city back to life.[11] The lively brushstrokes of green, red, purple, orange, yellow and blue, the squared and rounded shapes on buildings, the patched, quilted look of facades is both pleasing and intriguing to the eye. From a city in ruin, Tirana has turned into a city of colour.

The Painting Tirana Project was a bold statement not only for a collapsed city, but also for Albania, a country ranked as the poorest in Europe, struggling with the effects of the Yugoslav wars, the incoming Kosovo refugees, and its own emigration problem.[12] The image of thousands of illegal Albanian immigrants piled up in boats heading for the Italian coast was replaced by one of a lively, revived city that for the first time in decades managed to attract tourists and its own elites that had moved abroad. The new look of the city managed to shift both the mood and attitude of the population, as well as the political debate on to the spatial, cityscape arena, opening up the door to a new kind of communication between, in this case, the local government and the inhabitants of Tirana. By fulfilling people's expectations that social change should be reflected (positively) in the surrounding material environment, Edi Rama gave the citizens of Tirana a reason to believe, a material proof, that although superficial, was clearly visible and held the promise of more.[13]

Financed with no more than US $67 million (Walt 2005), the project instilled hope in an otherwise largely apathetic population, resulting in a surprising vote that made Edi Rama the winner of the World Mayor 2004 contest.[14] The comments posted by his voters showed that this was an over-whelmingly positive response to his 'city renaissance' policies, and particularly the Painting Tirana Project. Voters saw hope, stability, identity and pride in him and his projects. They saw the ability to fulfil promises, and thus to rehabilitate politics and politicians to a can-do status.[15] They also saw Edi Rama as someone other than a typical politician, an artist who governed under no ideological or party doctrine, but rather under the belief that society needed to look and feel different in order to embrace the change brought about by the fall of communism:

> Edi Rama is something else altogether from your average politician, in fact the reason he is so successful is that he is NOT one. He represents a new generation of Albanians, one that has no more time to waste, and no doctrines to experiment with, no 'great fathers' to listen to and follow. I find him arrogant, at times unpleasant, I have never felt he can give an interview, but above all I can see the city I love, and was born in, and I know how much he had to do with the way it looks and feels these days. Edi Rama, thank you![16]

Even his enemies could not deny the important role that he has played in changing the face of the city for the better. Despite being blamed for his arrogance and his tendency to turn the city into his own canvas (Walt 2005), Edi Rama has managed to achieve in good part his initially stated goal: 'My real project is to try to resuscitate hope, so that people will start looking on their country not as a transfer station, but as a place where they might want to live' (Edi Rama quoted in Woodward 2005). The uniqueness of his approach lies not only in his urban revival strategies, something that urban planning policies and architects everywhere have long upheld as positive and essential, but rather in his prioritising of these strategies above the usual employment and economic revival promises. His genius was to recognise the importance of the short-term and not just the long-term, the need to change the 'look and the feel' of the city immediately, even at the risk of doing so with a superficial coat of paint.

By changing the way in which people look at their own city, by drawing their attention towards the possibility of change, by giving them a glimpse of what their city could look like one day and allowing Albanian emigrants to take pride in it even from abroad, the artist-turned-politician tricked the 'natural' aesthetic of change, manipulated the look and feel of the change, reframed the horizons of the visual and literally moved the city into a new temporality – the potential long-term future. All this was achieved through a mere creative repainting of facades. The structures behind them are still corroded and slowly collapsing, the pipes and infrastructure is still old, the over-population problem is still there and yet things 'look and feel' different, and positively so.

Unlike the freshly painted facades of the old towns of Prague, Budapest or Warsaw, Tirana changed the look of the entire city, and did not shy away from painting over old communist flats or meagre looking three story buildings at the outskirts of town. The aim was to change the aesthetic experience of the everyday flâneur walking to work, the local supermarket or heading back home, and not just the tourist, the businessman or the investor that inhabits the city centre. Change needed to be felt in a uniform fashion, equally accessible and with similar transformative possibilities. The colours are not just paint on a canvas, an artefact, a visual trick, but rather an organic part of the material environment, a new visual frame through which otherwise little changed structures can be perceived differently. As Rama himself explains, the colours are means to replace the old, rotting, organs of the city – they may appear superficial, an easily erased make-up, but they constitute a significant intervention (Rama quoted in Kramer 2005).

The colours have significantly changed the walking/flânerie experience of the everyday inhabitant of Tirana.[17] As Edi Rama himself notes, 'there is perhaps no other city in Europe, be it the richest, where people discuss so passionately and collectively about colors. The hottest discussion in the coffee bars, in homes, in the streets was what are the colors doing to us' (Sala 2007[18]). The photographs of Tirana walk us through a city that is definitely changing. The colours add contrast, bringing out the new air-conditioners, double-glazed windows and satellite dishes, the publicity banners, shops and neighbourhood bars. They help to confirm, silently, yet powerfully, that things are indeed changing, and that the myriad of promises after the fall of communism will not all drown in boats heading for the Italian coast.

Anri Sala, another Albanian artist and former roommate of Edi Rama in Paris, put together a video montage entitled *Dammi I Colori* (Give me Colour), showcasing the colours of Tirana and its mayor in a drive-by interview that juxtaposes Tirana's freshly painted buildings with Rama's presentation of the project. The video montage was shown at the TATE London, as well as several well-known galleries in Paris, Hamburg, New York and Chicago, and has appeared in two Venice Biennales.[19] The video sought to (re)present the changes that the Tirana flâneurs were experiencing on an everyday basis, and thus juxtaposed images seen through the movement of the car, with verbal commentary, reproducing both the relationship between the body in movement and space as well as the visual and the verbal narrative. It sought to present Albania, and Tirana in particular, as a state of mind and a particular experience of space that can only be reproduced visually and materially – as directly opposed to the textual and verbal narratives that have always dominated 'discourses' of change.

By exposing the relationship between social and material change through the careful manipulation of the aesthetics of change, whether willingly so or not, Edi Rama is also exposing the manipulative power of projects such as his, as well as other mechanisms of 'painting' the city, perhaps more common in the general cityscape of post-communist Europe in the publicity panels, the colourful posters, the new brands and the fashion stores. The quick transformation of the Tirana cityscape also challenges the process of normalisation of change through the acceptance of often insignificant and temporary change as radical change. It underlines how easy it frequently is to misread 'progress' in the material environment, and to represent it, visually, in places where only its promise exists. It challenges the nature of our expectations that change should be immediately visible and more importantly, that it should follow a particular model of 'progressive' transformation.[20]

More importantly however, it opens a new space of analysis, in which politics becomes embedded in the transformation of the material environment, the silent engagement with that environment, and the possibilities that new ways of seeing old spaces open up. While the popularity of Edi Rama the mayor was indeed expressed through a voting process, his promises were not made on a standing platform addressing the crowd, but rather on the city as a canvas, on the buildings of Tirana, on that blue, or red or yellow patch of paint that reframed the way in which people looked at collapsing buildings, the corner of the street, the neighbourhood shop or the park by the river. What became visible was not only the 'new' but what was already there – the decrepit, the old, the temporary, suddenly turned endearing and less threatening in its failure to meet expectations.

One subjective reading of the spatial transformation of Tirana, while acknowledging the impossibility of recognising each and every flâneur of Tirana, relies on deductions concerning what the effects of collective flânerie might be. In the case of Tirana the appeasement of the need for the senses to feel something different, led to an acceptance of the present for what it was. The spectacle of colours resulted in an unexpected catharsis that suddenly implicated everyone in the process of change. The city appeared not just as a stage on which politicians could act, but rather a space in which collective practices of seeing and walking became visible gestures of approval or disapproval, of collaboration or rejection, of social and political communication. Moreover, by swiftly moving the temporality of the city into the future, the colours not only put the past behind, transforming communism into an allegorical time, a once-upon-a-time, but also helped to temper expectations that social change should necessarily translate into material change, and that the visibility of some material change is necessarily a sign of 'progress'.

The Painting Tirana Project demonstrates the extent to which a simple act of repainting can transform an entire city and its inhabitants, by using the temporary, freshly painted facades both as a material promise that change is on the way, as well as a manner of reframing the visual experience of everyday flâneurs and engaging them in the larger political transformation of the country. Space thus becomes much more than a canvas on which history and change leave their trace, but also a board on which promises can be pinned, an arena in which the visual replaces verbal and written communication.

From consumerism to flânerie in Prague

Much further north from Tirana lies another post-communist city, Prague, a city that has been praised for its outstanding economic performance as well as for its beauty and ability to attract tourists from all over the world. Prague has experienced a different type of aesthetics of change. Much more successful in its ability to replicate the 'Western' look, and to distinguish itself as a favourite capital of Europe, the Prague cityscape is struggling with the appearance of radically new structures such as hypermarkets and malls that in turn pose new dilemmas to the process of aesthetic change.[21] While facades in the centre of Prague have also been painted over, there has been no equivalent to the Painting Tirana Project. Another project however has revolutionised the way in which the local inhabitants of Prague visualise and frame the material changes taking place in their city – the Czech Dream documentary.

Directed by two young Czech film-makers – Vit Klusak and Filip Remunda – as their final project for their film school, the documentary tracks the publicity and opening campaign for a hypermarket, symbolically named *Czech Dream*, a hypermarket that would never be built outside of the imagination of the two film makers, but that managed, notwithstanding, to attract over 3,000 people to its fictional opening. Claimed to be by far the largest publicity and consumer hoax the Czech Republic ever experienced, the documentary made waves in the film world, winning a number of different awards, both at home and abroad, from the student Oscars nomination by the Film Academy in Prague to the Golden Gate Award for Best Documentary Feature at the 2005 San Francisco International Film Festival and the Best Nonfiction Film Award at the Michael Moore Traverse City Film Festival. *The Economist* called it the funniest European film of the year, the *New York Times* called it the comedy of capitalism while the British Film Institute, *Sight and Sound* magazine, called it unclassifiable (Klusak and Remunda 2004).

Inspired by theatre director Petr Lorenc, whose original idea was to advertise a fictional out-of-town hypermarket to trick people into going for a walk in the countryside, the film focuses on the extent to which images, brands and publicity can fool people into action, that is, visiting a non-existent hypermarket and enjoying a beautiful day out in an open field with nothing but a wooden prop that stands as the façade for the so-called hypermarket. Celebrated as a critique of consumerism and the entire apparatus that supports it, the film gains a different perspective in the eyes of its actors. These are not just the two directors who have to 'sell' the idea to the publicity company, but also the main actors – the over 3,000 people who showed up for the opening – and the city that they inhabit, Prague. The film is not so much a farce on capitalism, but a farce on the visual illusion of change and spaces where change can be experienced first hand – such as hypermarkets.[22]

The special television and radio spots, the 400 illuminated billboards, the 200,000 fliers, the advertising song, the website and the newspaper and magazine advertisements used to publicise the non-existent hypermarket all shouted mixed messages from the 'Don't Go, Don't Rush, Don't Spend' message on the billboards to the 'It will be a nice big bash, and if you got no cash, get a loan and scream, I want to fulfil my dream!' (Spencer 2005) message in the advertising jingle. The signs and posters that invaded the cityscape and visual-scape of Prague in the two weeks prior to the supposed opening of the hypermarket, were meant to guide the consumer and flâneur towards one particular path – the Czech Dream hypermarket. Situated at the margins of the town, the hypermarket lured its clients with unbelievable prices and promises of a much better life on the cheap.

Informed by the latest technology that helps to identify the colours, fonts, products, and prices that are most attractive to Prague customers, classified by gender, social standing and age, the publicity campaign, as followed throughout the documentary, seeks a precise manipulation of the vision of Prague flâneurs, one that guarantees results and can be easily tracked and assessed. The framing is simple: we sell you your dream – the Czech Dream – the ability to own everything you ever wanted to own. A quick scan through the crowd that did turn out at the opening, reveals a not unexpected mix of people – the old, the poor, the deal hunters and the hopeful. Those who turned out believed in the 'too good to be true prices' not only because the advertising was so good, but perhaps because they needed to, because those were the only prices that they could afford to pay.

Yet it is not the critique of capitalism aspect of the documentary that this case study would like to focus on, nor the meaning and inner-workings of the publicity campaign, but rather how this documentary and the visual tools employed to guide it, have helped to alter the way in which the changing material environment of Prague is to be perceived and interpreted. While the documentary, just like the publicity poster, is no doubt a representation, a visual tool as well as a visual technological manipulation, its props – the fake hypermarket facade, the paper on which the posters were printed and the walls on which they were placed – as well as its protagonists – the people who came and the hypermarket as a structure in general – were a part of the material environment of the city, and a part of the aesthetics of change as read into this material environment. With a message more precise than the colours of Tirana, the posters and the fake facade did, however, do much more than fool people into believing a hoax. They lead not only to a fake hypermarket, but also to an abyss, to a breaking of patterns, or at least a questioning of hypermarkets as both a material as well as a symbolic place.

The appearance of hypermarkets has been, no doubt, celebrated as the triumph of change, the completion or near completion of the transition from communism to capitalism, as the material confirmation of years of political and economic promises and reform (Garb and Dybicz 2006). If social change can indeed be read into the material environment, then hypermarkets would be the proof that significant change has taken place. As the Tesco manager interviewed in the documentary points out, things have changed from the time when he was a little boy, standing in a long line for bananas – a sparse commodity in communist times – feeling humiliated by the Japanese tourists filming him. For he now makes a good living, and has access to any goods that his heart desires, right there, in his store. Yet the Czech obsession with hypermarkets, as noted by the two documentary directors, may not be entirely healthy. In a 2004 interview, Klusak and Remunda explained why they chose to focus their documentary on hypermarkets:

> In the course of a mere five years, foreign investors built 126 of them. In Holland, a country the same size as the Czech Republic, it took them quarter of a century. The Czechs started shopping in these hyper-markets more than people in the other post-socialist countries, and the new edition of the Czech dictionary of neologisms features words like hypermarketománie – a pathological addiction to shopping in hypermarkets, the worship of hypermarkets.
>
> (Klusak and Remunda cited in O'Conner 2004)

The obsession is thus both material, as a result of the mushrooming of these structures to a point where they start to dominate the visual-scape of the city, as well as psychological, to a point of physical addiction. Yet the fetishism with commodities may not be the only explanation for this addiction. Hypermarkets could perhaps also be seen as a refuge, a confined, celebratory space, in which change for the better is indeed visible and radical, in which there are no contradictions and doubts, in which the material confirms loud and clearly that the transition has now been completed. The escape to hypermarkets is thus an escape from other visual horizons, the ones that do not so easily confirm the completion or success of the transition such as the grey suburban areas, the old blocks of flats, the dirty buses and streets, the begging homeless or the neo-nazi marches.

Unlike the painted facades of Tirana, hypermarkets appear as far from being superficial structures, a mere colour that promises more. They are the 'real' thing, the sound, the permanent, the non-temporary. And yet, perhaps the main point of the visual prop, the fake facade of the imaginary hypermarket, is to show that these permanent structures may not be as stable as they appear to be, and that an imaginary act of erasure opens up a space for roads that would otherwise not be taken, for destinations other than the market, for the beauty of non-inscribed, natural material. Looking for change in the material environment, trusting material change as confirmation of larger social change, is thus potentially deceiving not only in cases where superficial change is visually manipulated to appear as radical change, but also in cases where actual radical change appears more stable, permanent and positive than perhaps it is.

If the painted facades of Tirana are an appeasement of expectations of more radical change, and yet to be fulfilled promises, the hypermarkets of Prague are an appeasement of the sometimes disappointing effect of the actual fulfilment of those promises. Both superficial facade colours and sound structures such as malls and hypermarkets ultimately have to rely on a certain element of suspension of disbelief. They are both props and decorations that seek to suggest a particular kind of change or development, that have a distinct way in which they are supposed to be read. A mere change of lighting, or re-framing through new technologies of seeing, such as photography or film, is enough to blur (or sometimes focus) the 'text' on the walls.

As the repainted facades of Tirana served to open up public spaces and encourage a different kind of communication between the local government and its citizens, the hypermarkets of Prague had perhaps the opposite effect. They closed down exploratory spaces, guiding flâneurs towards an exact, enclosed target, in which the wonderworld of goods and diversity made everything seem possible. Just as in Vaclav Havel's *Power of the Powerless*, where the grocer places amongst the onions the sign 'workers of the world unite' (Havel 1985), the publicity and fake hypermarket in the *Czech Dream* documentary also metaphorically and ironically place among the Prague cityscape the sign 'consumers of the world unite'.

The imaginary hypermarket in the *Czech Dream* documentary proposes a different kind of evasion of temporality, stepping back in time as opposed to leaping forwards, imagining a space where hypermarkets do not yet exist, where choices are made differently, spaces are explored unguided and patterns of flânerie do not follow a set path. This evasion serves to challenge the idea that change can be normalised through the achievement of a set final goal or the meeting of particular material expectations, thus challenging the idea that processes of change are necessarily based on a continuum whereby one moves from point A to point B. The breaking of patterns of a particular flânerie (walking with the aim of reaching a particular space or goal) is also a symbolic breaking of the particular pattern or linearity of time.

Conclusion

This chapter has looked at how a unique thirst for consumption across post-communist Eastern Europe led to the emergence of a capitalist consumer culture that significantly changed the surrounding environment, taking over public spaces and commodifying all aspects of communal life. By tracing the foundations for this obsessive consumption in the communist culture of shortages and an indiscriminative fondness for anything 'Western', the chapter has argued that the problematic commodification and privatisation of all public spaces has largely been met by an unbounded, uncritical optimism by the majority of the Eastern European population. The radical transformation of space associated with this fast commodification has slowly but surely led to the creation of increasingly segregated spaces and the cultivation of a cherished sense of elitism that everyone strives for.

Examining the evolution of the tight relationship between consumption and its sustaining architectures, the chapter has traced the transition from seemingly impermanent structures of open-markets and garage architecture to established shopping malls and gated communities. Each marks an important step towards increased segregation and discrimination based on income and ability to consume, yet also points to continued naïveté about its social and political effects, with the majority continuing to embrace this radical transformation of space as positive. The chapter has argued that this collective blindness in the face of radical changes that have left many in increasingly vulnerable positions, denying them access to some of the most basic infrastructures, is largely the result of a continued obsession with appearances and association of progress with looking 'Western'-like.

Employing the nineteenth-century concept of the 'flâneur' as key to unlocking critical possibilities in the visual, spatial and architectural dimensions of change, the chapter has also explored the potential for transforming post-communist communities into more actively reflective twenty-first-century flâneurs. By focusing on two main case-studies – the Painting Tirana Project and the *Czech Dream* documentary – the chapter pointed to the emergence of new spaces of critical reflection that play with some of the same strategies employed by consumer culture in order to create possibilities for change. While pointing to an increasingly sophisticated approach to the meaning and implications of new consumption practices, these case-studies also serve to underline the undeniable importance of visual aesthetics to understanding the 'transition'.

The 'aesthetics of change' as represented by the material environment of Tirana and Prague thus suggest clearly that the post-communist transition is negotiated not only through economic reform packages, elections and integration into the European Union, but also through different forms of visual, spatial and architectural manipulations meant to legitimise individual and collective expectations of the 'transition', and show a clear 'progression' towards the 'West'. As the case-studies show though, both superficial/temporary and seemingly permanent facades can be deceiving. The illusion of the 'West' might in the end not reveal itself until we have not only become the 'West' but perhaps even surpassed it in its consumerist glory.

Notes

1 For a more detailed discussion of the implications of shock in transition societies, please see Pusca (2007).
2 Opened by neighbours and friends often forced into entrepreneurship by lack of other job opportunities, these bars and neighbourhood kiosks maintain an important sense of community and simplicity, where people can gather, drink and shop at reasonable prices as well as exchange favours and learn about new opportunities. These observations are mainly based on ethnographic work in Timisoara, Romania.
3 These 'temporary' structures, due to their un-kept aspect and association with drunkenness and wastefulness, have often been seen as shameful spots on the otherwise positively changing face of the city. Those located close to or even within the city centre and city parks were seen as particularly threatening due to their high visibility and seedy 'membership', leading local governments to campaign

heavily for their destruction. President Basescu of Romania led a very successful 'cleaning-up' campaign in Bucharest, demolishing thousands of structures in the city centre and erasing along with them the visibility of poverty, disillusionment and despair under the fighting corruption banner (the claim was that many of the kiosks in the city centre were illegally run by a number of corrupt nouveaux riches). Although the corruption charges are likely to have been right, the move contributed to the further marginalisation of those who did not fit the positive image of transition – the unemployed, the few remaining factory workers, the homeless and even the seedy entrepreneur.

4 The Iulius Group has been one of the first largest developers of shopping real estate in Romania.

5 More information about the Palas Project, as well as the residential project next to the Iulius Mall in Timisoara is available at: http://www.iuliusmall.com/en/cluj/despre_noi.

6 Romania's population is 22 million people.

7 The House of the People was an essential structure of the communist party, providing an important social and cultural space where people could gather and share ideas. Currently transformed into museums or re-allocated for new uses, they have lost their initial popular appeal, at least in Romania. For an interesting examination of the role of space and the House of the People in communist ideology, see Kohn (2003).

8 Timisoara is my home town.

9 The film *Goodbye Lenin* captures this very nicely through the metaphor of the grandmother who is protected from the shock of change through a preservation of the material environment that she inhabits as stable and unchanged. Brands, objects and newspapers are used to maintain that stability.

10 See more on the Situationists in Bonnett (2006) and Zweifel, Steiner and Stahlhut (2006).

11 See official site for the municipality of Tirana: http://www.tirana.gov.al/?cid=2,10,23. Downloaded 7 June 2007.

12 For a more detailed examination of the wider context of the Albanian post-communist transition see de Waal (2005) and Saltmarshe (2001).

13 One of the biggest challenges to the post-communist transitions has been the ability to spread and make visible the positive 'material' transformations outside of the city-centres. By recognising the importance of making change visible everywhere in a more equal as well as friendly, incremental manner, Edi Rama embraced the superficiality and temporary nature of colours as an efficient way of signalling change as an interactive process in which everyone is an equally important participant.

14 See featured article on the World Mayor webpage: http://www.worldmayor.com/worldmayor_2004/comments_rama.html. Downloaded 6 June 2007.

15 While the on-line voters are certainly not representative of the entire population of Tirana, they do show both the extent to which Edi Rama has managed to mobilise a majority of Tirana's inhabitants (enough people needed to vote in order to make him World Mayor) as well as the clear positive impact that he has had on wide-spread attitudes towards the city both at home as well as abroad.

16 Quoted from the City Mayor's site: http://www.citymayors.com/gratis/city_mayors.html. Downloaded 6 June 2007.

17 Interviews cited by both local and international media, on-line testimonies as well as email communication with inhabitants of Tirana support this claim. While the flânerie experience of each individual is certainly subjective and difficult to portray, the overall examination of the change in visual horizon suggests that the collective flânerie of the everyday inhabitant of Tirana has generally taken a more positive turn.

18 For a more recent discussion on the topic based on Sala's exhibit at the TATE modern in London, see http://www.tate.org.uk/context-comment/video/architectureart-crossover-and-collaboration-edi-rama-and-anri-sala.
19 For more information see: http://www.artnet.com/Magazine/reviews/douglas/douglas11-4-04.asp
20 This expectation was largely supported by a 'discourse' of a return to 'Europe' that encouraged most post-communist states to not only dream of European Union membership but also imagine themselves as a 'physical' part of the West – the transition was thus popularly assessed through the extent to which one adopted the 'look' of the West. Thus, the transition will be over when post-communist cities 'look and feel' like Frankfurt, Paris or London.
21 Often presented as a model city and country in the post-communist transitions literature, Prague and the Czech Republic appear as a miracle of capitalist transformation, along with Hungary and Poland. For a more detailed analysis of the implications of this 'miracle discourse' as well as a wider analysis of the Czech context of post-communist change see Weiner (2007) and Vecernik (1997).
22 The documentary is also a backhanded critique of some of the material motivations and interests underpinning spatial change in post-communist Europe. Most of these material motivations are supported not only by foreign investors seeking to provide a beautiful facade for their profit-making investments but also by the European Union structural and development funds which seek to invest in long-term infrastructure that will facilitate turning its new post-communist members into a new booming market for its products as well as cheap suppliers of goods, workers and creative potential.

Bibliography

Aumont, Jacques. 1997. *The Image*. London: British Film Institute Press.
Backes, Nancy. 2004. 'Reading the Shopping Mall City'. *Journal of Popular Culture* 31(3): 1–17.
Baudelaire, Charles. 1985. *Les Fleurs Du Mal*. Edited by David R. Godine. New York.
Benjamin, Walter. 1968a. *Illuminations*. New York: Schocken Books.
Benjamin, Walter. 1968b. 'The Work of Art in the Age of Mechanical Reproduction'. In *Illuminations*, edited by H. Arendt. New York: Schocken Books.
Benjamin, Walter. 1970. *One-Way Street*. Frankfurt: Suhrkamp Verlag.
Benjamin, Walter. 1999 (1982). *The Arcades Project*. Trans. H. Eiland and K. McLaughlin. Cambridge: Belknap Press of Harvard University Press.
Bonnett, Alastair. 2006. 'The Nostalgias of Situationist Subversion'. *Theory, Culture and Society* 23(5): 23–48.
Buck-Morss, Susan. 1977. *The Origin of Negative Dialectics: Theodor W. Adorno, Walter Benjamin, and the Frankfurt Institute*. New York: The Free Press.
Buck-Morss, Susan. 2000. *Dreamworld and Catastrophe: The Passing of Mass Utopia in East and West*. Cambridge: MIT Press.
Chelcea, Liviu. 2002. 'The Culture of Shortage During State-Socialism: Consumption Practices in a Romanian Village in the 1980s'. *Cultural Studies* 16(1): 16–43.
Creed, Gerald. 2002. 'Consumer Paradise Lost: Capitalist Dynamics and Disenchantment in Rural Bulgaria'. *Anthropology of East Europe Review* 20(2): 119–125.
de Certeau, Michel. 1984. 'Walking the City'. In *The Practice of Everyday Life*, 91–111. Los Angeles and London: University of California Press.
Debord, Guy. 1994. *The Society of the Spectacle*. New York: Zone Books.

Garb, Yaakov and Tomasz Dybicz. 2006. 'The Retail Revolution in Post-socialist Central Europe and its Lessons'. In *The Urban Mosaic of Post-Socialist Europe*, edited by Sasha Tsenkova. Champaign, IL: University of Illinois.

Gecser, Otto and David Kitzinger. 2002. 'Fairy Sales: The Budapest International Fairs as Virtual Shopping Tours'. *Cultural Studies* 16(1): 145–164.

Havel, Vaclav. 1985. *The Power of the Powerless: Citizens Against the State in Central and Eastern Europe*. New York: Palach Press.

Hirt, Sonia. 2006. 'Postsocialist Urban Forms: Notes from Sofia'. *Urban Geography* 27(5): 464–488.

Hirt, Sonia. 2014. 'The Post-public City: Experiences from Post-Socialist Europe'. ACSA Annual Meeting: Globalizing Architecture – Flows and Disruptions.

Jinaru, G. 2008. 'Mall-urile cuceresc Timişoara' (Malls Conquer Timisoara).31 March,*Banateanul*.

Jovanovic Weiss, Srdjan. 2007. 'Evasion of Temporality'. Available online at: http://www.holcimfoundation.org/T463/TemporaryUrbanism.htm. Accessed 9 November 2007.

Klusak, Vit and Filip Remunda. 2004. *Czech Dream*.Prague: Irena Kovarova/Schwarz Smith and Taskovski Films.

Kohn, Margaret. 2003. *Radical Space: Building the House of the People*. Cornell: Cornell University Press.

Kramer, Jane. 2005. *New Yorker* 'Painting the Town'. *New Yorker*, 27 June 2005. Available online: http://www.newyorker.com/magazine/2005/06/27/painting-the-town. Accessed July 2015.

Kreja, Karina. 2006. 'Spatial Imprints of Urban Consumption: Large Scale Retail Development in Warsaw'. In *The Urban Mosaic of Post-Socialist Europe: Space, Institutions and Policy*, edited by S. Tsenkova and Zorica Nedovic Budic. Heidelberg: Physica-Verlag.

Lefebvre, Henri. 1984. *Everyday Life in the Modern World*. New York: Transaction Publishers.

Maclaran, Pauline and Stephen Brown 2005. 'The Center Cannot Hold: Consuming the Utopian Marketplace', *Journal of Consumer Research32*(September): 311–323.

Manrai, Lalita, Dana-NicoletaLascu, AjayManrai and Harold Babb. 2001. 'A Cross-cultural Comparison of Style in Eastern European Emerging Markets'. *International Marketing Review* 18(3): 270–285.

O'Conner, Colin. 2004. 'Interview with the Directors and Producers of Czech Dream'. Available online at: http://www.ceskatelevize.cz/specialy/ceskysen/en/index.php?load=ofilmu_iw. Accessed July 2015.

Pusca, Anca. 2007. 'Shock, Therapy and Postcommunist Transitions'. *Alternatives* 32(3): 341–360.

Rancière, Jacques. 2005. 'From Politics to Aesthetics?' *Paragraph* 28(1):13–25.

Sala, A. 2007. *Dammi I Colori*. Transcript at https://drosier.wordpress.com/2006/11/13/dammi-i-olori-transcript.

Saltmarshe, Douglas. 2001. *Identity in a Post-Communist Balkan State*. London: Ashgate Publishing.

Serazio, Michael and Wanda Szarek. 2012. 'The Art of Producing Consumers: A Critical Textual Analysis of Post-communist Polish Advertising'. *European Journal of Cultural Studies* 15(6):c 753–768. doi: 10.1177/1367549412450638.

Sinclair, Iain. 1995a. *Downriver*. London: Vintage.

Sinclair, Iain. 1995b. *Lud Heat and Suicide Bridge*. London: Vintage.

Sinclair, Iain. 1997. *Lights Out for the Territory*. London: Granta Books.

Smigiel, Christian. 2013. 'The Production of Segregated Urban Landscapes: A Critical Analysis of Gated Communities in Sofia'. *Cities* 35: 125–135.

Spencer, Liese. 2005. 'Reviews: *Czech Dream*'. *Sight and Sound* 15(7): 46.

Staeheli, Lynn A. and Don Mitchell. 2006. 'USA's Destiny? Regulating Space and Creating Community in American Shopping Malls'. *Urban Studies* 43(5/6): 977–992.

Svab, Alenka. 2002. 'Consuming Western Image of Well-Being: Shopping Tourism in Socialist Slovenia'. *Cultural Studies* 16(1): 63–79.

Vecernik, Jiri. 1997. *Markets and People: The Czech Reform Experience in a Comparative Perspective*. London: Avebury Publishers.

Waal, Clarissa de. 2005. *Albania Today: A Portrait of Post-Communist Turbulence*. London: I.B. Tauris Press.

Wall-Street Online. 2007. 'Iulius Mall Timisoara isi va dubla suprafata' ('Iulius Mall Timisoara will double its surface'). *Wall-Street Online Business Journal*, 4 October. Available online at: http://www.wall-street.ro/articol/Real-Estate/33852/Iulius-Mall-Timisoara-isi-va-dubla-suprafata.html. Accessed 6 October 2008.

Walt, Vivienne. 2005. 'A Mayoral Takeover'. *Time*. Available online at: http://www.time.com/time/printout/0,8816,1112793,00.html. Accessed July 2015.

Watson, Ben. 2007. 'Iain Sinclair: Revolutionary Novelist or Revolting Nihilist?' Available online at: http://www.militantesthetix.co.uk/critlit/SINCLAIR.htm. Accessed July 2015.

Weiner, Elaine Susan. 2007. *Market Dreams: Gender, Class and Capitalism in the Czech Republic*. Ann Arbor, MI: University of Michigan Press.

Woodward, Colin. 2005. 'Trendy Tirana? Mayor Invigorates a Backwater Capital'. *The Christian Science Monitor*, 23 March 2005. Available online: http://www.csmonitor.com/2005/0323/p01s03-woeu.html. Accessed July 2015.

Zweifel, Stefan, JuriSteiner and Heinz Stahlhut. 2006. *In Girum Nocte Et Consumimur Igni – the Situationist International (1957–1972)*. Zurich: JRP/Ringier.

5 The 'aesthetics of violence'

Roma/Gypsies visibility and the re-partitioning of the sensible

Anti-Roma violence

Roma communities across former communist spaces have gained increased visibility in recent years, yet more often than not that visibility has had negative connotations. Whether covering issues related to Roma western migration, the demolition of Roma settlements, Roma poverty or violence against or by Roma, the popular press has painted a bleak image of the state of one of the most marginalised minorities across Europe (Dancea 2010; Plesa 2010; Vidican 2010). From the 1990s onwards, instances of violence against Roma have been on the rise, with a noticeable peak around 2008–2010, when both the number and violent nature of attacks against Roma communities across Europe grew exponentially.

In western Europe, countries like Italy, France and later on the UK and Northern Ireland mobilised to deal with the so-called 'Roma problem': in May 2008, Italian Prime Minister Silvio Berlusconi declared a state of emergency in relation to Roma 'nomad' communities and ordered the fingerprinting of all Roma living in 'nomad camps', including children, and later, the forceful evacuation and dismantling of several of these camps (Picker 2012). After a failed attempt to pass legislation that would allow the forceful repatriation of EU citizens, Italy continued to pressure Roma migrant communities to return 'home' and even enlisted the help of Romanian police forces to do so (Plesa 2010).

Later in 2010 France followed suit and dismantled more than 40 Roma camps across the country with over 700 residents scheduled to be returned to Romania and Bulgaria (Barbulescu 2012). In June 2009, the houses of several Roma families of Romanian origin living in Belfast were attacked with rocks and bottles thrown through the windows. Over 100 of them were forced to leave their homes and take shelter in a church and later a leisure centre before being sent back to Romania (Clark and Rice 2012).

Similar attacks on Roma houses took place in Romania. In May 2009, in the village of Sanmartin, 40 houses belonging to Roma families were attacked by over 400 ethnic Hungarians. Accused of stealing from the local villagers, the Roma houses were broken into, windows, doors and roofs destroyed, television sets and aerials broken, cars damaged and dogs killed. A Roma house was also set on fire, leaving many Roma families to sleep out in the cold for fear of further attacks (Toma 2012: 191).

The Czech Republic also saw a worrisome increase in anti-Roma political movements, particularly through the rise of the National Party and the Worker's Party, as well as the increased profile of neo-Nazi movements, which culminated in the Litvinov riots of November 2008. For the 2009 European Parliament elections, the Czech National Party ran on an anti-Roma platform featuring a campaign video that incited anti-Roma violence by promising the 'Final Solution to the Gypsy Question' and featuring a white sheep kicking a black sheep off the Czech flag (Albert 2012: 139). On 17 November 2009, a national holiday in honour of the Velvet Revolution, neo-Nazis gathered in front of the Janov housing estate where many of the local Roma live, and threatened to attack chanting anti-Roma slogans. Over 1,000 riot police officers had to be dispatched to protect them. The violence resulted in 17 injuries, many of them amongst police officers. No one was arrested (Albert 2012: 147).

The list could go on with anti-Roma violence present in most European cities. Isolated instances of anti-Roma violence are certainly not new: what is however different about these new strings of attacks is how quickly they become part of a wider discourse surrounding the so-called Roma 'problem' and help feed stereotypes of Roma criminality, petty theft, and poverty. Increased awareness of this so-called Roma 'problem' across Europe creates the illusion that not only are Roma groups a 'problem' everywhere but also that there is no real solution to this 'problem'.

As Horvath and Albert explain, Roma groups seem to be mainly guilty of having become increasingly visible: 'The Gypsy left his/her customary place, became visible, occupied a new place, and became a synonym of the changes and problems of an increasingly unpredictable world' (Horvath 2012: 120); 'The Roma, it would seem, are essentially hated merely for having become an increasingly visible presence on the streets of the town' (Albert 2012: 163). This chapter seeks to explore this newfound visibility of Roma groups across Europe, how it is expressed, why it often carries negative, even violent connotations, and how this negativity may be reversed.

By exploring the rise of a so-called 'aesthetics of violence' that builds on historic practices of Roma fetishisation, othering and exoticism, the chapter argues that current instances of violence are extreme reactions to an Eastern European identity crisis fuelled by the fall of communism and all the changes that it brought about. The political nature of this crisis is explained in terms of a 're-partitioning' of the sensible, to use Rancière's words: in essence, the new-found visibility of the Roma represents an attempt to claim new spaces, occupations and rights to a political discourse, that is causing significant distress across majority groups not only 'at home' but also across Europe.

The chapter engages with a series of prominent representations of Roma groups in photography and film in order to capture some key negotiating moments that mark the transition from one partition of the sensible to another. First, the chapter zooms in on Koudelka's now classic photographs of Czechoslovakian Roma which serve to mark a specific moment in time: the forceful settlement of the Czechoslovakian Roma during communist times, and along with it, the tacit acceptance of a tolerated marginality as an acceptable settlement of an unequal partition of the sensible. Second, the chapter takes us on a tour of striking new photographs of Roma castles, a unique post-communist phenomena that marks the rise of new economic opportunities for Roma and their not so subtle attempt to flaunt their wealth in the face of a dismayed and increasingly outraged majority. The castles, while lie in deep contrast to images of Roma camps and extreme poverty, capture some of the extreme results of the post-communist partitioning of the sensible. Third, we are introduced to a series of new Roma-focused Reality TV shows which point to new forms of Roma fetishisation, 'self-exoticism', and the partitioning of the Roma identity into an acceptable virtual/celluloid entertainer/performer versus a more problematic off-screen reality. And last, but not least, we look at the rise of Roma rights photography and its limited ability to present a new 'face' of the Roma, and in the process re-negotiate a more equal position in society on 'their' behalf.

An 'aesthetics' of violence: the coming into visibility of post-communist Roma

Increased violence against Roma is premised upon a series of important changes in how the group is 'seen' by the rest of the community. During communism, Roma minorities were loosely integrated into the wider community either through their participation in state-sponsored jobs or through their forceful settlement and intentional dispersal – which in many ways secured a sense of invisibility. After the fall of communism many Roma groups became increasingly visible largely due to the loss of state jobs and benefits and increased reliance on the black market, informal selling of second-hand goods, begging and an increased internal and external economic migration. As Horvath and Albert explained earlier, their customary place in society changed, with Roma families now much more present in the everyday dealings of the majority community.

In addition to this, the EU accession process emphasised the need to accord new rights to minorities, including Roma minorities, and insure equal treatment under the law, and the provision of social services, in particular healthcare and education. This also served to increase the visibility of Roma groups, as their status and treatment became a condition upon which the fate of the rest of the country depended: if Roma poverty and discrimination was too visible, this would significantly undermine the country's chances of joining the EU within the allocated timeframe. The flurry of new laws and provisions which targeted Roma groups that were largely inspired by the need to prove that the state was equally concerned about the fate of its Roma citizens resulted in an increased public resentment and backlash that saw this as 'special treatment'.

Roma groups were thus increasingly perceived as having gained special privileges and protections, which were not always afforded to other members of the community also in need. They were also perceived to be much more astute at managing and profiting from the black market that dominated post-communist economies in the 1990s, and at amassing wealth by working abroad. This combination led to the creation of a series of misconceptions that saw Roma as profiting from the transition at a time when most other groups only stood to lose, leading to further resentment. The reality, for the most part, was quite different: the fall of communism led to an increased immiseration of most Roma communities (Ruzicka 2012), many of which lost their only sources of income, and oftentimes, their home. Some were forced to return to living off the land and find shelter in abandoned homes at the edge of villages, while others were forced into urban ghettos and abandoned buildings.

The gap between the perception of gain and profit from the 'transition' versus the reality of misery was increasingly 'explained' by the popular press either in terms of an uncanny ability of most Roma to 'hide' their wealth and live publicly 'as if' they did not have it, or to flaunt their wealth 'at home' while pretending to be poor 'abroad' (Stefan 2008). Either way, as far as most Romanians were concerned, Roma communities were 'faking' their poverty. In this context, wider discussions of Roma rights, EU funding and support for Roma, Roma political representation, often became simply a facade to be taken seriously only by 'foreigners' who simply did not know any better and could more easily be 'duped'.

Hopes that regime change would create strengthened opportunities for dealing with Roma marginalisation, were often seen as dependent on the success of the democratic transition (Barany 2002). What many however failed to take into account was that democratic transitions, like most processes of regime change, are ultimately processes of massive displacement from which, in a majority of cases, minorities and marginalised groups stand to suffer. While many celebrated the increased visibility of Roma groups as the first step towards the provision of rights, what they failed to see was the direct connection between this increased visibility and further vulnerability.

The 'aesthetics' of violence thus refers to, in this case, a unique coming into visibility of Roma communities across post-communist spaces in Europe, and the majority's resentment that often accompanied that newfound visibility, giving birth to a dangerous social context in which violence against Roma became not only acceptable but also justifiable. Appadurai refers to this as the majority's 'fear of small numbers', fear that can become increasingly predatory and even ethnocidal when 'minorities [and their small numbers] remind these majorities of the small gap which lies between their condition as majorities and the horizon of an unsullied national whole, a pure and untainted national ethos' (Appadurai 2006: 8).

Placed under the microscope of outside communities – from the USA, to the European Union, as well as its own internal microscope of purification from its communist legacy, post-communist Europe became obsessed with its self-image. The need to present itself as belonging to the 'West', forward looking, modern, and open to new opportunities, did not fit well with the continued existence of extreme levels of poverty. While Roma groups were certainly not the only ones 'guilty' of being poor, they often took the blame for it, especially when their poverty pushed them into external economic migration. Roma migrants became not only the EU's 'Roma problem' but also the 'great stain' on their nation of origin (Efremova cited in Stewart 2012: xx). The removal of this 'stain' often involved violent tactics: from bulldozing of Roma settlements, to the building of walls separating Roma communities from the rest of the neighbourhood, to setting legal restrictions on Roma travel and settlement, as well as on accessing state benefits.

It is not that post-communist Eastern Europe simply cannot 'imagine' its Roma minorities as an integral part of its wider community – much of local popular culture and film in particular proves that it is certainly capable of doing so (Dobreva 2007) – but that it struggles to imagine them as 'equals'. It is the place that Roma occupy in society – both the 'physical' space as well as its more classical meaning of 'class' – that many take issue with. Inherent in this, is a deeply imbedded conviction of Roma inferiority, that means Roma groups can be tolerated, but only to the extent that their 'inferior' status in society is respected. With this assumption of inferiority deeply imbedded in local traditions, language and expectations, many of which have only been kept dormant during the communist period, a renewed nationalist revival has often meant that in the process of dusting off and uncovering the past, these old convictions have once again resurfaced.

The 'spaces' that Roma generally occupy in traditional European societies have certainly changed over time. What history seems to have taught us though is that periods of calm coexistence or relative toleration are generally periods where Roma groups were well integrated into the local economies with clearly defined roles and specialised skills that made them useful yet did not threaten to take anything away from majority groups. Their 'visibility' meant that they generally occupied set spaces and were expected to perform only specific jobs: in the early 1900s that may have been either seasonal agriculture jobs, masonry and brick making, wood work and tin making, or work as musicians (Lucassen and Willems 2003); while during communist times it often meant allocated state jobs, many of which generally involved the cleaning of streets or public spaces (Silverman 1986), often complemented by side-jobs within the fields of traditional occupations of the 1900s (Cvorovic 2005).

This is not to say that a Roma elite did not exist early on: it is this elite that fought to have Roma rights recognised and Roma professionals accepted into all sectors of the economy. They did, however, generally represent only a minuscule portion of Roma society and were perceived to occupy a special in-between space: during the early 1900s they were the allies of the modernising intellectual elite that sought to do away with Gypsy slavery (Achim 1998), while later, during communism, they became key translators of the communist integration policies and shapers of Roma men, women and children into 'new citizens' (Donert 2008; O'Keeffe 2013).

The changes brought about by the post-communist period propelled Roma groups into new spaces creating both new economic opportunities as well as new political spaces where they could create and affirm new identities. No longer tied to specific jobs or locations, Roma groups became more visible by increasingly inhabiting spaces that simply were not available to them before: main city squares, steps of major government buildings, concert halls, shopping malls, as well as the new open air bazaars that dominated so much of the early 1990s everyday life. Newfound legal and rights protections required by the European Union and part and parcel of the wider reform process meant that a police force that was equally disturbed by Roma's new found visibility had to at the same time find ways to protect them. This led, not surprisingly, to countless altercations whereby Roma groups often found themselves dependent for protection on the same police forces that harassed them on the street for public loitering and begging.

The post-communist 'aesthetic of violence' thus refers to a particular coming into visibility of Roma groups that did away with a historically accepted partition or distribution of the sensible, to use Rancière's terms. In his discussion of the essential role that this distribution of the sensible plays in politics, Rancière underlines the extent to which power dynamics are neatly tied to certain aesthetic expectations, which, when disrupted, can cause a great deal of unrest:

> The distribution of the sensible reveals who can have a share in what is common to the community based on what they do and on the time and space in which this activity is performed ... it defines what is visible or not in a common space, endowed with a common language, etc. There is thus an 'aesthetics' at the core of politics [...] It is a delimitation of spaces and times, of the visible and the invisible, of speech and noise, that simultaneously determines the place and the stakes of politics as a form of experience. Politics revolves around what is seen and what can be said about it.
>
> (Rancière 2004: 12–13)

This particular 'aesthetics of violence' thus refers to Roma politics as ultimately a dispute over what they can do and the spaces they can inhabit in society. The redistribution of the sites of the sensible, according to Rancière, is essential for the establishment of a real democracy. The community of equals that Rancière evokes is dependent upon equal access to the sensible, the visible and the discursive. The post-communist transition to democracy has thus, not surprisingly, meant a deep and continuous struggle and negotiation over the partition of the sensible, which posited not only Roma groups against non-Roma, but instead involved a complete renegotiation of the sensible by the whole of society. What appears to be an economic struggle over resources is, at its core, also a struggle over a historical sense of entitlement that non-Roma communities have over Roma groups.

The fight over the partitioning of the sensible, and more importantly, what is at stake within this often violent renegotiation, becomes perhaps most visible in certain forms of contemplative art and popular culture, such as photography and film. As Walter Benjamin argues, the rise of photography and film as public forms of art increasingly enjoyed by wider audiences, has created a series of new collective contemplative spaces – the art gallery and the cinema – in which the glimpses of society, captured either intentionally, or not, by the camera, flicker in front of our eyes revealing, in slow motion, evocative instances of change (Benjamin 1970, 2008), and along with it, the very (re)distribution of the sensible that Rancière refers to.

As such, the remainder of this chapter turns towards examining how this unique partition of the sensible becomes visible in key photographic and film endeavours, which have now become part of popular culture. In the process, along Benjaminian lines, the chapter points to both the revealing potential of these unique pieces of art, as well as their power to re-inscribe and enforce new forms of distribution of the sensible: what Benjamin refers to as the politicising of art versus the aesthetisation of politics (Benjamin 1968).

Koudelka's Gypsies: tolerated marginality

Josef Koudelka started photographing Gypsies in the context of 1960s Czechoslovakia, a time of forced settlement for the Gypsies – which tied many of them to rural isolation and poverty – as well as a time of great unrest in the country – particularly after the 1968 Russian invasion, which Koudelka also photographed. Koudelka is not a Gypsy, and although he had a rural upbringing, his village did not have any Gypsies. The choice of Gypsies as a subject, as he explains it, was quite arbitrary at first, mainly as a result of his love for Gypsy music and his personal friendship with several Gypsy musicians and poets. He saw his photographs of Gypsies in Slovakia as being directly connected to his own identity as Slovakian and has always argued that his photographs of Slovakian Gypsies were better than those he took of Gypsies elsewhere, suggesting that he experienced a different kind of connection not only to the subject of his photographs, but also the familiarity of the setting. His photographs were not meant to be 'news', to 'inform others' or support particular causes. They were 'for himself', taken with almost an instinctual approach to the subject (Farova 2002: 122).

Koudelka's photographs, mainly portraits, reflect his particular initial training, as a theatre/stage photographer and focus on his subjects as performers. Having learned to carefully control the way in which they portray themselves to the outside, his subjects are indeed performing, with Koudelka allowing them to direct him towards a particular perspective, object, or frame. The Gypsies in his photographs appear to have carefully mastered the photo-graphic process and are not afraid to show their power as subjects. The horse whip, the violin, the hat, the proud stance, the bent over in pain stance, the coffin, the dead, children's play, the cold, the heat, the simplicity and poverty of the households, all came together to form a carefully arranged yet organic ensemble that reminds us of a theatre stage. As Anna Farova explains: 'for him this, too, was a sort of theater – the actors here played themselves, while the exteriors and interiors that changed in spaces almost like stage scenery also manifest unbridled real life' (Farova 2002: 8).

In talking about the role of his photographs, Koudelka and his critics emphasise that he took most of his photographs 'for himself', that most of them were never meant for a particular audience other than a close circle of friends and that they represented a very personal diary of his trips and experiences that was never meant to serve as a 'document', a 'statement to the world', or even something open for public and collective interpretation (Koudelka 2007). And yet, once his photographs were printed and distributed, once he reached a certain level of fame – particularly after his affiliation with Magnum – once people started paying for his photographs, his photographs did become very powerful documents, featuring as some of the most prominent imagery of Gypsies in photography up until today. This prominence has put new pressures on the 'meaning' of his photographs, particularly at a time when human rights groups and state agencies for the protection of minorities are increasingly aware of the power of representation and seek to employ it in order to promote less discrimination and equal treatment. Perhaps the biggest challenge in representing Roma is being able to directly engage with the way in which they choose to represent themselves.

Although forced to settle into marginal rural communities that insured that Roma/Gypsy 'integration' into communist society would not disturb an 'equal' yet clearly divided society, Koudelka's Gypsies show a clear sense of resilience in the face of rising adversity: they inhabit their humble spaces proudly, fill them with cherished objects that remind them of traditional skills and occupations; they look straight into the camera and are not afraid to show pain, death and a sense of powerlessness when faced with police arrests. Koudelka captures, what I call a sense of tolerated marginality: the newly settled Gypsy groups are carefully guarded by the police to insure that they do not cross into majority territory, and as such, their settlement is somewhat tolerated. Their clearly inferior status in society, despite claims of equality, pacifies increasingly embittered majorities. This forceful partition of the sensible, whereby Gypsy groups inhabit a carefully scripted marginality within which certain traditions can be tolerated as long as they are carefully contained within the group, while majority groups are guarded against potential predatory behaviour, suggests an unequal but tolerated social pact.

Koudelka manages to cross over the invisible border between Gypsy and Gadje or majority groups, and catch a glimpse of the normality of life on the other side: for anyone familiar with rural life in communist Eastern Europe, this reality is not that much different, albeit perhaps a bit poorer. The Gypsies on the other side turn out to be just as human, just as religious and often adherent to similar cultural traditions. Although physically separated from the rest of the community, they are still, in many ways, very much a part of it. Evidence of crossover impregnates Koudelka's photographs: the Gypsies are involved in village activities such as agricultural work or as blacksmiths, musicians and horse dealers. In the photographs, they stare back in confidence because they trust the author and are willing to share some of the most intimate moments of their lives with him: the death of family members, baptisms, weddings, arrests. This level of trust is unique and almost unprecedented, creating representations that stand out not for their ability to depict Gypsies as 'different', but quite the opposite, for their ability to depict them as in many ways living a life similar to other Czechoslovakian peasants.

Koudelka captures the 'pain of others' subtly, in the eyes of a handcuffed child walking out on his own with his community as well as the police standing behind him at a distance; in the frozen stillness of a group of mourners around an open casket; in the coins carefully placed on the eyes of the deceased. Everywhere there is a strange sense of calm and acceptance. His subjects have accepted their pain, and their place in society. There is no sense that anything is out of the ordinary. The viewer/spectator has nothing to offer them. Instead, each photograph appears to be a silent conversation between the subject and the photographer, which we simply happen to witness. We are not a part of that conversation nor are we really meant to be.

The key to the success of Koudelka's photographs lies not only in the performance of his subjects, but in the fact that he gives his subjects complete control over their performance. He does not seek to impose a particular message, the photographs do not serve any particular purpose, they are not 'documents' as Koudelka argues. Unlike many other representations of the Gypsy community, many of which are carefully staged to achieve particular desirable results and call upon particular stereotypes and emotions, there is a certain honesty to Koudelka's photographs: not in the sense that they reveal the 'true' identity of his subjects, but in the sense that they are able to somehow 'disperse comfort rather than aggravate pain' (Koudelka 2007).

> The closest to his intention was direct photography, straight-ahead, simply and clearly composed, free of excessive detail, with the centripetal placement of the figures in frontal view against the simplest possible background. Static figures stood motionless in the center, yet were full of excitement, tension and internal expressiveness.
>
> (Farova 2002: 8)

His camera does no violence to the subject. His presence is accepted because he is a traveller himself, because he does not have a specific agenda, because he is more than just a photographer, because he lets himself be directed by the subject, because he lets his camera become part of a larger conversation. He does not promise anything, his photographs are not there to achieve a particular goal, to bring any kind of deliverance. There is only a sense of humility that allows the subjects to simply say: here we are, like any of you, in our proud and our sad moments. They do not call out for help, they do not seek to appeal to our sympathy, empathy or sense of giving, they do not seek to put themselves on a political platform, or shame anyone. They are just claiming the recognition of their presence, there, in a particular space, at a particular point in time, to whoever is willing to look.

It is not much to ask, and yet it is something that different Gypsy and traveller communities have been refused time and time again. As Dobreva points out, the 'celluloid Gypsy' has taken over the 'real Gypsy' to a point where the representation is the only place where the community becomes acceptable. Yet these representations have to adhere to a strict performance that fits into the comfort zone of the majority: the Gypsy musician, dancer, dressed in traditional clothing and behaving in unacceptable yet predictable ways, was until recently the norm (Dobreva 2007). Any attempt to deviate from this scenario and the celluloid Gypsy loses its appeal. Documentaries on Gypsy beggars, Gypsy camps and demolitions, evidence of violence by and against Gypsies, spark little interest in the wider community, their appeal lying largely with a small human rights community that often uses and manipulates these representations for very specific purposes. The 'real Gypsies' that they represent have little to offer: they do not entertain, do not always fit stereotypes and often demand the seemingly unacceptable: that they are already very much a part of the broader community.

If Koudelka's photographs encapsulate a very particular social reality, and social pact, that governed Gypsy-Gadje/majority relations during communism, what follows seeks to point to the deep sense of rupture that the end of communism brought to this reality: with no-one left to police the strict border between Gypsy-Gadje society and the opening up of the economy, the need to maximise new economic opportunities propelled Roma/Gypsy groups into new spaces. New economic opportunities meant new wealth for some Gypsies, and along with it, an opportunity to re-inscribe the spaces they inhabited with visible opulence, while at the same time, extreme new forms of marginality for other Gypsies, who were increasingly forced into the squalor of Gypsy camps. This contrast of extreme wealth and poverty captures a new chapter in the partition of the sensible, whereby Gypsy/Roma groups could no longer be easily classifiable along similar lines or ascribed to similar spaces.

Roma camps versus castles: the horror stories and fairytales of capitalism

Depictions of extreme poverty in Roma camps are not uncommon today. A majority of Roma images that populate the internet are indeed depictions of the extreme poverty often associated with these camps. The very popularity of the word 'camp' in association with Roma groups is indeed something relatively new, often connected to the fall of communism, and along with it, the increased internal and external migration of Roma groups. Roma camps are a reality both 'at home', with many Roma from rural areas having migrated to larger urban areas; as well as 'abroad', with Roma families taking advantage of their new found freedom of movement within the EU to look for new economic opportunities. The 'camps' represent an extreme visualisation of a new kind of spatial and social marginalisation that has seen Roma groups pushed into completely segregated communities that are increasingly treated as suspended from national territory and national law and thus susceptible to abominable treatment (Aradau 2007, 2009).

These new camps signal yet another partition of the sensible: one that, paradoxically, has seen Roma economically propelled into increasingly visible spaces generally populated by majority groups only – begging on wealthy public streets or in front of public institutions during the day, while at the same time pushed into extreme marginality with not even a semblance of protection at night – upon returning to the camp. This odd new form of marginalisation, that sees Roma more present in the everyday life of the majority, yet at the same time, further separated from them, shows the friction created by, on the one hand the perceived visibility of Roma groups in spaces where they 'do not belong', and on the other, the rising squalor of constantly growing camps that encroach upon the poor and lower class Gadje groups.

Although the border between Roma and non-Roma groups is much more porous today, the relationship between the two is perhaps at its worst. The crossover of Roma groups into spaces where they are more difficult to police, as well as the extreme separation of their camps from majority communities – whereby, unlike in the past, Roma groups no longer play an visibly active party in the economic activities of the majority community – has caused perhaps the deepest rupture in Roma/non-Roma relations in centuries. The inability to contain Roma communities to certain spaces and negotiate inter-actions on the terms of the majority has caused a deep sense of unsettlement which has spilled over into uncontrollable violence. The desire to re-ascribe Roma groups to specific spaces has resulted in the creation of increasingly isolated camps, the refusal of authorities to provide any services to many of these camps, and the increased tendency to visibly separate the camps from neighbouring communities with walls, and in some cases, police stations that enforce curfew.

Roma camps today are increasingly designed as ultimately terrains of invisibility. As Fabrizio Floris explains 'the principle characteristic of these settlements is not poverty, violence, unemployment, or even architectural decay. Their fundamental characteristic is their invisibility' (Floris 2010: 55). Pushed literally to the edge of society, the Roma camps are often surrounded by fences that seek to physically separate them from the surrounding local communities. The presence of the camps is tolerated only as long as the invi-sibility is maintained. It is not surprising then that the dismantling of the camps often comes at times where the increasing visibility of the Roma com-munity gains negative connotations: often a crime committed by a member of the community.

Unlike the Roma caravans of the past, the Roma camps of today maintain little of the aesthetic appeal of the former. Makeshift homes in the camp are rarely decorated maintaining a purely functional, yet temporary style. Put together within a matter of days, the homes come apart just as easily. While the inside of the camp homes remains intensely colourful (Orta 2010) and decorative, it remains invisible to the outside world. The camp, as Mariana Celac explains, is not a place where one can find

> a wealth of exotic folklore, a quest for identity or regional expression [...]
> The new urban poverty is uniform, non-specific, highly banal, and non-ethnic. The determinants that bring ghetto people together are always similar: being born in a ghetto, having been left out in the process of economic restructuring and pushed into poverty by a consumerist and segregative urban society.
>
> (Celac 2010: 101)

While alternatives to the camp often translate into 'box-like blocs of minimal flats or monotonous aseptic alignments of identical pavilions' (Celac 2010: 101) a new type of Roma architecture is on the rise throughout Central and Eastern Europe: Roma 'castles'. These striking Roma palaces show a remarkable vitality of creativity, expression and identity: 'gigantic houses, with their unmistakeable stylistic features: roofs with turrets and overlapping cornicing, a vague mix of Chinese pagodas and the gingerbread palaces of Bollywood melodrama' (Andresoiu 2007: Preface). Funded mainly through remittances from abroad these palaces function as intricate displays of wealth that are not uncommon amongst groups that have recently come into money (Petcut 2008).

A phenomenon closely connected to the economic migration of Roma groups abroad, the castles, although they stand apart in their unique aesthetic style, represent a similar desire of all those who have found new wealth to show it. Less ornate, yet similarly imposing villas built by non-Roma economic migrants are testament to a similar kind of opportunistic social climbing that allows the previously poor to re-inscribe/re-write themselves into visibility, in this case through architecture. What makes Roma castles particularly controversial is not only their extreme flaunting of wealth, but also their ability to turn a previously imposed marginality on its head: the castles are now the centre of a community of their own, standing proudly apart yet clearly dominant of the skyline. The often empty or seemingly abandoned castles are meant to act as effective stand-in props for their owners, often absent while travelling abroad.

This increased visibility remains however, in many ways, guarded by a highly selective access to the inside of these palaces. Two recent collections of photographs: Renata Calzi, Patrizio Corno and Carlo Gianferro's *Gypsy Architecture* (Calzi, Corno and Gianferro 2007) and Igloo Patrimoniu Press's *Kastello* (Andresoiu 2007) offer for the first time a view of the inside of the palaces and a glimpse of the lifestyle of an otherwise very private group of people. The grandiose rooms are for the most part sparsely furnished and hardly ever used, with the outdoor space continuing to play the most important role in the life of the family. The inside space, like the facades, is for the most part used to make a statement as opposed to actually 'house' the family. The community remains closely guarded despite its increased visibility. Perhaps what the castles – facades and interiors – provide is a sense of visibility that does not necessarily increase the community's vulnerability. They are a clear sign of the community's desire to establish its own terrain not only of visibility but also of settlement.

Each palace has a meaning of its own, made in the image of its creator, a collection of decorative and architectural fairytales mixed with coded messages that symbolise the owner's source of wealth and oftentimes their actual trajectory during the foreign travels that allowed them to gather such wealth: Mercedes and dollar signs, lions, stags, even a model of the Brandenburg Gate. The roofs often list the family names of their inhabitants, and decorative elements such as exterior stairs, terraces, turrets or new tiling are constantly added and changed in an effort to maintain visibility and compete with neighbouring palaces.

Although imposing in their appearance, many of the palaces are not professionally built, often supported by a weak foundation that isn't able to withhold the many structural additions tacked on in time. A majority of the palaces thus often appear unfinished, a constant construction site that risks to suffer significant setbacks as parts of them collapse while others are added. The fragility of these castles defies the stability and longevity that most buildings aspire to, baffling architects that are growing increasingly interested in them. It is clear that this new kind of Roma architecture is something 'new', defiant of previously established architectural categories. As Mariana Celac beautifully writes:

> Their penetrating spirit, dynamism, cumulative expressivity, the numerous challenges they pose, the attraction for distinctive features of various sources, the vitality and the large sums invested together with a social success that exceeds ethnic boundaries, the territorial dispersion and critical mass achieved – all these together have removed the kastell from under the sign of the picturesque. Kastells are supported by a substratum that can be compared, metaphorically speaking, with that which facilitated the journey of Jazz from the margins to a sub-species of high music with equal rights: hunger for identity, irreverence for what went before and authority, but an active mimetic spirit, freedom to take control over anything that can be used to realise your own design, the capacity to resonate with a growing audience, but also exclusion, sarcasm and negative publicity – as a vulgar, aesthetically crude, anti-cultural phenomenon. All with the advantages of uproar as a vehicle of fame.
>
> (Celac 2008)

While Celac's optimism is infectious, it marks perhaps the perspective of an architect discovering a radically new approach to 'settlement'. The reality of the economic crisis, slow growth at home and abroad has however clearly caught up with even the wealthy Roma communities, leaving an increasing number of their palaces unfinished or in decay. The ultimate expression of post-1989 capitalist growth mixed with a unique desire to reshape and control the way in which their community becomes visible, these castles could easily be seen as 'the symbolic expression of a minority group's search for legitimacy' (Stefan 2008). How successful this new visibility has been remains to be seen.

If anything however, this newborn Roma architecture has established a clear terrain of social visibility under which the Roma were able to impose their own vision of themselves and their post-1989 experience. As Petre Petcut argues: if 'the ability to switch between social visibility and invisibility was the main weapon wielded by nomads faced with constant controls by local and national authorities', today this has given way to a permanent visibility (Petcut 2008), perhaps a sign of a fearless defiance that clearly states: we are, and have been, here to stay and the sooner you acknowledge our presence, the better.

The shock that this newfound visibility of Roma groups has caused majority groups should not be underestimated. Despite the creation of much more liberal legal and political regimes under which the equal rights of the Roma are clearly recognised, the reality is that this renegotiation of the spaces that Roma groups can inhabit and of their increased visibility within traditionally non-Roma spaces has led to a series of extreme behaviours, and sadly, to an almost complete spatial and social separation of Roma and non-Roma groups. More recently popularised depictions of Roma castles, only recently available to a Western audience, capture some of the extremes to which the newly wealthy Roma have gone to in order to re-inscribe the traditionally marginal spaces they inhabited into new community centres, and their almost desperate desire to be 'seen' while maintaining anonymity.

This paradoxical newfound and often extremely perverse visibility of Roma groups which coincides with some of the most dramatic forms of separation of Roma and non-Roma groups is also found in the rise of a newer representational form: Reality TV. Through it, the 'Gypsy' is able to appropriate yet another kind of space in the popular imagination, creating a false sense of 'closeness' – through the highly intrusive gaze of Reality TV – and yet managing to put the 'Gypsy' question on the popular agenda in a much less openly 'political' or controversial way. While this new space of popular entertainment is often faulted for serving to further exoticise and stereotype Roma groups, it does open up a series of new ways of thinking of Roma groups as very much part of our everyday life and our communities.

Gypsies in Reality TV: the 'other' performs itself

The recent rise in Roma/Gypsy focused Reality TV has been spurred by the unexpected success of *My Big Fat Gypsy Wedding UK*. Copied in the USA, with *My Big Fat Gypsy Wedding US* and *American Gypsies*, the show also found different Reality TV spin-offs across Central and Eastern Europe: the *Vijelie Family* in Romania and the *Gyozike* show in Hungary, both modelled after the Osbournes. Unlike the ordinary Roma, 'the Roma media star is a new phenomenon, who has transformed the figure of the traditional Roma musical entertainer from tolerated exception into admired, albeit ambiguous celebrity' (Imre 2015: 104). Produced by 'an industry that treats cultural identities as commodities' (Tremlett 2014: 316), the shows depict the rise of a new kind of Roma/Gypsy: the middle and upper class Roma with disposable income and a lifestyle that is in many ways closer to the middle and upper class majority.

While *My Big Fat Gypsy Wedding UK/US* continue to fetishise certain traveller traditions with regards to communion and weddings, shows like the *Vijelie Family, Gyozike* and *even American Gypsies* depict Roma families who are in many ways integrated into mainstream society, although still playing to the stereotypes of the loud, fun-loving, rule dodging, palm reading Gypsy. The wide audiences that each of these shows enjoy, while riding the wave of the success of Reality TV in general, might also be explained by the need to find alternative ways of looking and understanding the so-called 'Gypsy problem'. With most Roma communities still very much maintaining a tight grip on their private lives, these shows allow curious majorities to peek behind the very walls that they have helped erect and reconfirm the fact that even 'rich' Gypsies are still Gypsies.

These reality shows do however open up a series of new 'virtual' spaces that the Gypsies are welcome to inhabit and claim as their own. While some argue that they are nothing but 'Gypsy circuses', these virtual performance spaces, through their unexpected popularity, increasingly play a very important role in bringing Roma groups into our everyday life. Unlike the exotic paintings of the past, or Gypsy performers and musicians on stage, these Reality TV characters claim to be representing the contemporary everyday life of a group of Roma and Travellers that is otherwise largely absent from our sight: the Roma/Traveller entrepreneur who has lifted his family out of poverty and could be, for all we know, our next-door neighbour.

The perceived 'virtuality' of these characters allows for a 'let's pretend' – to be accepting, to be neighbours – attitude that is much more difficult to replicate in real life. It also allows for a different kind of division of the sensible: one in which the Roma can make a claim to 'prime' spaces without this being seen as necessarily controversial or intrusive. The ability to control when and how they inhabit these spaces – through the simple use of the remote control – might explain this seemingly odd openness. As Aniko Imre explains, 'Gypsies are tolerable on reality shows as long as they are passive victims, for whose exploitation the medium can be blamed' (Imre 2015: 120). Virtual spaces however are also prone to deep violence. While audiences clearly find these shows fascinating, given the constantly high numbers of viewers, the online comments around the shows are often 'outright vitriolic' (Imre 2015: 116).

This 'love–hate' relationship captures the extent to which the Gypsy 'other' is both closer and further apart at the same time in contemporary reality. Each of these shows captures this love–hate relationship – and closeness yet distance inherent within it – in different ways.

Produced by Firecracker Films for Channel 4, *My Big Fat Gypsy Wedding* initially aired on February 2010 in the UK as part of a one off show in the Cutting Edge series. Following Irish and English traveller families as they prepare to celebrate their daughters' communions and weddings, and the fanfare that comes with that, the first show recorded unexpectedly high ratings which triggered the creation of an entire series. The second episode reached a peak of 7.4 million viewers at one time. Firecracker Films' moto of *shows designed to make a lot of noise* certainly lived up to expectations. Featuring prominently on their homepage is a still from the show: two traveller beauties, a blond and a brunette, decked out in bubblegum pink puffed-up gowns, hats and arm decorations, with sparkling fake diamonds on them (BBC 2011).

The show's main narrator is Thelma Madine, dress-maker extraordinaire for the traveller communities in Ireland and England. Based in Liverpool, Madine's shop Nico has catered to these communities for over 15 years creating decadent, over the top outfits fit for fairytale weddings and their dress-rehearsals, communions. Her latest creation includes a dress made out of 250 meters of colorful hair extensions which she offered to Lady Gaga for her latest tour. Riding her new-found fame, Madine becomes the unlikely traveller expert introducing the viewer to their unusual habitat (or at least the habitat in which they celebrate their weddings). Moving away from stereotypes of poverty and isolation, the traveller community emerges as what looks like a successful community, ready to invest what most people suspect are significant sums – though carefully never revealed, in over the top dresses, cakes, limousines and carriages. The theme is fairytale glamour, with Disneyland and its characters' dresses and settings as inspiration.

The show straddles a tough line: a reality show clearly meant to entertain, it also seeks to address some of the problems surrounding the traveller communities in Ireland and the UK, including the provision of services in caravan sites, evictions, early marriages and the status of women in the community, education, tradition and the role of secrecy in managing discrimination. Although highly criticised for its failure to clearly distinguish between Romani Gypsy traditions and Irish traveller traditions, as well as for its exclusive focus on what appear to be particularly well-off families, the show does offer a unique look into some of the most intimate moments in the lives of young traveller girls and their families as they prepare the get married.

As the first reality show to focus on traveller communities, at a time when tensions between traveller communities and the wider community ran particularly high – especially with the evictions from Dale farm as well as increased police pressure during the Appleby Horse Fair, which the show does briefly address – the source for the surprising appeal of the programme seems to lie in the promise of an intimate encounter with a community which has mainly been known for its well-guarded secrecy.

As Ruth McElroy and Rebecca Williams argue, reality television in general seeks to exploit 'its promise of intimacy' by bringing the outsider gaze as close as possible to the subject's body (McElroy and Williams 2011). For anyone familiar with any Romani Gypsy or traveller groups, it is surprising that this extreme kind of intrusion would not only be allowed but to a certain extent encouraged. The community's visibility during the show however remains carefully guarded and controlled, with many heads of the family and grooms-to-be choosing not to have their identity revealed for fear of reprisals and the effect it might have on their business and public persona. The intrusive gaze focuses instead mainly on the young girls, their friends and their mothers.

To the extent that one has to assume that such a closely guarded community could only agree to participate in a show like this to encourage and promote a particular view of themselves (as well as perhaps the economic benefit, although whether and how much these families were paid remains unknown) the show, while seemingly focused on 'big weddings' also serves to showcase the extent to which the community has changed: most of the families on the show are settled despite many of them still living in caravans, the children and young couples are perfectly able to blend into their wider communities when they choose to and live in many ways a similar 'modern' life as many of their generation – they shop in malls, meet people on facebook, go out with friends and look forward to finding a partner, getting married and settling down. Despite the over-the-top outfits and 'exotic' rituals such as 'grabbing' – which many Romani Gypsies have criticised – many of these traveller communities appear to have carefully adjusted to settled life. While grandmothers mourn the freedom of the life on the road, the young brides are more concerned with the kind of life they can provide for their future children, and talk about their desire to see them be better educated, get stable jobs and live 'normal' lives.

Although clearly located within 'modernity', the traveller families in the show are still deeply steeped in tradition: couples marry young yet girls have to carefully guard their image and virginity until marriage, most of the girls are expected to leave school at an early age and help care for their younger siblings, cleanliness at home is extremely important with girls cleaning the caravans for several hours a day, and once married, the girls appear to be completely under their husband's control, with few if any allowed to keep jobs outside of the household. The show fixates itself on this contradiction between the extreme glamour of the girls' wedding day and their everyday life once married as if to say that marriage appears as the celebrated entrance to a time warp that sucks the girls away from their otherwise 'modern' lives into a different time and space altogether. As Jensen and Ringrose explain, 'the Gypsy girl is constructed on a trajectory of backward immobility', often depicted as bride in captivity (Jensen and Ringrose 2014: 377).

With the show's audience largely formed of non-Romani or travellers, the message is clearly aimed at the wider majority. The experience of the spectacle as image is a collective one, one that is clearly meant to renegotiate – not necessarily for the better – our attitudes towards this community, the stereotypes that we attach to them, and in many ways, bring the carefully crafted historical image of the traditional 'Gypsy' into the twenty-first century. These are the 'modern' Gypsies and travellers who can no longer afford to guard themselves from the gaze of outsiders in a society where everything is increasingly visible, and are much more acutely aware of the need to direct and control their visibility. The show is to a certain extent such an attempt. Despite criticism from some of the Romani Gypsy communities who are less comfortable with the intimate access and visibility of the girls; bodies, the show has served to propel the traveller community in Ireland and the UK to the forefront of the collective imagination much more efficiently than any news story or documentary.

Alaina Lemon argued within the context of post-communist Russia that the Gypsy communities there were experiencing a 'crisis of representation' (Lemon 2000: 72). As more and more Romani Gypsy and traveller communities around the world are subjected to increased visibility, this 'crisis of representation' demands a readjustment of stereotypical Gypsy images cultivated until recently by film, photography and other forms of popular culture. Within the appeal of the spectacle of reality shows and other forms of popular culture and communication today, lies the opportunity for the Romani and traveller communities to renegotiate not only their visibility, but through it, their political positioning. Negotiating and gaining more control over their visibility is key, yet this process also runs the risk of unravelling an 'exoticised' frame that has carefully guarded the community from curious outsiders by providing them with the desired spectacle.

The increased realisation that, in the twenty-first century '"what's on" creates the context for what is known and hence finally for what "is"' (Ginsgurg 1994: 365) makes their visibility much more a question of physical and political survival. Perhaps the point of shows such as *My Big Fat Gypsy Wedding* is less to provide 'realistic' portrayals of all aspects of Romani and traveller lives and more to begin to re-negotiate the collective imaginary when it comes to these communities and the social projects that follow, or not, from them (Buck-Morss 2000).

Building on the success of the UK series, *American Gypsies* began airing in the USA during the summer of 2012 on the National Geographic channel with Ralph Macchio as executive producer. Extensively advertised throughout New York, the reality show follows the life of the Johnses, a family of Gypsies long settled in New York, as they pursue their American dream. The Johnses run several businesses across New York and Florida, and function within a close knit circle of other Gypsies in the USA. They go to Gypsy doctors, use Gypsy real estate agents, do business with other Gypsy families, fight to maintain their traditions and convince their children to do the same, but they are also integrated within the wider community, do business with outsiders, speak fluent

English, are proud of their hyphenated identity 'American-Gypsies' and the young Gypsy men are keen to date and meet Gadje (non-Gypsies).

Unlike *My Big Fat Gypsy Wedding, American Gypsies* takes a closer look at how Gypsies in the USA sustain themselves both as families as well as a wider group: how they maintain traditions, including the so-called Cris (Gypsy court) which is depicted in one of the episodes; how they run their businesses (the Johnses have traditionally run palm reading shops but are also involved in the scrap business – stereotypical Gypsy traditions, although the show makes clear that other Gypsy families make their living in other businesses as well), and how they develop their business acumen (the young boys of the family start their own Gypsy food stall in Union Square, which generates quite a bit of interest, with many New Yorkers stopping to ask questions about their identity as Gypsies as much as to order the food).

The Johnses are loud, they fight a lot with each other and others, their actions are dramatic and exaggerated, appearing more as modern day *Sopranos* than anything else. They do not claim to be representatives of the Gypsy community in the USA, although they do appear to come from a prominent Gypsy family, well respected in the community. They are certainly not afraid of their newfound visibility, but seem to, on the contrary, thrive on it, play to it. They appear proud of who they are, despite the verbal and sometimes physical violence captured on film – for which the show has already been heavily criticised (*Huffington Post* 2012; Lloyd 2012) – claiming *The Osbournes* and their crazy yet loving family as inspiration for appearing on the show (Salamone 2012). This is a family who loves Reality TV and is not afraid to use it as a medium to increase their exposure.

Although the show, just like the UK one, plays on well-established stereotypes, it also introduces these mass audiences for the first time to the existence of many Roma families amongst them and to their sometimes curious attempts to combine a modern lifestyle with changing traditions. Both shows undoubtedly point to the slow erasure of tradition, particularly for the new generations of Roma, and the violence that sometimes ensues in trying to desperately preserve it. This desperate and unusual attempt on the side of some Roma and Traveller families to 'open-up' and offer an extreme sense of exposure, points to a significant shift in how some of the Roma communities think of their visibility: with invisibility no longer providing a sense of security and protection, extreme visibility on the side of wealthy and powerful families becomes a strategic tool to re-negotiate their perception, to claim their right to co-exist within specific spaces and communities and to express the strong sense of crisis that the community is currently undergoing.

The *Vijelie Family* and *Gypzike* shows also play in many ways with the idea of 'modern' Gypsies. Anika Imre argues that the mixed reaction to the shows – large television audiences which suggest unexpected popularity but also vitriolic attitudes towards the shows online and in the press – is largely explained by continued resistance to the idea that a national culture – particularly an Eastern European one – can be racially mixed. Despite attaining middle-class status, the Vijelie and Gyozike families, although entertaining on screen, are still not seen as an acceptable part of the 'nation'. She goes on to argue that: 'Brought together in the hybrid media space created by Gypzike, the normative responses of public intellectuals and the anonymous comments of ordinary viewers reveal the interdependency between race and cultural value in defining the Eastern European nation as a family' (Imre 2015: 124).

Even the 'modern, virtual' Gypsies do not belong: their culture is too 'low' to help build the much-desired Westernised self-image that much of Eastern Europe has fought so hard to paint for itself. The spaces that they inhabit, do however open up a series of interesting debates and the possibility of conceding a less marginal presence of the Roma in everyday life.

Roma rights photography: picturing a 'different' Roma

One of the most recent trends in Roma photography is that of finding ways to resist a constantly negative portrayal of the group, while at the same time finding ways to capture the struggles of the community with poverty, isolation, marginalisation and abuse. The idea behind this new trend is that by creating a photographic space in which Roma groups can regain their dignity, the overwhelmingly negative representations of Roma groups in popular press will lose some of their grip or at least be increasingly questioned for their approach, which often instigates violence. Sponsored by Roma Rights groups such as the Open Society Foundations, Roma rights photography acts as an openly political tool aimed at creating positive spaces and frames through which Roma groups can be 'seen' and claim 'visibility'. Its success is however mixed, as, unlike Reality TV shows, its audiences are not only significantly smaller, but also generally part of an intellectual elite that already accepts the legitimacy of Roma groups to claim positive spaces.

Photographer Chad Evans Wyatt recently embarked on a project to portray a different kind of Romani people: the middle and upper class professionals who are often thought to not exist. The result, www.romarising.com, collects black and white photographs of over 250 Roma professionals from across Europe and Canada, which seek to 'engage the viewer in an unfamiliar conversation, an honest discussion between equals' (Wyatt 2014). They represent respect, calm, formality, intelligence, human ambition, as opposed to the most common 'ingredients' of Gypsy photography: exoticism, otherness, 'a theatre of grotesque characters, irremediably different, without redemption, often emphasizing poverty, unbridled ecstasy, rootlessness, irresponsibility' (Miroslav Vojtechovsky cited in Wyatt 2014). The photographs identify those depicted not only by their full name, but also with a short paragraph which describes their achievements and current role. They are an eclectic group of incredibly accomplished, proud citizens.

The popular circulation of these images however is almost non-existent. For someone not familiar with Chad Evans Wyatt's work or with a rising human rights based movement that seeks to show a different face of Roma communities, these images would not in any way be connected with a Roma identity. Wyatt is amongst the few photographers who have managed to disconnect images of Roma from images of 'trash' and 'poverty'. The struggle for most photographers who are looking to fight negative and often violent portrayals of the community, is how to address and portray the struggles of the community without inciting violence.

The meaning of images and photographs is difficult to control, and their effects can be unpredictable: the same image could incite violence in one context and empathy in another. Livio Mancini's now famous photograph of a Roma boy holding a toy gun in a run down camp in Kosovo (Mancini 2012) is a case in point: originally taken in the context of the post-war reconstruction work done by the Italian NATO contingent that had come to keep the peace in Kosovo, the picture was later used by a Swiss magazine to draw attention to the rise in robberies by Roma in Switzerland, using the caption: 'The Roma are coming' (Goodman 2012). Cropped so that the boy and gun are up close with the gun pointing to the viewer, the picture is highly confrontational. The gun appears to be real, despite the fact that Mancini assures us it was in fact a toy gun the boy had found in a pile of trash. The boy's face is dirty but appears serious and his grip is strong, fearless, almost as if he wouldn't even blink if a shot were to be fired. Silly playfulness was easily turned into perceived aggression through a mere change of context, caption and crop. The remainder of the photos taken by Mancini show Roma children playing games, showing off, laughing and making the best of their 'playground': a trash collection site.

The misuse of photography is not new or uncommon. Ed Kashi, who has also photographed Roma communities in the context of a wider project on ethnic profiling, argues that photographers, representing agencies and the wider media have a responsibility towards the appropriate use of photographs: making sure they are not taken out of context, that captions and descriptions are accurate and that permissions are always sought and discussed. Laif, the agency that represented Mancini's work, called for a 'visual ethics', in the case of the egregious misappropriation of his work.

As Kashi however explains, maintaining this 'visual ethics' is difficult, particularly when photographic assignments are becoming increasingly specific, demanding that photographs take a particular line. The photographer is thus expected to 'find' that line amongst the multitude of stories available and often ignore or keep to themselves the wider context of their encounter that is not necessarily present in the photograph (Kashi cited in Cohen 2012). The civil contract of photography, that Azoulai (2012) argues invariably exists in all photographs, does not necessarily give agency to all those represented. While photography does indeed create a political space through which the photographed person can potentially also speak (Carville 2010), there is no guarantee that the spectators will necessarily listen.

Even attempts to 'look past the poverty' (Frohne 2013) and go 'behind the Roma walls' (Leung 2014) inevitably end up capturing a background of 'trash', dirt and poverty. The appeal for alternative representations in these cases often focuses on the face as somehow separate and set apart from this back-ground. The faces are often very expressive: proud, laughing or serious, posing, pensive. They seek to show a deep sense of humanity amongst the challenges that surround them. Sonia Tascon argues that while there is an intrinsic con-nection between the face, its representation, and humanity, certain faces are easier to show than others, particularly within sensitive contexts.

Turning to Sontag's argument about representing the pain of others, Tascon reminds us that it is often much easier to show the faces of others amongst extreme poverty/violence: 'the others provide the "spectacle of suffering" for the privileged who can choose to be unaffected' (Tascon 2012: 872). While most of those 'others' generally tend to be far removed from the 'privileged', in the case of European Roma, that is often not the case at all. This closeness, which is often implied in many of the photographs, scares and incites at the same time. The idea that a civilised Europe could contain such poverty loads these photo-graphs with intense emotions that, when coupled with a series of problematic stereotypes about Roma communities, can result in highly volatile situations.

Sarah Parsons, talking about Sontag's *On Photography*, argues that: 'It is the dialog between what we know and what we see in the powerfully constructed photographs that lends emotional force to them. In photographs of trauma, this emotional force is evident and often intentional on the part of the photo-grapher' (Parsons 2009: 292). At the same time though, 'photographs also deaden our emotions and promote emotional detachment' (Parsons 2009: 293). This paradoxical emotional inflammation and detachment is quite emblematic of most portrayals of Roma communities in popular media. The shocking lack of empathy in the face of often traumatic events, such as the drowning of two Roma girls in Italy which left sunbathers unfazed for the over two hours the bodies laid on the beach (Hooper 2008), shows the extent to which current popular representations of Roma communities have managed to erase their humanity.

Whether Roma humanity is visible or not, is once again dependent on the context in which the photographs are presented: taken out of context by the popular press seeking to incite particular responses, the humanity can easily be wiped off their faces; placed within the neat frames of an elite exhibit on the walls of one of the richest foundations in the world – see for example the Moving Walls collections by the Open Society Foundations: http://www.openso cietyfoundations.org/moving-walls/collections/by-topic/roma – their humanity suddenly comes back alive. As Sharon Sliwinski reminds us: 'The meaning of a photographic image is never fixed, never guaranteed, and never to be trusted. Like all implements of violence, this medium will lend its signifying powers to the highest bidder' (Sliwinski 2009: 308).

Conclusion

This chapter has argued that there is an intricate connection between increased incidents of Roma violence and the new spaces that Roma groups increasingly occupy. Using Rancière's idea that space is inherently political and that aesthetics deals in many ways with the, sometimes violent, re-appropriation of space – division of the sensible – the chapter has looked at some of the interesting new ways in which Roma groups have appropriated new spaces for themselves, or have had others do so on their behalf. By comparing and contrasting the spaces that Roma occupied during communism versus the ones they are claiming today, and, more importantly, the way in which that change has been captured in a series of more prominent forms of representation – such as Koudelka's photography, depictions of Roma camps versus castles, Roma Reality TV and Roma rights photography – the chapter hopes to have shown the difficulties in resisting spatial, and along with it, political marginalisation, and the critical role that the space Roma occupy plays in their ability to affirm themselves politically as part of the 'nation'/community.

The chapter points to an important transition from a tolerated marginality of Roma groups, that allowed nonetheless for constant contact with majority groups, creating a sense of symbiosis, albeit a controversial one, to an increasingly violent reaction to Roma occupying new, and often more central spaces in our communities. While the physical occupation of more central spaces is often more controversial than the virtual one, both forms of claiming new spaces and along with them, new political identities, have been met with significant violence. While new virtual spaces, such as Roma Reality TV, have been more open to a temporary sense of acceptance, they also continue to draw audiences less on the basis of a more 'positive' portrayal of middle-class Roma and more on the basis of an unlikely 'modern' Roma, who, in spite of his/her economic success, continues to fall into the stereotypical tropes of his/her race, thus re-affirming in some ways the impossibility of 'integration'.

The chapter does however argue that this transition from occupying marginal spaces to increasingly central spaces that have traditionally belonged to the 'majority' is an important move in the political 'affirmation' and 'redefinition' of Roma groups. The violence with which it is often met is perhaps a sign that it is working. By focusing on the 'aesthetic' aspect of this violence, the chapter argues that new representational forms, such as photography and film, are key to this renegotiation of the spaces that Roma groups inhabit, and along with it, their political positioning.

Bibliography

Achim, Viorel. 1998. *The Roma in Romanian History.* Budapest, New York: Central European University Press.

Albert, Gwendolyn. 2012. 'Anti-Gypsyism and the Extreme-Right in the Czech Republic 2008–2011'. In *The Gypsy 'Menace'*, edited by Michael Stewart, 137–165. New York: Columbia University Press.

Andresoiu, Bruno. 2007. 'Kastello, Palate Ale Romilor din Romania: Castelul si maneaua' (Kastello, Palaces of the Roma in Romania: The castle and the manele). In *Kastello: Palate ale Romilor* (Kastello: Roma Palaces). Bucharest: Igloo Patrimoniu.

Appadurai, Arjun. 2006. *Fear of Small Numbers: An Essay on the Geography of Anger*. Durham and London: Duke University Press.

Aradau, Claudia. 2007. 'Law Transformed: Guantanamo and the 'Other' Exception'. *Third World Quarterly* 28(3): 489–501.

Aradau, Claudia. 2009. 'The Roma in Italy: Racism as usual?' *Radical Philosophy* 153 (January/February): 2–7.

Azoulai, Ariella. 2012. *The Civil Contract of Photography*. Cambridge, MA and London, UK: The MIT Press.

Barany, Zoltan. 2002. *The East European Gypsies: Regime Change, Marginality and Ethnopolitics*. Cambridge: Cambridge University Press.

Barbulescu, Horia. 2012. 'Constructing the Roma People as a Societal Threat: The Roma Expulsions from France'. *European Journal of Science and Theology* 8(1): 279–289.

Benjamin, Walter. 1968. 'The Work of Art in the Age of Mechanical Reproduction'. In *Illuminations*, edited by H. Arendt. New York: Schocken Books.

Benjamin, Walter. 1970. 'A Small History of Photography'. In *One-Way Street*, edited by W. Benjamin. Frankfurt: Suhrkamp Verlag Press.

Benjamin, Walter. 2008. 'The Work of Art in the Age of Its Technological Reproducibility'. In *The Work of Art in the Age of Its Technological Reproducibility and Other Writings on Media*. Harvard: Belknap Press of Harvard University Press.

Buck-Morss, Susan. 2000. *Dreamworld and Catastrophe: The Passing of Mass Utopia in East and West*. Cambridge: MIT Press.

Calzi, Renata, Patrizio Corno and Carlo Gianferro. 2007. *Gypsy Architecture*. Stuttgart and London: Edition Axel Menges.

Carville, Justin. 2010. 'Intolerable Gaze: The Social Contract of Photography'. *Photography and Culture* 3(3): 353–358.

Celac, M. 2000. 'An Elite that Did Not Take this Country for What it Really Was'. *Revista* 22(4): 6–7.

Celac, M. 2008. 'Tinseltown'. In *Kastello: Palate ale Romilor* (Kastello: Roma Palaces). Bucharest: Igloo Patrimoniu.

Celac, M. 2010. 'Archipelago on the Move'. In *Mapping the Invisible: EU-Roma Gypsies*, edited by L. Orta. London: Black Dog Publishing.

Clark, Colin and Gareth Rice. 2012. 'Spaces of Hate, Places of Hope: The Romanian Roma in Belfast'. In *The Gypsy 'Menace'*, edited by Michael Stewart, 167–190. New York: Columbia University Press.

Cohen, Will. 2012. 'The Roma are Coming: Ed Kashi on the Misuse of Photography'. Available online at: http://www.opensocietyfoundations.org/voices/roma-are-coming-ed-kashi-misuse-photography. Accessed July 2015.

Cvorovic, Jelena. 2005. 'Gypsy Oral History in Serbia: From Poverty to Culture'. *Oral History* 33(1): 57–67.

Dancea, D. 2010. 'Ţiganii Repatriaţi cu Scandal la Timişoara' (Gypsies repatriated to Timisoara make a fuss). *Adevarul*. Available online at: http://adevarul.ro/locale/timisoara/Tigani-repatriati-scandal-timisoara-romii-i-au-scuipat-injurat-jurnalisti-galerie-foto-1_50ae683c7c42d5a6639c7007/index.html. Accessed July 2015.

Dobreva, Nikolina. 2007. 'Constructing the "Celluloid Gypsy": Tony Gatliff and Emir Kusturica's "Gypsy Films" in the Context of New Europe'. *Romani Studies* 17(2): 141–154.

Donert, Celia. 2008. 'The Struggle for the Soul of the Gypsy: Marginality and Mass Mobilization in Stalinist Czechoslovakia'. *Social History* 33(2): 123–144.

Farova, Anna. 2002. *Josef Koudelka*. Prague: Foto Torst.

Floris, Fabrizio. 2010. 'The Population of the Slums in Italian Cities.' In *Mapping the Invisible: EU-Roma Gypsies*, edited by L. Orta. London: Black Dog Publishing.

Frohne, Lauren. 2013. 'Looking Past the Poverty: Life in Roma Ghettos'. Available at: http://www.opensocietyfoundations.org/voices/looking-past-poverty-life-roma-ghettos. Accessed July 2015.

Ginsburg, Faye. 1994. 'Embedded Aesthetics: Creating a Discursive Space for Indigenous Media'. *Cultural Anthropology* 9(3): 365–382.

Goodman, David. 2012. 'Cover of Swiss Magazine Draws Accusations of Racism'. Available online at: http://thelede.blogs.nytimes.com/2012/04/12/cover-of-swiss-magazine-draws-accusations-of-racism. Accessed July 2015.

Hooper, John. 2008. 'Gypsy Girls Corpses on Beach in Italy Fail to Put Off Sunbathers', 21 July. *The Guardian*.

Horvath, Kata. 2012. 'Silencing and Naming the Difference.' In *The Gypsy 'Menace'*, edited by Michael Stewart, 117–135. New York: Columbia University Press.

Imre, Aniko. 2015. 'Love to Hate: National Celebrity and Racial Intimacy of Reality TV in the New Europe.' *Television and New Media* 16(2): 103–130.

Jensen, Tracey and Jessica Ringrose. 2014. 'Sluts that Choose versus Doormat Gypsies'. *Feminist Media Studies* 14(3): 369–387.

Koudelka, Josef. 2007. *Josef Koudelka*. London, New York: Thames and Hudson Photofile.

Lemon, Alaina. 2000. *Between Two Fires: Gypsy Performance and Romani Memory from Pushkin to Post-Socialism*. Durham, London: Duke University Press.

Leung, Chuck. 2014. 'A Photographer Goes Behind the Roma Walls'. Available at: http://www.opensocietyfoundations.org/voices/photographer-goes-behind-roma-walls. Accessed July 2015.

Lloyd, Robert. 2012. 'Television Review: "American Gypsies" Follows a Formula'. *Los Angeles Times*. Available online at: http://articles.latimes.com/2012/jul/16/entertainment/la-et-st-american-gypsies-20120717. Accessed July 2015.

Lucassen, Leo and Wim Willems. 2003. 'The Weakness of Well-Ordered Societies: Gypsies in Western Europe, the Ottoman Empire and India 1400–1914'. *Review (Fernand Braudel Center)* 26(3): 283–313.

Mancini, Livio. 2012. 'A Completely Different Picture: Inciting Hatred Against Roma'. Available online at: http://www.opensocietyfoundations.org/voices/completely-different-picture-inciting-hatred-against-roma. Accessed July 2015.

McElroy, Ruth and Rebecca Williams. 2011. 'Remembering Ourselves, Viewing the Others: Historical Reality Television and Celebrity in the Small Nation'. *Television New Media* 12(3): 187–206.

O'Keeffe, Brigid. 2013. *New Soviet Gypsies: Nationality, Performance, and Selfhood in the Early Soviet Union*. Toronto, Buffalo, London: University of Toronto Press.

Orta, Lucy. 2010. *Mapping the Invisible: EU-Roma Gypsies*. London: Black Dog Publishing.

Parsons, Sarah. 2009. 'Sontag's Lament: Emotion, Ethics, and Photography'. *Photography and Culture* 2(3): 289–302.

Petcut, Petre. 2008. 'Tranzitie cu Turnulete' (Transition with Turrets). In *Kastello: Palate ale Romilor* (Kastello: Roma palaces). Bucharest: Igloo Patrimoniu.

Picker, Giovanni. 2012. 'Left-Wing Progress? Neo-Nationalism and the Case of Romany Migrants in Italy'. In *The Gypsy 'Menace'*, edited by Michael Stewart, 81–94. New York: Columbia University Press.

Plesa, Carmen. 2010. 'Italia il sustine pe Sarkozy si vrea sa intreaca Franta la expulzari' (Italy supports Sarkozy and wants to surpass France in terms of numbers of Roma sent back home). *Jurnalul National*, 23 August. Available online at: http://m.jurnalul. ro/stiri/externe/italia-il-sustine-pe-sarkozy-si-vrea-sa-intreaca-franta-la-expulzari-55260 5.html. Accessed July 2015.

Rancière, Jacques. 2004. *The Politics of Aesthetics: The Distribution of the sensible.* London and New York: Continuum.

Ruzicka, Michal. 2012. 'Continuity or Rupture? Roma/Gypsy Communities in Rural and Urban Environments under Post-socialism'. *Journal of Rural Studies* 28: 81–88.

Salamone, Gina. 2012. '"American Gypsies" Focuses on a New York Family and its World of Feuds and Fortune Tellers'. *New York Daily News.* Available online at: http://articles.nydailynews.com/2012-07-17/news/32717910_1_romany-people-gypsy-culture-tina. Accessed July 2015.

Silverman, Carol. 1986. 'Bulgarian Gypsies: Adaptation in a Socialist Context'. *Nomadic People* 21–22: 51–62.

Sliwinski, Sharon. 2009. 'On Photographic Violence'. *Photography and Culture* 2(3): 303–316.

Stefan, Dorin. 2008. 'In Gramada Deschisa a Kitsch-ului Imobiliar Romanesc' (The Sprawling Mass of Romanian Real Estate Kitsch). In *Kastello: Palate ale Romilor* (Kastello: Roma Palaces). Bucharest: Igloo Patrimoniu.

Stewart, Michael. 2012. 'New Forms of Anti-Gypsy Politics: A Challenge for Europe'. In *The Gypsy 'Menace': Populism and the New Anti-Gypsy Politics*, edited by Michael Stewart, xiii–xxxviii. New York: Columbia University Press.

Tascon, Sonia. 2012. 'Considering Human Rights Films, Representation, and Ethics: Whose Face?' *Human Rights Quarterly* 34: 864–883.

Toma, Stefania. 2012. 'Segregation and Ethnic Conflicts in Romania: Getting Beyond the Model of "The Last Drop"'. In *The Gypsy 'Menace'*, edited by Michael Stewart, 191–213. New York: Columbia University Press.

Tremlett, Annabel. 2014. 'Demotic or demonic? Race, class and gender in 'Gypsy' reality TV'. *The Sociological Review* 62: 316–334.

Vidican, C. 2010. 'Romii care au fost expulzați din Franța sustin că nu îi prinde iarna în Bihor' (The Roma thrown out of France say they will go back before the Winter in Bihor). *Adevarul*, 21 August. Available online at: http://adevarul.ro/locale/oradea/romii-fost-expulzati-franta-sustin-nu-prinde-iarna-bihor-1_50ae67767c42d5a6639c68 19/index.html. Accessed July 2015..

BBC. 2011. 'My Big Fat Gypsy Wedding: Why is it a hit?' 28 January. BBC Online. Available online at: http://www.bbc.co.uk/news/magazine-12311604. Accessed July 2015.

Huffington Post. 2012. '"American Gypsies" Premiere: Families Throw Down Over Gypsy Law in New York City' (Video). Available online at: http://www.huffingtonp ost.com/2012/07/18/american-gypsies-premiere-gypsy-law-video_n_1682152.html. Accessed July 2015.

Wyatt, Chad Evans. 2014. 'Romarising'. Available online at: http://www.romarising. com. Accessed July 2015.

6 The end of 'transitology', the end of 'post'-communism, the end...

The end of most things generally elicits a sigh: it is done, over, time to move on to something else. Declaring an 'end' of something, at least in academia, generally does not coincide with any 'actual' end, other than a desire to conclude, to reflect looking backwards, to justify the move towards a new idea, new paradigm. The end of 'transitology', as declared by many post-communist intellectuals, started in the early 2000s and is still going on (King 2000; Carothers 2002; Ray 2009; Petsinis 2010; Rupnik 2010; Tichindeleanu 2010; Plattner 2014; Shleifer and Treisman 2014). 'Transitology' and along with it 'post'-communism have been ending for over 15 years now.

The 'end' has come to refer to a number of different things:

1 the emergence of a relatively stable new social contract in post-communist countries (Mungiu-Pippidi 2010);
2 a general sense of exhaustion, disappointment and nostalgia for the past, along with the realisation that there is no alternative to 'democracy' (Rupnik 2010);
3 the closing of a historic window of opportunity which saw some nations join the 'West' and others locked outside of it – see Ukraine, Moldova (Mungiu-Pippidi 2015);
4 the maturing of the infantilised East European nations, which often coincides with the realisation of historical powerlessness (Buden 2010);
5 the need for a new intellectual paradigm through which to analyse different post-communist trajectories that do not necessarily assume democracy as an end goal (Carothers 2002); and ...
6 the recognition that, at least for now, the era of democratic transitions is over and unlikely to be matched in the future (Plattner 2014);
7 the hope that 'democracy consecrated will become democracy contested' (Schmitter 2015);
8 the realisation that the desire for 'a state of being in which problems presently confronted are [permanently] removed or resolved' is yet another form of utopia (Ray 2009: 325);
9 that despite a generally sombre mood, 'the post-communist transition does not reveal the inadequacy of liberal capitalism or the dysfunctions of democracy (Shleifer and Treisman 2014);

10   that it is time to stop thinking within the narrow matrix of the region and start thinking about the wider European and global implications (Petsinis 2010);

11   that despite its end, communism remains quite actual as a horizon of thought, one that cannot be pronounced definitively 'dead' yet one that recognises the 'impossibility of its return' (Tichindeleanu 2010: 32).

The 'end' in this case means too many things to too many people. The 'end' is exhausting, precisely because it is confusing. The 'end' is the realisation of a perhaps falsely premised beginning, of a radical change in expectations, or perhaps the 'death' of those expectations. The 'end' is the slow descent into irrelevance, and indistinctiveness. The end of 'transitology' is not only the declaration of the end of a paradigm but also the acceptance that, academically speaking, but also politically, at least on the US side of the Atlantic, the interest in post-communist Central and Eastern Europe has slowly vanished, and that new paradigms of change, focusing on Asia, the Middle East and North Africa have taken its place. It is an undeniable signal that now is the time to jump ship. Those of us still writing about post-communist Central and Eastern Europe need to find new ways of staying relevant, need to insert ourselves into new paradigms that carry a more global, or at least wider European, sense of relevance.

The end of 'post'-communism refers perhaps to a slightly different thing, or at least this book interprets it as something different: it marks the slow closing down of a window of critical reflection on communism, a slow erasure and removal of both the material and mental marks that communism left behind. This book has tried to capture some of the interesting reflections that arose during this narrow window when the erasure of communism is not yet complete, when acts of resistance are still possible, when people still have something concrete/physical to hold on to, to remember, to confront. As former communist spaces are increasingly privatised and new architectures take their place, as film makers and artists are increasingly forced to focus on more global concerns in order to stay relevant, as spaces of resistance eventually give in to change and erasure, and bodies decay and eventually die along with the memories they carry, communism becomes history. A history that is much more difficult to recover, to engage with, a history that slowly sinks below the surface, that takes effort to dig out, that dissipates into fragments that can never be precisely reassembled.

As one approaches the realisation of the 'end' and gains enough of a sense of distance from the often confusing point(s) of origin, a spur of creativity usually occurs. This book has argued that this spur of creativity reached its peak in the early 2000s and is now slowly approaching its end. Capturing this critical sense of creativity is an important endeavour, not only because it marks a critical intellectual point of coagulation of a certain experience of change, but also because it represents a side of everyday history that often gets overlooked. The material marks that trigger this creativity will soon be gone or permanently transformed: the images captured during the 1989 Revolutions will no longer be recalled by a generation that was not even born at the time – they will never speak to that experience the same way; the former industrial platforms will be either razed down to the ground or transformed beyond recognition, and the workers who once inhabited them will soon all be gone; the open markets and garage architecture are already disappearing, while shopping malls no longer represent anything 'new' or 'unusual' but rather are the expected 'normal'; the Roma populations of Eastern Europe will slowly continue to lose their unique identifiers – from language to cultural traditions, and although they will likely remain on the outskirts of social and political life for a while, violence against them will be based on a fragmented memory of traditions of 'nomadism' and 'criminality' that although long gone, remain written into the law and the wider majority consciousness.

There is no way of capturing and re-assembling this period of intense creativity so that it continues to speak into the future as it does today. Post-communist aesthetics is an intellectual experiment that is uniquely relevant now. The painted walls of Tirana will not mean much to future generations once they have faded. The *Czech Dream* Documentary will take its place into the film archives only to be perhaps rediscovered by an eager academic seeking to describe the disturbing early enchantment of hypermarkets to a generation of students who probably do most of their shopping online and have long forgotten what hypermarkets are. Street performances will have been forgotten, theatre plays briefly remembered as one uncovers an old flier or script, and monuments will have long lost their meaning. Precautious post-communist artists like Dan Perjovski are already incorporating this element of unavoid-able erasure into their work: his drawings, often in 'permanent' marker on museum, collectives and art gallery walls, never last more than six months before they are erased. New drawings incorporate old ones, with new messages, and re-appropriated meanings that increasingly go from the narrow/local towards the global.

Perjovski represents in many ways the future of post-communist artists and creators that are slowly recognising the 'end' of communism, or even of 'post'-communism, as a powerful and meaningful point of reference, and along with it, the 'end' of a particularly inward way of looking that seeks to uncover something unique or different about those who underwent the experi-ence of the post-communist transition. Having tattooed the word Romania on his arm in the early 1990 during one of the first collective art performances organised in post-communist Romania – Perjovski is a Romanian artist[1] – he then went on to publicly remove it during a later performance in 2001. In the process, his locality, his focus, his relevance, his context had changed: Per-jovski is now an international artist, drawing on the walls of the MOMA and some of the most established museums in the world. His drawings no longer deal with the post-communist context alone: they place Romania's and the wider post-communist region's concerns squarely within wider global concerns. His text is multilingual.

The closing of this critical period of creativity, which I have tried to briefly capture through a wider theory of post-communist aesthetics, should not necessarily be mourned. It is in many ways inevitable. Creativity will certainly continue, but its object and mechanics, at least in this case, will necessarily change. As Groys has so effectively argued, the twenty-first century will bring about a completely new way of seeing in art and beyond: the architectural panoramas of the nineteenth century which signalled the rise of the perspectival view in which the individual was faced with an opening of space; will give way to the rise of collective panoramas in the twenty-first century: in which individuals will increasingly experience themselves as part of a wider collective brought together not by history but by the spaces that they (temporarily) inhabit together (Groys 2013).

The most recognisable of these spaces themselves will no longer carry unique connotations to locals, but rather be integrated into a wider, global circuit of tourism, monuments, images, that will increasingly carry similar connotations to all. The symbolic territory left behind by the experience of communism will soon be consumed and exhausted, and post-communist art will move on. Post-communist aesthetics at that point will carry a completely different meaning: unlike today, it will have become history itself. For now though, while we can, we should enjoy these creative engagements with the aftermath of communism while we can still relate to the more subtle references that they make. We can, for just a little bit longer, live with the illusion of being different, special.

Note

1 For more information see the artist's official website: http://www.perjovschi.ro.

Bibliography

Buden, Boris. 2010. 'Children of Postcommunism'. *Radical Philosophy* 159 (January/February): 18–25.

Carothers, Thomas. 2002. 'The End of the Transition Paradigm'. *Journal of Democracy* 13(1): 5–21.

Gans-Morse, Jordan. 2004. 'Searching for Transitologists: Contemporary Theories of Post-Communist Transitions and the Myth of a Dominant Paradigm'. *Post-Soviet Affairs* 20(4): 320–349.

Groys, Boris. 2013. *Art Power*. Cambridge MA and London UK: MIT Press.

King, Charles. 2000. 'Post-Postcommunism: Transition, Comparison, and the End of "Eastern Europe"'. *World Politics* 53: 143–172.

Mungiu-Pippidi, Alina. 2010. 'The Other Transition'. *Journal of Democracy* 21(1): 120–127.

Mungiu-Pippidi, Alina. 2015. 'The Splintering of Postcommunist Europe'. *Journal of Democracy* 26(1): 88–100.

Petsinis, Vassilis. 2010. 'Twenty Years after 1989: Moving on from Transitology'. *Contemporary Politics* 16(3): 301–319.

Plattner, Marc. 2014. 'The End of the Transitions Era?' *Journal of Democracy* 25(3): 5–16.

Preda, Caterina. 2012. 'Art and Politics in Postcommunist Romania: Changes and Continuities'. *Journal of Arts Management Law and Society* 42(3): 116–127. doi: 10.1080/10632921.2012.726550.

Ray, Larry. 2009. 'At the End of the Post-Communist Transformation? Normalization or Imagining Utopia?' *European Journal of Social Theory* 12(3): 321–336.

Rupnik, Jacques. 2010. 'In Search of a New Model'. *Journal of Democracy* 21(1): 105–112.

Schmitter, Philippe. 2015. 'Reflections on 'Transitology' – Before and After'. Available online at: http://www.eui.eu/Documents/DepartmentsCentres/SPS/Profiles/Schmitter/ReflectiononTransitologyrev.pdf. Accessed 11 July 2015.

Shleifer, Andrei and Daniel Treisman. 2014. 'Normal Countries: The East 25 Years After Communism'. *Foreign Affairs* 93(6): 92–103.

Tichindeleanu, Ovidiu. 2010. 'Towards a Critical Theory of Postcommunism? Beyond Anticommunism in Romania'. *Radical Philosophy* 159 (January/February): 26–32.

Velicu, Irina. 2012. 'To Sell or Not to Sell: Landscapes of Resistance to Neoliberal Globalization in Transylvania'. *Globalizations* 9(2): 307–321.

Index